Past, Present and

Discover through first-hand experiences
How you create your present circumstances
In past lives and how you can change the present
And manifest a new future.

Come to KNOW:

Every human soul experiences cycles of birth and rebirth over and over again for hundreds of lifetimes until each soul fully realizes and KNOWS the truth of who they really are and actualizes their Divine Nature.

Everything that exists is, in essence, Love. Love is always tempered with truth. The realization or recognition of Love and Truth in relationship with another person is the experience of "True Love".

Love is eternal and lasts forever. Once "realized," love never dies, though it may go underground, become hidden and seem to disappear. Love is forever present and all encompassing.

Once you have experienced Love with someone, that Love will resurface life after life and the recognition of that Love will grow into an instant attraction that is often called: "Love at First Sight".

You repeat good and bad experiences (karma) life after life until all experiences become good and then, even good experiences must be transformed into divine…

You can know the past, present and future. Each reveals itself in the right time. All is revealed in the moment you are "ready" to know each truth. It is our destiny to know the truth that will set us free.

In actuality, the past, present and future are all occurring at the same time. Most individuals see these in a progressive sequence. That is why many people fail to recognize that all of these are intertwined, accessible and changeable this moment.

There is an answer to every question and it is possible for anyone to access these answers, once they discover one of the many ways available to tap into the universal source of all knowledge.

BOOKS BY JEANNE MARIE MARTIN

FOR THE LOVE OF FOOD
The Complete Natural Foods Cookbook

THE ALL NATURAL ALLERGY COOKBOOK

HEARTY VEGETARIAN SOUPS AND STEWS

EATING ALIVE with Dr. Jonn Matsen, N.D.

VEGAN DELIGHTS / Gourmet Vegetarian Specialties

201 FAT BURNING RECIPES with Cathi Graham

THE SUNRISE TOFU COOKBOOK
with Sunrise Tofu Company

RETURN TO THE JOY OF HEALTH
with Dr. Zoltan Rona, M.D.

JEANNE MARIE MARTIN'S LIGHT CUISINE
Seafood, Poultry and Egg Recipes For Healthy Living

COMPLETE CANDIDA YEAST GUIDEBOOK
with Dr. Zoltan Rona, M.D.

THE POWER OF SUPERFOODS with Sam Graci

RECIPES FOR ROMANCE / Passionate Poetry,
Aphrodisiacs and Menus For Loving

YOUR NATURAL MEDICINE CHEST

FLOWER POETRY / GODDESS POETRY

SOULMATE REALITIES

WEBSITE www.jeannemariemartin.com

DEDICATION

For all who hunger for the truth and seek to know
Why their life is how it is.

This book is also especially for my mother,
My beloved Mom-o.
Your love and support are invaluable.
You have grown and opened to seeing some of the
purposes behind and beyond this life.

ACKNOWLEDGEMENTS

My heartfelt thanks and appreciation for my friends
at the Edgar Cayce Center: The Association of Research
and Enlightenment
and the Heritage Store in Virginia Beach,
John and Melissa Goodheart,
and especially Gloria Siegel.
You helped me through my accident
and helped turn a devastating life incident
into a healing journey of discovery
and an opportunity to complete this book.
Also special thanks to my dear Aunt Betty
who has given me loving support.

IMPORTANT NOTE

All the poetry in this book not attributed to another author
was written and copyrighted by Jeanne Marie Martin.
The actual names of most people in this book
have been changed to protect them and their privacy.

THE RIVER DAUGHTER

I am the River Daughter.
I am the Joy of Spring.
I am the Song of Heart's Love,
Of me the Poets Sing.

Oh, Let the River Flow over me.
Oh, BE that Joy Divine.
I am forever growing.
It will all soon be mine.

I stand upon a green, green hill
And from it I can see –
The city and the River Flow.
They're one in Harmony.

My feet are rooted to the hill.
My hair blows in the breeze.
My arms are branches dancing.
I am living with the trees.

Oh, Heart cannot contain this Love,
This Beauty that so shines.
Forever I will let it flow
To creatures of all times.

To everything that has the hope,
The seed of Life within –
This is but a taste of it.
Now Heaven just begins!

First Words – Prelude

"I know your life has been hard,
But you are what you are because of it.
The best steel must go through the fire.
Being Loving, Beautiful or Talented is not enough.
We must be Strong."

Charles Dickens
David Copperfield

Generally, I do not like Forewords or Prefaces, but these "First Words" are a powerful key and an intricate part of my journey in this story. This may be the most important chapter in this book. So read on...

I believe God wants me to write this book. There is nothing else to do! I have been lying in my queen-sized bed that I bought in anticipation of getting a boyfriend, after I moved into a new living space. Instead of getting a boyfriend, I am wearing a large neck brace that stretches from the middle of the back of my head to the top of my shoulder blades and it curves up, around and over the sides of my lips, stretching down to my breasts. I have a broken neck.

2 THE RIVER DAUGHTER

It doesn't take a Louise Hay to sense the irony in this situation. Perhaps as much as I want a new boyfriend, I see him as a-"brace"-ive (abrasive), confining and limitating? Perhaps this view of my situation is incorrect and I have chosen to be too hard on myself? There are other circumstances in my life more confining at this time: finances, deciding what city to live in, what direction to travel in next and what aspect of my career to pursue? Realistically, the later items are more relevant, but the boyfriend idea got you thinking, I'll bet, and seemed far more exciting. It is the writer's prerogative to shift the reader into a multitude of perspectives!

Let's get back to my broken neck. It was broken from the top to the bottom of vertebrae – C1. I've had frequent dizzy spells, headaches, pain, some nausea and more. I found out who my real friends are and they fed me, drove me to the doctors, bought me food, cleaned my house and gave me loving support and encouragement. My doctors say I could be, and indeed should be, paralyzed from the neck down. It is a miracle I am not dead say the car crash investigators. My car is totaled and one of the main reasons I am not – is God wants me to write this book. I "see" this. I know it is the truth.

Even my friend Virginia, who is a psychic reader, says my accident happened in order to push me into writing this book. I had put off writing my personal story to pursue some new career goals. Now I know that nothing is more important for me to do right now than to write this book. I am not allowed to die until I tell my life story. There are lessons and insights provided by my lifetime journey that I am meant to share with others. God still has work for me to do, and that includes inspiring people to live life fully. Life is a precious gift and not a bit of it should be wasted.

Tonight, I watched *The Pianist* starring Adrien Brody and I was thrown back into images and memories of my last lifetime as a Jewish woman in a German prison camp. Just watching that movie was more devastating than any memory I have from this present life incarnation. Some past life remembrances make a more lasting impression on the psyche than others.

I have discovered that everything is connected. I am on the verge of "seeing" how this car accident is related to my last incarnation as a Jew. I was beaten, raped, tortured and finally torn apart by two German shepherds while trying to escape a nightmare I did not know how to wake up from – then.

Now I know that:

1. I create my own reality.(What I believe, I make true.)
2. I get what I concentrate on. (I have the power to change my reality.)
3. I am unlimited.
4. My moment of power is now.

These power statements are from the Huna – Hawaiian Philosophy and are included in similar words in many other of planet earth's sacred texts.

I intend to show "how" these principles work in my life and ultimately in every life, within the pages of this book. My present life purpose or karma (1) is to tie up loose ends or complete bits of karma left over from hundreds of past lives.

My dharma (spiritual life purpose) is to share what I have learned about the value and messages that past lives can bring us to help everyone who is ready to know, understand, and expedite the completing of their past karma. Then each individual who wants to proceed can more speedily fulfill their life's purpose and be ready to live their destiny.

All our destinies are intertwined. Every victory in life – every act that elevates a single consciousness, affects the entire human race and lifts everyone a notch closer to our shared destiny.

All of our destinies are to live in our highest consciousness as sons and daughters of the Divine and as spiritual beings without beginning or end. When we wake up to this knowledge that has always been, when we fully accept our immortality – there will no longer be a need for delusions of lifetimes, pain, suffering and longing. We will be the very fullness we pretend to seek, here on this earthly plane. We will be – awake!

Footnote: (1) Karma is the law of "what you do comes back to you." Therefore: "Do onto others as you would have them do unto you." Karma is reward or punishment in the form of a good or bad experience that is the result of past thoughts and/or actions. It can be the result of this life – a moment, a day, a year or a decade ago – or a past life. The Old Testament version of karma is: "An eye for an eye. A tooth for a tooth." There is also a higher perspective on karma as a law of balance as talked about in the New Testament. Karma, an East Indian term, can also be a lesson in soul growth. Even if someone is murdered, if the killer completely repents and has fully learned the lesson of: "Thou shall not kill," then Grace enters the karmic picture. By Grace, what comes backs to a killer or any other person who creates karma can then be lessoned considerably. Return lessons, by Grace, have the opportunity to be milder, lighter and allow for speeded up or even "instant karma." According to John Van Auken in *Past Lives And Future Relationships*, the purpose of the karmic or universal law is: "not retribution or punishment but education." He states: "The intention of the law is to provide each soul with an insight into just how its desires, actions, thoughts and words affect itself, others and the Whole."

"Through every thought of goodness, a wicked person becomes better, a wild animal less savage, and a poisonous plant less dangerous. There is a rise and fall woven together in everything, and the whole of creation… is striving together upward to the light…"

Manfred Kyber, The Waldorf Press
The Three Candles Of Little Veronica

THE ROAD TO REALITY

It's a long road back,
When you finally wake up
To the fact that you're asleep.
All this life does seem
To be a dream to me
And every bit of truth,
A wakened memory,
Of a life more real
Than real of earth can ever be.
The road to my true home
Is walking back
Through all the things I've been.
Till I become the things I AM
And was in the beginning
And will be in the end.

Dwelling on the past is not how I live my life today. The present usually keeps me busy along with occasional hopes for future achievements. "NOW" takes up my power, presence and determination to make every moment as full and rich with the flavors of life as possible. When I teach or write, play or work – I usually give 100% and that makes what I do deeply satisfying and rewarding in ways that multiply my joys.

I have not always been this way. I used to spend months, even years, regretting one mistake or one moment that I wished I could do over and make perfect. Perhaps I wanted to control the outcome of my interactions – with friends, family and especially lovers. But I have learned – to surrender, to let go and to know that the best I can do each moment is enough.

"Don't cry over spilled milk." Just clean it up and get on with what matters most. Part of my ability to get on with life comes from the knowledge that some things cannot be changed or rather should not be. The best things in life have a way of working themselves out.

Some things "are" or they "become" consistent to a certain degree, if they are meant to stay in our lives. What is truly possible and best has a way of sticking around if it is right for a person. If, with all my efforts, I can not find a way of making something or someone stay in my life – then something else must be better for me. I find as I remove what I do not really want or need from my life – what I do want or need has room to manifest.

Sometimes, the past plays an important part in securing the present. Old baggage, or karma from this life and past ones, has a way of presenting itself over and over again – like multiple ripples in a lake after a stone is thrown in – until with effort, these past karmas are dissolved and the ripples dissipate into a clear lake. Only then can I see my real self and avoid the cycles of rebirth and death or reincarnation that cause each of us to live many, many lifetimes in search of the perfection that actually lies within us. We relive the "ripple effect" time after time, life after life, until we progress and often we only progress because we are tired of doing it again and again, and we cannot stand to "not proceed."

I started writing these last pages today because I caught myself watching a TV rerun and halfway through it – I was bored. I had just seen it too many times and decided not to drag myself through it again. Why do people watch TV reruns? Or for that matter – see a favorite movie over and over again? I think it is because we have not quite absorbed all the information we want or require from that experience yet. There is still something "new" to see in that show we feel drawn to repeat. If there were nothing new to perceive in it we would turn it off. It would be boring. But every time we grow and change as human beings, which is hopefully a steady process, we can repeat an experience – with a show, a book, a person or an event – because we do see it differently each time. Something that first escaped our notice becomes visible, or as I've stated often, to any who would hear me: as our consciousness rises, we see old situations in a new, more profound light and we derive something – an energy if you will

– that gives us juice. It feeds us, supports and sustains some part of us that wants, or perhaps needs to be, fed.

Ever watch a sci-fi show like *Star Trek*, the *X-Files* or *Charmed* or a movie like: *"12:01"* or *"Ground Hog Day"* and seen the heroes repeat a day over and over again until they realize what is happening: "Hey this looks familiar. I think we've done this before." But why is this repetition happening? Time repeats until the outcome – the destiny is changed! We are destined or doomed if you prefer to believe, to repeat the past (at least the essence or lessons of it) until we can change – our attitudes, our way of seeing or perceiving as well as our way of approaching and resolving a situation.

Thus I have shared with you insights into my own life – and your own. I am one of those rare individuals who from early childhood has earned, or been given by grace, the ability to "see." I believe that I gained this vision in a past life (one as a nun). I have seen, in dreams and waking visions, my past lives: my biggest mistakes, my dearest loves, my greatest joys, my worst tragedies, and I have been given the capacity to change the past and ultimately the present and future – in this lifetime, and eliminate the detrimental effects of bad karma, that is to burn the "seeds of karma" – once and for all.

Have I succeeded in these endeavors? In many ways – yes! Overall, I have accomplished what few see, feel, experience and have the opportunity to change. In some cases, I suppose I may have failed as I still have a lot to learn before I can love – my experiences, others and myself – completely and unconditionally in each moment of my earthly experience. To love completely and unconditionally in each moment is a true sign of spiritual realization. My spiritual astrologer says that this lifetime for me is one of the most difficult a human can face. He says I experience in one year what most people experience in twenty and I feel twenty times more deeply what others feel. I have traveled a long, long, hard way. And there are "miles to go before I sleep…" or rather: before I rest in the divine consciousness. Many schools of spiritual thought view this in an opposite light. They would actually call this "awakening" to divine consciousness and our lifetime experiences here on earth: dreams or maya, which is illusion.

Not everyone is ready to handle the karma of seeing (or feeling) past lives. There are many, many individuals who find this lifetime alone, to be far too challenging, so they turn to:

overeating, alcohol, cigarettes, drugs, excessive sex or TV, over-shopping/working/playing, sugar, chocolate or any one or more of an endless array of addictions to hide in. This way, they can delay the realizations and lessons this life provides and avoid moving ahead in consciousness. The above substances can dull the senses, block our acceptance of what is truly real and also interfere with natural perceptions of other lifetimes, higher realities and even divine ecstasies. These spiritual realities can become faint dreams and distorted traces or remembrances of our true identities. We are divine creatures trapped in human skins or more notably we are trapped in human dreams that have become our mistaken realities. Our dulled senses have been trained to believe in the nightmares of human existence and to ignore the echo of our true heritage in the Divine.

What we perceive as intuition, a faint essence of Divinity or universal/cosmic consciousness, is indeed 99% of our true "beingness." We're lost in the one percent dream of earthly, human living. We have created a dream that we have added physical substance to and made so real that we generally prefer to accept our everyday worldly awake state as reality when in truth – our true reality only escapes for most individuals as distant dreams when we are in the sleep state. So we are actually asleep – dreaming that we are awake! The conscious mind controls our view of reality in the daytime, but at night as we dream, what is really true begins to surface and we, trained in earthly pursuits and pleasures, keep stuffing down our faint remembrances of our reality of divinity each morning just as good boys and girls who live as mommy and daddy taught us, rather than in the consciousness that is available to all children until they are "conditioned" to think as other human adults have been taught.

Every true mystic has spoken of this, in his own way – from Krishna, to Buddha, to Moses, to Jesus, to Mohammed. Even modern spiritual teachers like: Edgar Cayce, Paramahansa Yogananda, Swami Satchidananda, Mother Teresa, Alan Cohen, Shakti Gawain, James Redfield and Neale Donald Walsch have urged us to pay attention to messages hidden in dreams and to realities beyond the physical senses.

We are divine beings dreaming that we are limited to human conditions. God cannot save us from earthly wars, famines and catastrophes – he did not create these – we did.

Therefore we have to rise up spiritually in consciousness to a place where these worldly torments dissolve and no longer exist. We, alone, can transform our outer worlds by first transforming our inner worlds to focus on the divine.

Those who cannot accept the realities of this life, are not given insights into past lives. There is an amazing intensity to the experience of witnessing former incarnations that would "fry" some individuals and make living in this lifetime with any degree of sanity, an impossibility. Until an individual can accept the responsibility of dealing with present life circumstances and clear these situations amicably, the past will not be stirred up – consciously – for you to resolve. We're never given "more than we can bear."

Karmic patterns, however, will continue to repeat like ripples from that stone cast in a clear lake. The karma is inevitable. The difference is that more conscious individuals or souls get a faster return on their karma – like "instant karma" whereas less conscious souls may not see a return of their karma for years, decades or even a lifetime or more after an act has been committed. Both bad and good karma are possible. Eventually, one must even overcome the good karma. Good and bad, like hot and cold, are physical dualities that must be transcended so our true divine nature can be made manifest.

All the roots of past karma need to be dug up, like roots of a dandelion, or else a life pattern or ripple may return again and again. All good gardeners know that a dandelion has many deep roots and the plant will grow back unless all the roots are removed from the soil or the plant is killed completely. In the book: *Illusions*, by Richard Bach, the hero Messiah, tells a little girl that the reason she fears flying is because she died in a plane crash in a past life. Once the little girl knows the whole truth and exactly where her fear comes from, she then becomes empowered to totally erase the fear. (That is – get rid of all the dandelion roots.) This she does almost instantly upon knowing the truth, and then she immediately gets on a plane and flys without fear.

All present circumstances do have roots in the past – whether it is many lifetimes ago – when an event originally occurred or just seconds ago when a thought was created. We open the doors of our individual and collective consciousnesses to make our thoughts, wishes, dreams, desires and actions – a reality.

The River Daughter may require more than one reading to obtain all the hidden messages it contains. I have included poetry throughout this book, mostly my own, because I have been writing poetry continually since I was eight years old. Poetry is who *I am!* My life has been poetry. Most of the poetry included here was written when it is given in the story or written later about the time period I am talking about. The poetry is my life and portrays it as much as the story does. Had I the time and inclination, I would put music to my story as well, as I have sung throughout my life, about my life. There have been moments like in all musicals, that I have burst into song at appropriate moments while dancing in the woods, parks or fields or when crying in my room.

This book is one woman's view of what I created in the past and how I deal with it in the present. For better or worse, thankfully, mainly for the better – I have cleaned up old karma from hundreds of past lives and I know that there are less than a few lives to go before I reach my ultimate goal of union with: "God, universal or cosmic consciousness, infinite or innate intelligence, the force, the one, nirvana, satori, samadhi or heaven," if you prefer. I am well on my way to completing the cycles of birth and death and will soon become a true Daughter of the Infinite – *The River Daughter* – awake and alive with the current of energy that flows through all life.

Buddha, when asked if he was a teacher, healer, great saint or a god, answered: "I am awake."

The past is a dream and when we fully awaken – we will have no need to sleep – or to interpret dreams. When the dreamer awakens – reality he finds…

DISSOLVING THE DREAM
All that is of earth must fade,
All the things and creatures made.
What is flesh and blood and bone,
What is leaf and soil and stone –
All are but substance of a dream.
All the five senses real as they seem,
Are maya, illusion, a moment in time,
A wish born of making that cannot abide.
When the dreamer awakens, reality he finds.
The truth of his being has waited inside.
When it comes forth – when all is told,
The essence – man's divinity – is all he can hold.

A longing pure
And not to be described,
Drove me to wander
Over woods and fields,
And in the midst
Of hot abundant tears,
I felt a world arise
And live for me.

Goethe

Chapter One – The Dance Begins

– Childhood –

"Child, child, love while you can…
Never fear though it break your heart –
Out of the wound new joy will start…"

Sara Teasdale

Peacocks strutted with their tail feathers spread in full array, flashing bold eyes of iridescent blues, greens, purples and gold. Nearby drooped heavily laden date palms and fruit trees amidst lush tropical gardens cascading with bold, brilliant, multi-colored blossoms and melodious songbirds. Angels sang and the heavens resounded with joy. Here a lavish feast, of exotic fruits was decked upon a long, richly draped table spread before Divine Beings, dressed all in gold, who were celebrating a great day.

Before my birth, my mother had frequent dreams of these scenes and she knew that I would be a remarkable child.

My mother was a lovely, blonde, American beauty of Finnish, Swedish and Slavic decent. She was born and raised on a farm in Minnesota with her five sisters. She met my father when he was serving in the United States Army.

My French father wanted at least one of his children to be born in his birth land, in his parent's home. I alone, among our family's five children, was born in the same house, laid in the same cradle and delivered into the world by the same midwife as my father, in Port-au-Prince, Haiti, the French West Indies. This Caribbean isle of tropical beauty and poverty is a land of former French possession with a little Spanish and Creole intermixed. The majority of Haiti's population is black with many mixed mulattos and a very small percentage of whites. It has been a land of turmoil and political upheaval for many, many decades.

I was born Jeanne (Marie) Martin (nicknamed Jane), on March 7, 1951 around 3:40 p.m. For less than a year I grew up in this island home before my family returned to the United States and settled in a suburb of Detroit, Michigan. My father was more than a little disappointed that I, his second daughter, was not a son. This, I believe, was one of the foremost reasons I was his least favorite child. This and the fact that he said "I was too much like him." Indeed I had his olive complexion and dark brown hair (unlike my two sisters who were blond at birth and looked more like our mother) and my father and I both had the same strong personality, yet I had a gentler, quieter disposition.

The fourth child (actually third in line) was a boy, which pleased my father greatly until it became evident that he was born sickly with severe asthma and eczema. Not exactly the perfect son he had hoped for to carry on the family name. This later became another thorn in my father's side and another reason to blame God for his burdened life. Despite underlying seeds of discontent, our family of six appeared somewhat average and felt comfortable enough in those early years.

Outside of a number of childhood illnesses, my life was happy and idyllic until the age of seven. I was a bright, intelligent young student who always excelled in school and I was the favorite of teachers, classmates and my home neighborhood as well. Life was simple, poor, and rich with contentment. My parents seemed happy and life was good and full of promise.

Probably one of the worst experiences of my young life was being chased up a fence by a Doberman Pinscher around the age of five. I sat on a chain fence, clinging desperately to it while screaming and crying for what seemed like forever. (It was actually about fifteen to twenty minutes.) Finally, a neighbor lady spied me and ran to rescue me. I clung to her for my dear life. This was the beginning of my fear of dogs in this life.

I recall having visions and guiding dreams from my angels as early as age four. At the age of seven, I had a very disturbing dream. My angels came to me and told me that my happy existence would soon change forever. They showed me pictures of my new life and told me that my family and I would be moving soon into a new house and neighborhood. They showed me visions of how I would suffer there. They told me to be strong and that they would always be with me. My angels assured me that I would be all right and in the end all would be well.

I was devastated and cried inconsolably for several weeks. My mother was at a loss trying to comfort me. How was I aware of our family's move before I was told and why was I so sure I would be unhappy in our beautiful new home?

The angels' predictions came to pass just after the move. We moved from a racially mixed inner city school district to an all white suburb school zone and my lovely tanned complexion and pride at being born in my tropical island – Haiti – brought insults from the other children. According to them I was black and a "nigger." For seven years I was tormented, beaten and misunderstood by other school children. My outgoing personality became withdrawn and I became shy and fearful of children my own age and older. So, I turned to younger, neighborhood children for friendship.

As early as age seven, I have had recollections of experiences that I knew were mine, yet I was different – I was somebody else. I was sure I had been black during some time period. I felt it. I just couldn't understand when it was. I did not understand anything about past lives at this early age, but I had dreams and vague visions of myself in other bodies as someone else. Looking back from the present, I believe I have lived several lifetimes as a black person and during them I had been taught to be ashamed of who I was. In this lifetime, after feeling shamed, belittled and unworthy because of my skin color, I eventually developed a strong sense of myself, a pride in my Haitian heritage and an appreciation of the beauty of my lovely tanned complexion. With this came a love and acceptance of people from all ethnic and racial backgrounds.

Dreams, nightmares and mental pictures of prison camp life also haunted me intermittently from this early age of seven and for many decades beyond. I envisioned a fat German lady barking orders while brutality and severe punishments including physical blows were dispensed freely. German Shepherd dogs patrolled a dismal, brown, muddy courtyard surrounded by menacing rows of barbed wire. In this camp I was starved, beaten, raped and eventually torn apart by two German Shepherds as I tried to escape. This violent death ended that lifetime in the early 1940s for me. Because I was previously starved, I've gotten in the habit of stockpiling food in this lifetime. I always keep a several month supply on hand and get nervous if I have less. Also, I have had a terrifying fear of dogs from a very young age. I have seen previous lifetimes (before the prison camp one) where-in I feared dogs as well. Two huge, larger-than-life, iron dogs on the steps of a Hindu temple petrified me in one life.

The prison camp pictures or "visions" haunted me early in this life. I did not understand what I saw. It was the 1950s and my family did not yet have a television that projected these kinds of pictures. Why did I see these images? Where did they come from? Though these images confused and frightened me, I kept them private as I had a greater fear of how others would perceive them and me.

Later, much later at age nineteen, the reasons for these experiences began to unfold. My young childhood was a "reflection" or "ripple in a stream" of these prison camp visions. I eventually learned that problems of other lives repeat continually in a similar form until they are overcome. Past lives are like ninety percent of an iceberg that are underwater (subconscious) and the present is the ten percent of the iceberg above the water line (conscious) that is a remnant or reflection of past lives. The present ten percent part continues or repeats, projecting bits of past life reflections until all of the past surfaces and becomes conscious knowledge like a "melted" iceberg and the complete past experiences have been resolved or healed.

For me, my prison camp in this life was living with my dad.

After I turned seven and my family moved into our new neighborhood, my father took over running our family household and he did it with a terrifying iron fist. Family problems: money, infidelity, child-care and work constraints burdened my parents and their relationship became strained and eventually distant. One night I sneaked a peek at my parents rolling on the floor, having a fight. My father struck my mother and she got a kitchen knife and told him if he ever touched her again, she would kill him. As far as I know, he never hurt her again. My mother worked full time and my father worked part-time occasionally while attending university.

My father was rigid and exacting in his treatment of us children and punishments were plentiful, painful and humiliating. One wrong word, gesture or inappropriate action – such as eating the last donut in the house, could warrant four to six hours standing up straight with your nose in the corner. Slouching brought sharp lashes with a leather belt and huge red welts formed on the buttocks and legs that lasted for days.

If my father was in a particularly foul mood, he would shout personal and political statements that I and/or my other transgressing siblings had to repeat – word for word – and reply to. The answers had better be what he wanted to hear. During and after, even the most severe punishments, we were frequently required to say: "I love you daddy."

There were other tortures. A severe lashing of leather on a bare bottom of a dozen strokes or more from "the whip," left me or a brother or sister too bruised and bleeding to sit properly for days. Part of the torture included his request for us to bring his belt for our punishments. How I dreaded the sight of a leather belt lying on a bed – even to this day it sends a shudder through me. He used all his strength, with each stroke of the belt on our bare bottoms, to teach us lessons like: never lie – always tell the truth – or else... He said he did it for "our own good." My mother often tried to reason my father out of hurting us but he was relentless and I believe she was just thankful he no longer struck her.

We children lived in constant fear. I would often hide in closets, outdoors, or under the covers – in or under my bed, shivering with fear and terror at the thought of my next punishment.

My two sisters and then one brother and I were also dad's little servants: "make me tea, bring me milk (he had a stomach ulcer), draw my bath, clean the bathtub, clean the house," or "everybody drop to the floor and collect dust balls from the carpet" (so dad would not have to vacuum before mom got home from work), for up to an hour. Mom still did the major housework and ironing.

Once, on Christmas morning when I was about five or six years of age, my father, in an angry fit, threw me down the basement stairs. I personally still have no recollection of this incident, but I bear the scars on both knees to this day and my head has more stitches in it than a baseball.

Later, around the same age, my siblings and I were with my father, visiting one of his friends and I climbed up on a kitchen counter to get more treats for all of us. I remember that I had on my favorite bright green dress with tiny white polka dots. My father's friend spied me leaning over with my little ruffled panties and pulled them down and bit me very hard on my bottom. I cried inconsolably as the bite was quite painful and the scar lasted many days. My father brushed aside my complaint as an innocent gesture on his friend's part but I was deeply hurt and humiliated. As retribution, father's friend tried to give me an Aunt Jemima doll he received from his mother that sat over the toaster as a cover. I loved that doll but my father would not let me have her. That act of his, ignoring my pain and upset, lost my father all future trust from me. I also grieved a long while over the doll that I was quite attached to and wanted very badly.

Another time, around age eight, it had been my turn to draw my father's bath and it was not hot enough to suit him. He raged at me from the bathtub (unknown to my mother who was then working) and after he was through, he made me sit in his dirty, cold bath water for a full hour to punish me and teach me to "do a better job next time." Afterwards, I got to clean the bathtub. In my naiveté, I was certain for weeks after that I was pregnant. I felt dirtied, humiliated and defiled by my father's treatment of me, but I dared not complain or tell my mother or anyone.

Sometime in between these events, my father, older sister Trixie and I were in a major three-car accident on an icy hill. We were in the last car and my head plunged into the front windshield as it shattered. Miraculously, I was only slightly injured with minor cuts and bruises. My father and sister were not harmed.

In the midst of this hell, there were happy moments. During childhood, I loved wandering alone in nearby woods and fields, dancing, playing with wildflowers, collecting miniature shells and sitting in trees or beside the local Rouge River. Here I dreamed of happier lives I saw small glimpses of. I spent hours gazing into the Rouge River – remembering. I was absolutely certain that if I could just concentrate hard enough I could remember something – I knew – that I "used" to do with great frequency. I had memories of diving into bodies of water and all the cells of my body dividing and going off in different directions within the waves. Then these many particles of myself would rise up into the sky and collect together again and I would be this – creature, this gorgeous being of light, energy, stars and incredible power. I envisioned myself as some sort of star creature or nature spirit who ruled earthly elements of water, air, earth and fire – and encompassed them all.

I was positive I could be this creature again if I just thought hard enough and long enough. If I could only just remember how I used to do this! (In later years, I had extensive perceptions of this lifetime of mine as a "nature being" and wrote numerous poems about this past life reality.) My exact feelings at this young age are epitomized in this poem written in my mid-twenties:

MEMORIES OF "GROWING PAINS"

Before…
I sat by the river
Hour after hour,
Day after day –
Waiting, watching, wishing,
Hoping –
By the river,
Flowing, flowing.
Wanting to jump in.
Praying that I might
Jump in and just dissolve
Within the waves,
Be one with it all
And never rise again
To mortal life and lies –
To a life I do not understand
And realities I despise.
I seek oneness, beauty and love.
Where does truth lie?
In the river, endless river –
Flowing by.
Let me mingle with the river
– The river of real life.

Like little Veronica in the book: *Three Candles for Little Veronica*, I eventually put these thoughts behind me and concentrated on worldly things. Such "visions" were fantasies I was told. Real life included the five senses, not my many daydreams. I was supposed to live in "the real world".

ELUSIVE

Do you hope to know me?
– To hold me within your limited grasp?
It would be easier if you tried to harness a cloud
And keep it for a pet.

One of the things I loved above many others was tending the over 100 rose bushes in our back yard. I was so in love with nature and so content among the roses in the garden, and in the woods surrounded by wildflowers. Like a nature goddess, I belonged close to these. These roses were a reminder to my father of his boyhood home in Port-au-Prince, Haiti. When dad was in a good mood, he and I also shared working on a large stamp album and took great pride in our unique collection of nature and fairy tale stamps from Haiti and Hungary in particular.

You could always tell what kind of mood my father was in by the type of music he played on the stereo. If he was angry or in a foul mood, he played the "*War of 1812.*" In between times, he played opera and in good moods he played: Debussy, Tchaikovsky, Mozart, Bach or Wagner's *Tristan and Isolde.* I learned to love all kinds of classical music from his vast record collection. He had a tendency to be spend thrifty (on himself).

On the days when my father was in an especially good mood, all the children and he danced all over the house and on the furniture, to French and Spanish Latin music. The girls wore long, old satin, thrift store skirts and we all shook maracas and tambourines. Twirling and gyrating to the rhythms of French and Spanish West Indian music, we danced for hours until we were completely out of breath. My father had been a dance instructor with Arthur Murray for several years. After all, when dad was in a good mood, the whole world was smiling and there was great occasion for celebration. What better time to rejoice? Yet, the good times grew less and less with each year that passed.

Unknown in those days, my father had a chronic case of intestinal parasites from the French West Indies where he and I, alone from our family, were born. I, too, had these parasites that were not to be discovered until I was thirty-seven and he was dead. These parasites caused his ulcers and I believe, his extreme temper and radical mood swings from deep depression, sadness and regrets to elation.

For myself, these parasites contributed to anorexia, skin rashes, headaches, pains, memory problems, nausea, shyness, depressions, and extreme fears that would later take me through the gates of Hades to anxiety attacks, hallucinations and nightmares that took me into Dante's Inferno.

Beyond these childhood glimpses of heaven and hell, there was another lifetime – a happier one that surfaced between the dismal recurrent reflections of my last lifetime as a young Jewish woman in a German prison camp.

The second lifetime before the previous one, I was living in France as a nun for over fifty years. I had developed a profound inner awareness and unshakable confidence in a higher power – God. From a very young age in this present lifetime I prayed for many hours at a time. I sang hymns from my present Catholic upbringing and devoted my life to the service of God. I was steadfast in this faith and often had visions of angels, Mary, and sometimes of Jesus and God.

MEDITATIONS

Meditations in the night and
Dreams of Peace and Joy,
Last night in sleep
I tossed and turned in Bliss.
But now I can't remember why.
My soul was filled with strength,
My mind with healing.
O night of nights,
Your stars came out
To shine and fill me.
In the morning I rose
Like a sun of light.

I felt at one with God and the universe at these times and I knew – I knew throughout my being – that God was real and there was a Divine purpose for everything that happened in life. I knew I only had to ask God for answers and eventually I, too, would know the reasons why everything was the way it was and happened the way it did. The truth did not strike like lightening, it unfolded slowly, like the petals of a rose and it had layers upon layers of depths (like skins of an onion), each of which led to a greater understanding of how the laws of the universe worked and could be altered or mastered if one had proper knowledge of their intricate patterns.

My many hours of daily prayer, for sometimes two to four hours at a time, were a safe refuge from my tortured young life. I was truly happy and found tremendous peace in these hours I spent with God.

On occasion, I got several of the neighborhood kids to pray with me for short periods of time. We would wrap ourselves up in light blankets or sheets and play at "being nuns." This game did not go over very well with some of the kids' mothers who were Protestant and they would sometimes drag their kids home amidst their protests of "We were having fun".

When I made my first Holy Communion, I was so happy to be able to wear a lovely white dress and veil and I finally got to use, for one day, a darling little white lace purse my mother had saved over a year for me and said was mine. I only got to use it for one day, and then my mother said she'd put it away for me until I was a little older. Over a year later, I found out my mother had given the purse away to the next door neighbor's little girl, for her hope chest, as I did not have one.

I was so deeply wounded by this act of my mother. I was certain that she did not love me nor think me worthy of that precious little purse. I felt it was the dearest possession of mine. How could she give away something that was so special to me? It took me well over a decade to forgive this slight that said to me that I was not good enough.

From a very young age, I had the ability to find lost objects, make my sincerest wishes come true and even occasionally, predict the future. At age 10, I successfully predicted the birth of my youngest brother on a Friday night. I knew he would be a boy and our pregnant next-door neighbor would have a boy also.

With the birth of my youngest brother, Benjamin, my mother became seriously ill. She was weak and unable to care for herself or the baby. Her hands constantly dripped a clear fluid that looked a little bit like candle wax melting and my older sister, Trixie and I had to wrap them, help care for her and even wipe her after she went to the bathroom. This mysterious ailment of my mother's lasted several months. Though we had some limited outside help, we two older girls were relied on to also help care for the new baby. Trixie and I were happy to help our mother and the new baby. I developed an instant bond with little Benjamin. We adored each other and I became a second mother to him and loved him like my own. Later, at age nineteen, I realized that I had indeed been Benjamin's mother in a past life. We could not have been closer in this life. He brought me tremendous joy that dissolved many of the pains of my troubled, adolescent life.

My father loved Benjamin above all his other children. He never struck him, scolded him or hurt him in any way. He called him the love child and his nickname for Benjamin was "Love". This was the son he had always wanted. My other brother, who had been born with asthma and eczema, had to be tied to his crib so he would not scratch himself. This was a major disappointment to my father. In Ben, he had the precious, healthy son he had waited through four other children to acquire. Benjamin stood, like a trophy, on the front passenger seat of the car when my father drove. (Children's car seats were not lawfully required in those days.)

Once when I was playing with Benjamin, he fell and got a dark bruise on his forehead. I was beaten and punished for days until it healed. "How dare you hurt my child, my Love," my father said to me. "How dare you hurt my Love!"

My mother and I had been nuns together, lifetimes ago. Despite some of our differences, we have had an incredibly close bond from my birth. It was a great treat for me to go to work with my mother and spend the day with her at her business office where she was a secretary, for a day or so a month, during the summer months when school was out. I would get to sit in one of the empty offices and draw or do "pretend paperwork." Sometimes I read the office magazines. I felt very businesslike and important when I visited her office.

One time, at age eleven (about 1962), while I was in her office, I had a profound experience while reading a poem in *Look* or *Life* magazine. The main part of this poem has stayed in my memory my entire life. It began:

To live without love
Is like living on a desert,
Like dying of hunger and thirst,
Like crying alone in the dark,
Like ignoring why we were born.
To live after all is to love.
My friend, there are many kinds of love…
Prayer of a Vietnamese Soldier

This poem haunted me and made a profound impression on me. It has proven to be one of the most important poems of my life. I memorized this part of it and have never forgotten it. It epitomized for me, my lifelong belief that nothing that exists is more important than love.

My mother and I have shared many lifetimes. From youth, I seemed to have a sixth sense with my mother, or "mom-o" as I affectionately called her and I could always tell what she was feeling and anticipate her needs. I still treasure the many times my mother spent reading my siblings and me fairy tales and kids' stories. Some of the best ones she made up herself. We would laugh and laugh over the antics of one mischievous "Dennis the Menace" type little boy she wrote about and told us stories of over and over again. We never tired of them. Also, I'll never forget all the games she taught us and played with us whenever she had a free moment. Though she worked long hours as a secretary/office manager, and often bused back and forth to work an hour each way and there was laundry, ironing, cleaning, and cooking to do – she always found time to play games that all of us kids loved. We played board games, Go Fish and Old Maid. And from age eight, we learned to play canasta, penuche and rummy. Games we all still love to this day.

My father was jealous of our closeness and accused me of being my mother's favorite. This was one of his many reasons for beating me nearly twice as often as my other siblings. As I got older, my mother backed away from me to protect me and I felt more alone than ever.

Besides my psychic abilities during youth, there were special "treats" or visions for me to see as well. Once, before age ten, for seven consecutive nights, the angels took me all around the world to see all the sights – beautiful places and people from every culture and ethnic background. On this journey, I remember visiting Japan, Greece, Egypt, France and a multitude of exotic places. It was a week of unbelievable joy and excitement. Each night, I was anxious to go to bed and continue my promised adventures. I did not realize at the time that this was astral travel. (2)

Childhood was full of similar experiences. After age seven, I withdrew and became a quiet, shy, introspective child, afraid to talk to most people except for my family and younger children.

Footnote (2) Astral travel is out-of-body travel by a person's soul or spirit, which retains a silver cord connected to the physical body.

I often spent many hours alone, daydreaming and enjoying my many visions.

At the time, I never questioned the normalcy of such experiences. I had nothing to compare them with. Dreams and visions were as real to me as everyday life and usually they were much happier and safer than my present physical world.

Only later, around age nineteen and beyond, did I start to piece together the meanings of these abilities and visions in my present life. I began to comprehend that my positive spiritual experiences, astral travel and prophetic insights were gifts of the spirit earned in other lives or given to me by grace from God. My past life visions were recurrent patterns from other lifetimes that I needed to understand and to heal before they continued again in this life and incarnations to come.

But perhaps I am getting ahead of my stories here. Everything in my life has been explained to me in natural progression. I have found that there is an answer to every question. Nothing needs to remain a mystery – forever. In time, all secrets reveal themselves. "Ask and it shall be answered and given to you." Just be careful what you ask for. You will get it – eventually, but will you be glad you did? I've heard it joked about that: "There are long exchange lines at the Gift Return counter in Heaven."

QUESTION

To know so little
And yet so much,
To reach the sky
Yet the earth barely touch:
Why am I allowed
To see this much?

. . .

IF ONLY FOR A MOMENT...

Shake your hair down on me trees.
Cover me with leaves.
Might I lie with you
Upon the earth before you crumble?
Might I share in part your death,
If I might be so humble?

Chapter Two – The Awkward Years

– Adolescence –

"Be Strong!
We are not here to play, to dream to drift;
We have hard work to do, and loads to lift;
Shun not the struggle – face it; 'tis God's gift."

Maltbie Davenport Babcock
Be Strong

Both my parents were raised as strict Catholics and, before they met, my father had intended to be a priest and my mother wanted to be a nun. So, during the autumn of 1962, when I was eleven, (after my brother Benjamin's birth), my parents took me and my older sister, Trixie, out of public school and placed us in a private Catholic school. Despite the high cost of private schooling, my parents were determined to give us the benefits of a proper spiritual upbringing.

I was more than disappointed; I was crushed. I missed out on spending sixth grade in public school with one of the best teachers our local grade school had to offer. My older sister Trixie had a remarkable year with Mrs. Tamara the previous year and made a history scrapbook full of fascinating pictures and stories of Egypt, Persia, Greece, Rome and other ancient civilizations and now I could not do the same! I dreamed of making my own notebook and now, no amount of tears or pleading could keep me in Mrs. Tamara's class.

Instead, I had somber nuns to learn from and new class subjects in which I was far behind my classmates. I was already supposed to know how to diagram a sentence in Sister Mary's class. I had never done it before, yet she made me stand at the blackboard for what seemed like an eternity until she was convinced I actually had no understanding of the process.

SIMPLICITY

Simple I am.
Simple I shall ever be.
Would it bother you
If you don't need
A dictionary to find me?

With Catholic school, came daily morning mass, sometimes Holy Communion and bringing breakfast to school, prayer time, and a whole new set of problems with a new group of children my age. I left behind in public school: the taunting, teasing and being called "nigger," only to encounter – worse treatment.

The kids in Catholic school could swear up a blue streak, unlike the relatively mild-mouthed public school kids. Boys who went to Holy Communion every morning were the meanest and the most belligerent. My incredible shyness and flat-chestedness from sixth through eighth grade (ages 11-14), brought me insults for not being a "real girl." "Flat as a board" was one of the nicer comments; "No tits," was another. For three years, guys whispered to me behind the nuns' backs to "unwrap your lips from my scrotum," and to "stop licking my dick – you're too ugly." Those were the milder of their profanities. Nothing could induce me to repeat the more frequent of their verbal atrocities.

In this school too, I was picked on constantly and beaten by the girls rather than the boys as in public school. I remember once fighting off six girls at once in a deserted hall. I learned to fight like a "wildcat" and eventually, during the eighth grade, they left me alone rather than risk the mutilations of my kicking, biting and scratching – whirlwind line of defense.

There was one midget boy who always sat behind me those three years of parochial school because his name came behind mine alphabetically. He was especially cruel in his sexually-perverted verbal torture of me. He also kicked me brutally as his little legs just reached my buttocks in the desk before his. For years, he added to my father's black-and-blue belt lashes with his frequent kicks to my backside. I dared not retaliate as he was in cahoots with all the tough kids at school.

Finally, near the end of eighth grade, Sister Hope caught him in the act and horrified, she ordered me to hit him as hard as I could. I took great delight in smacking him as hard as I could with my textbook. It mattered little to me that it did not even come close to paying him back for three years of constant torment. I felt exonerated and triumphant. From that day forward, I never let him hurt me again. I threatened, "to tell". I would accept safety any way I could get it! Sister Hope found out this had been a regular occurrence and promised me safety. By God, I was going to take it!

Amidst the angst of parochial school, there were happier consequences and some benefits to attending a Church school. The school had an extensive religious library with hundreds of volumes of lives of every saint imaginable along with all kinds of spiritual Catholic books: songbooks, prayer books, stories of nuns and missionaries, as well as traditional classic and contemporary literature. This was a treasure I devoured with all the relish of a hungry aspirant with stars in my eyes and dreams of being a nun in foreign lands. (Obviously, in this "incarnational leak" my wanting to be a nun was partially a memory of being one in my past lives.) The lives of St. Patrick, St. Francis, St. Clare, St. Catherine, St. John, St. George, St. Therese, St. Agnes, St. Elizabeth and St. Cecelia, in particular, were nectar for my heart and soul. These books were a refuge from every storm in life, for me. Here I found solace, comfort, peace and joy.

I also learned to love the morning mass, especially because it was sung in Latin! It awakened memories of my previous lives (more than one) as a nun and I felt like a nun as I devoted myself to memorizing and perfecting each line I sang. Despite the problems of Catholic school, I dreamed of being a nun and sometimes resented that only boys could hold the special honor of being priests. My spiritual dedication to God grew stronger and deeper in these teen years from ages 11-14.

RAINBOW
Colors, colors, colors –
Vibrant delights!
I see myself a rainbow,
Gloriously bright.
Reds of fire and passion,
Blues of peace and coolness,
Greens that sooth and heal,
Yellows – light and joy,
Pinks of delicacy and delight,
Purples of regality and strength,
Oranges firm and true –
All of a paint box overturned
And spilling every hue.
All run from me in rivers –
Rivers of light, liquid colors –
Bold, Captivating, Illuminating,
Blinding mortal eyes.
Colors flow from me
In spirals and waves of energy.
Liquid colors –
Food and nectar to those who can taste,
Strength and healing to those who seek,
Love and fullness to those who feel.
Real, real, real –
Colors, colors, colors,
Oceans of light, bright hues,
Flowing from me to you.
Do you receive?
All you have to do is…Believe!

I also had the thrill of writing my first magazine article and sending it to *Catholic Digest Magazine*. My father said: "You'll never get anything for it. The world never gave me anything. Why should it give anything to you?" But it did! I received the tremendous payment of fifty dollars for the publishing of my article. This was a lot of money for a fourteen year old in 1965 and I was very proud and thankful. At least now I knew I did not have to share my father's fate when it came to publishing my writing. My father seemed shocked and a bit jealous when my check arrived. Perhaps, he mused, I would do things he could not? Soon after, I won the prestigious honor of receiving a rosary blessed by the pope for an essay about the church.

After eighth grade, I managed to persuade my parents that a Catholic high school was not only too much money, but not worth it for me. I did not want to follow in my older sister Trixie's footsteps and attend the same strict, all-girls parochial school. Those girls wore ugly plaid, pleated skirts and blazers with old-fashioned saddle shoes. Uh Uh! Not for me!

I triumphed when I succeeding in returning to public high school and was relieved to find that I was no longer a complete outcast. I was still perilously shy, but I was free to go unnoticed through the halls and that was a bit of heaven for me. I was finished with being beaten and tormented by my school peers. At last – no particular notoriety!

Until the age of fourteen, I played with dolls and I preferred the company of younger children (they were safer, more accepting of me and easier to understand), than the company of kids my own age. I taught most of the neighborhood children to read and write before they were five and I was their beloved ringleader who led them in songs, dances and games. We often put on musical shows and plays for each other. I taught them every name and story of all the Greek gods and goddesses before they were in the second grade. I organized lemonade stands, rummage sales, competition games and clubs for summer profit and fun. Their mothers loved me and they all thought I would become an exceptional schoolteacher one day.

Summer good times also included small pool parties in our back yard, trips to local public pools and the greatest trips of all, to the Michigan Great Lakes. These days were rare indeed and left an indelible impression on my young mind:

A DAY REMEMBERED

A day comes back to me of youth,
A day of sun and sand and sea,
Boat rides and friends –
A rare one spent with family.

The lake was all colors –
Blues, golds, pinks and greens.
The waves were ever calling me
And over and over in their arms I'd be.

The sand was warm and white and fine
And I built figures and castles high,
   That stood so very proud,
   Beneath the bluest sky.

And there were cottages empty –
Haunted castles to explore,
With ceilings high, windows wide
And oaken beams and doors.

Trees with rustling leaves
And many branches for to climb,
A tower and a fortress –
The grandest one was mine.

There were sand dunes plenty.
Down the hills we'd roll
Or pack across the "desert" sands –
The lake our goal.

There were laughing friends and family.
Food and drink tasted so good to me, to you.
With watermelon, lemonade and franks
And steaks to barbeque.

Best of all I liked to watch
Sandpipers in among the reeds.
Through grass and sand they ran from us
   – Mischievous indeed.

But sometime it had to be over.
The sun beat down upon that endless day.
Why it should be so remembered,
I cannot say.

Packed up we went, quite satisfied,
Into our float boat, taking us home.
But I shall remember that day,
No matter where in life I roam.

Age sixteen brought tears and reawakened fears. My angels and inner guidance told me it was time to learn to be an "adult" now, and I did not know how to interact with teenagers in my own age group. I was painfully honest and could not play the relationship games everyone else my age seemed to excel at. I was awkward, terrified and completely clumsy. I was shunned at school and considered one of the "nerdy" outcasts. So I kept quiet and to myself, hoping for a miracle to help integrate me into a life I did not want or understand. I always preferred the company of children and to this day I am perfectly at home with children of any age.

Another important event in my sixteenth year was my turning away from prayer and God to become an agnostic. I felt my parents and peers were hypocrites and I was disillusioned with my life. My old ways of seeking spiritual solace no longer worked, so I set aside my beliefs, hoping that they would someday resurface in a way that I could comprehend, accept and adapt to my teenage life.

Slowly, and in complete confusion, I attempted to integrate myself into high school life. My favorite classes were Art and English and I excelled at both, except when I had to make a speech. Sometimes I could choke out a sentence or two in front of the class, then I would return to my seat or rush from the room in tears, unable to continue. I preferred an "F" grade to the embarrassment of talking before a class. A firing squad would have been more desirable to me than giving a speech.

On the other hand, I was perfectly comfortable talking with and entertaining before children. I trusted children and felt their acceptance. In a classroom situation, I struggled not only with speaking before strangers, but I felt my classmates' thoughts, opinions and distain for my fearful incompetence. Around this time, I wrote the following poem that speaks for itself:

SOME

Somewhere not far from here,
Someplace I long to be.
Someday I'll find my place there.
Some say it can never be.

Sometime I know I'll find it.
Somehow I just know.

Someway I know I'll be happy.
Something tells me so.

Some may think it a foolish dream, yet
Someone still may know:
Somewhere, sometime, somehow,
Someway, I'll find someplace – I know!

Age seventeen, my junior year at high school, brought the biggest trials of all. This was the worst year of my young life. My father was angry now – every day. Each day brought multiple punishments: many hours standing in the corner and beatings every week, sometimes several times a week. My father ranted and screamed from early morning until late each night. He hated life and everyone. The whole world was "against him" and had "ruined his life" and he was going to make people pay. His children were first on his list for revenge. He hated me most of all because he said I was most like him.

My grades shot down from the occasional honor role to a D minus average. That year, one of my teachers suggested I seek help from a school-sponsored psychiatrist. My mother made fun of me for being her "crazy daughter," and embarrassing her. So I ended the much-needed sessions after these and other insults. My year in total hell continued. I learned to stand straighter in the corner and prayed to faint, as it was an occasional reprieve if my father felt sure it was not faked.

The annual Spring Fair at my Catholic Church brought my best friend, Darla, and I out for a rare evening of fun playing sideshow games and reveling in amusement park rides. For a few brief hours I was in heaven. She and I met a couple of boys and I enjoyed my first kisses. I walked arm in arm with my new guy friend and Darla followed close behind with her guy friend. I was more than content enjoying this innocent time together. I knew I did not have an early curfew, but little did I know that Darla did.

Her parents came looking for her at my house and my father headed the search party. He caught me receiving one of my first simple kisses. Right in front of the entire fair, with thousands of people around, he took off his belt and began beating me mercilessly amidst accusations of "American bitch, whore" and a procession of other words not fit to print.

I fell to the ground and he kicked me many times in the head and stomach as he continued to whip me savagely. I was screaming, crying and begging him to stop, while trying quite ineffectively to protect myself from the constant blows. People were gathering to stare and point. Kids I had gone to Catholic middle school with were looking on in surprise. I wanted the pavement to swallow me whole.

My girlfriend Darla was laughing – saying: "This is ridiculous, we did nothing wrong." I hated her for laughing as I was being beaten, and never spoke to her again from that moment. I would never return to this Church again.

My father continued to beat me and swear until he was tired and satisfied he had done a good job. A policeman finally approached and said that was enough. He said he would put my father in jail if he could. Back then, in the sixties, I suppose he had little authority to interfere between father and daughter. Child abuse was not a major issue in those days as it is today. Parents frequently beat their children under the guise of "discipline."

I spent three days in bed after that, with no doctor to tend the multiple wounds I received from head to toe. The verbal abuse continued throughout my recovery, but at my mother's insistence, he did not beat me again – until my present wounds were healed. Luckily, for my strong bones and me, nothing was broken; but there was bruised and bleeding skin with huge red, black and blue welts and cuts all over my body and head.

My father's rages and punishments continued for months more. Then one hot summer day, my father climbed on top of my sixteen-year old brother, Jonathan, and was punching him in the face. After seemingly endless minutes of ineffectively begging him to stop, my mother, sisters and I jumped on top of my father and dragged him out the front door. We threw him his car keys and locked the door behind him. He never lived in our house again. I refused to speak a word to him for over two years.

After this terrible family "incident," I resolutely vowed that no one would ever harm me again! I decided I would die before I let myself be hurt by anyone, and I have kept this promise and will, throughout this and every lifetime to come.

It was not until I was nineteen that I understood the underlying "karmic implications" (past life occurrences and present beliefs that contributed to these events) of this final brutal episode with my father and the painful beating at the church fair that tortured me throughout nearly two decades of psychotherapy and meditation sessions. It took spiritual understanding to finally rise above the pain and transform it to lessons that did not need to ever be repeated.

Also, two years later, at age nineteen, when I experienced a spiritual reawakening, I had visions of many past lives, including an extraordinary past life with my father. It was a Mayan or Aztec past life during which my father and I were married in primitive South America. (Family members have often been reincarnated together before in different relationships, for many lifetimes.) In one of my few lifetimes spent as "royalty," my father was a haughty, controlling and cruel ruler and I, his wife, was just as arrogant and temperamental. A great battle was being fought in our land and our people were victorious. I watched my father – my husband then – climb to the top of a tall pyramid in proud triumph as I walked behind him in flowing robes: cocky, willful and full of my own self-importance. I saw and felt the wildness of my personality and the blatantness of my emotions. My character was unlike most North or South American personality types found on these continents today.

In present time, it is almost as if the experiences with my father in this lifetime, happened in a movie or a distant past lifetime. Today, these memories are a faint recollection that I write about as a faraway reminiscence. They are water under the bridge of life that one views without emotion, only wonder. These experiences were like dreams and nightmares I could not awaken from when they were taking place. Other dreams, happier dreams, have replaced these old ones that no longer hold emotions or purpose. I have moved on.

Despite my complicated fears after my father's retreat, I began moving into a happier time. It was a time of self-discovery, healing and an exploration of girlhood and romance.

This poem was written in my mid-teens and reflects my youthful struggles with life.

THAT'S LIFE

In the morning
As I wake before the dawn,
I walk along the path
That takes me to the sun.

If he is hidden from my view
By clouds or rain,
It makes me sad to see him
So I cry and feel pain.

He sometimes casts the clouds aside
And laughs and says to me:
"For those who cannot face the day,
No one will weep."

It may bring sadness and pain,
But those who seek
Will find that happiness and love
Can conquer all.

Don't spend days crying.
Crying heals no pain.
Take care lest you be forgotten,
You who are weak and vain.

As I turn to go,
I smile and say I will be brave.
Now I can face the setting sun
And smile – I'll find my way.

COMMUNION

The quiet hills
whisper not a sound,
yet they draw me to them
with a yearning sigh
I cannot resist.
They still ring
with my laughter
and await with open arms
— my coming.
As I steal a bit of sun
and wildflowers
or play in the grass —
all of it is mine.
They gave themselves to me.
The hills hold my tears
and make me Love,
all that I see and feel.
They are a part of me
and in return
I give them a breath of spring.
I would gladly share with you,
one moment of my joy,
for the hills gave me
Unselfish Love
and it is yours for a time.
Tomorrow you may be gone,
but the hills are always mine.

(Written at age 17)

Chapter Three – First Love

"You are never given a wish without also being given
the ability to make it come true."

Richard Bach
Illusions

AND

"Imagination is more important than knowledge."

Albert Einstein

The summer my father left, I began to live. I was seven-teen. My parents had legally separated and it was a relief to feel I could explore the world and date without my father hovering in the background proclaiming, "I never dated a woman until I was nineteen, so why should you date?" That summer of 1968, my girlfriends and I visited the Rouge Pools, several large public swimming pools where the local kids hung out. I got a chance to wear my new leopard bathing suit and some people said I: "looked like a mermaid."

I wanted a boyfriend, but I was terribly shy and afraid of boys. I had shared a few, quick, stolen first kisses at the church fair with a boy, but now I wanted to learn to "make-out." All my girlfriends had done it and they knew how. I was still way

behind even the younger girls, including my little sister, Loni.
So I did my best to find a younger guy to make-out with – just
for practice, so I would not have to be embarrassed later. I
wanted some "experience" before my senior year at high
school, especially since I hoped to find a boyfriend that year.

It was a gorgeous, hot summer, free from my father's
influence. I relished my freedom and my chance to flirt and
explore romance without the fear of repercussions.

The first moment I saw him, I knew he was the right guy,
exactly who I was looking for, to "practice" with. Allen was
fifteen, short, dark haired, blue-eyed, very sweet natured and
exceptionally cute. Somehow, after a little shy flirting, I found
a way to get "make-out lessons" on one of the park picnic
tables with him. I had to hide him from my girlfriends, they
thought a younger boy was absolutely "immature, un-cool" –
being with such a younger boy was "just not done." When one
of my over-zealous friends found out I was making out with a
fifteen year old, I had to give him up, then and there. Allen
understood the pains of "peer pressure" and kindly stepped
aside. We wished each other well and I have always kept a soft
spot of thanks to him in my heart. But I had a couple days of
kissing practice before my friends found out, so I now felt
confident enough to move on to dating a guy closer to my
own age.

A couple months after these experiences, I wrote the
following metaphoric poem about my "hunting" experiences
at Rouge Pools, in my leopard bathing suit:

I AM THE LEOPARD

I prowled about
By hunger swayed,
For food was scarce.
I sought the spring.
Drank to pass time
But could not cause
The want to cease.
Soon on my way,

I joined the hunt,
Made my kill –
A child at play.
Then roamed in shade,
To my surprise
– Caught in a trap,
Captured by the game.

Before the summer was over, I was proud and excited to land a few dates with one of the lifeguards at the pools. I was certainly moving up on the dating scale ladder. I did feel I had a lot to make up for in my social life.

By fall, I was ready, well – at least a little more prepared for high school, for dating and for my greatly anticipated senior year. Without my father at home, I was anxious to do new things. My mother was now happier and freer to be supportive of my siblings and me, so we had a whole new world of privileges. Life was open to explore. Despite my extreme shyness, I was now ready to take chances.

There was still one thing missing in my education of "Boys 101." I now knew how to kiss, but I did not have a clue as to what sex actually was. I had previously changed my youngest brother's diapers and seen both brothers in the bathtub, but I had no idea what the sex act entailed. For years I had been too embarrassed to ask and with the limited information at my disposal – I had "pretended" I knew.

There were a few sex education books in our home hall closet, left by my mother, for my siblings and me, but I never did get beyond the boy and girl body parts section. It was imperative I find out the truth and now had to be the time! I mustered up all my courage and finally asked my best friend, Elaine, to explain it to me. She gladly played mentor and shared the secrets of sex information with her anxious pupil. I was amazed! It was nothing like I had imagined. Armed with this final bit of necessary information, I felt ready to enter my senior year and I was open to all the possibilities it held.

My mother had sewed a few new, simple, summer dresses for me and I wore one proudly on my first day back at school. In art class, I was assigned to a table with three eligible and nice looking guys who were alphabetically destined to sit with me. Only at the end of the school year did I find out that all three of these guys had their eyes on me all year, and were interested in me, and thought I was beautiful. Certainly, I had never thought of myself as pretty. I still saw myself as others had in the past as less than plain and far from attractive. It took some time before I accepted that I was attractive and desirable.

I was too shy to say much at school. Occasionally, a boy would approach me for a chat or to get to know me and I literally curled up and slid away. It was not until nearly spring, a few months before summer graduation, that I allowed a boy to get close enough to ask me out. Even then, I did not go out more than once or twice before my birthday.

For my special eighteenth birthday, in March, my mother gave me the magnificent present of a sleepover party for several of my high school friends. She even contributed a whole fifth of whiskey to the party. She said I was old enough – as long as my friends and I drank it under the safety of her own roof.

Mom let a couple of boys come over for a few hours of the party, in the evening only: Manny and another guy named Jim who was dating one of my girlfriends. Manny (short for Manfred) had been one of the three cute guys who sat at my art table the beginning of the school year. We took an instant interest in each other that night and enjoyed a great make-out session. Before 11:00 p.m., the boys left and we girls got out the negligees and candles and danced and drank much of the night away.

My party pictures shocked the school as everyone erroneously assumed the boys spent the night. After the party weekend, when I returned to school, Manny was out sick for two weeks, so I got caught up with another guy who approached me that first Monday back. It seemed like he was waiting for me and anxious to get to know me.

Ron was one of my most important high school loves for me. He was the first guy who really seemed to like me for who I was. Ron treated me like I was special and very beautiful. I had never truly felt that I was that attractive or desirable before I met him.

He was a handsome, blond, blue-eyed, popular eleventh grader – a whole year younger, which did mean a lot in high school. One year was a huge difference in maturity at that age. Ron was a real James Dean look-a-like. It was hard for me to believe and still harder to accept his overwhelming affections. He wanted me to be "his" girl and was jealous if any other guy even looked at my legs. Ron walked me to all my classes – "for protection." In two weeks, he bought us a set of matching diamond rings with three diamonds on each ring, all for the expensive price of about $100 for the set. It was a hefty price to pay for a high school student, with only a part time job at a gas station, in 1969.

Ron was definitely one of the sweetest guys I have ever known. Sadly, both his parents had died in an auto accident on the way to a movie he vowed never to see. Perhaps that's why he was so over-zealous in his affections for me.

After a few weeks of smothering attention, I had enough and broke off our entire relationship. I felt caged and I wanted to be free. I did not know how to say this nor did I have a clue about how to express any of my feelings at the time. My emotions seemed to be all bottled up inside me. I was not used to listening to my feelings and thinking about what I wanted, I was used to being told how to feel by my father.

But I wanted "out." So I broke it off with Ron and had no more serious boyfriends for the rest of the school year.

TO CATCH A BUTTERFLY

If you try to catch a butterfly, and succeed;
You will either crush its wings in your grasp
Or it will slip free through your fingers.

If you just Love that butterfly
And it feels and knows you will not hurt it,
It will light upon you and take delight
In fluttering around you.

I did, however, continue to date. There were a few men I dated then who still stick out in my memory because of their distinctive qualities.

There was soft-spoken Ray, a "frat" who on the first date pledged me everlasting love and gave me some kind of copper ring to wear, which I returned on the second and final date. If diamonds could not keep me in a relationship, no lesser ring could in those days.

Next was Don, a gentle, lovable, bad boy. He was an easy-going "greaser" with slick, combed back hair and a great motorcycle. I loved riding with him. He carved my initials in his arm with a pencil and got lead poisoning. He probably still has my initials on his arm today.

Last and most intriguing, was Jack, a real Patrick Swaze type with a hot rod GTO and all the charm and charisma a girl could ever dream of. He was well mannered, strong – and elusive. Not the type too many girls could tame. I did not try. He blew away with the wind.

I found out much later that I had completely broken Ron's heart. Over a year after I left high school, he ran into my younger sister, Loni, and told her: "Your sister broke my heart. Now I just love-um and leave-um." That surprised me and saddened me. I was then too disconnected from Ron to have visions of our past lives together but it had to be a strong love bond to elicit such a long-term reaction from him regarding our break-up. In my heart I wished him well and hoped that he would have the strength to move on with his life.

About a month before graduation, my mother and an aunt took my older sister, Trixie, her friend Ellen and me to a popular supper nightclub in Windsor, Ontario, just over the Detroit/U.S. border. We enjoyed an all night concert with Sonny and Cher. Our table was right near the stage and we got to meet them, shake hands and chat with them personally between their songs which featured: "*I Got You Babe.*" This was certainly one of the thrills of my young life, never to be forgotten.

I was dressed in a short black evening dress edged with black feathers, like a sophisticated lady that night. I wore my then traditional Natalie Wood flip hairdo. Not surprisingly, many people told me frequently in those days, and especially that night, that I looked very much like Natalie Wood. This was a high complement indeed for me. That night, I even drank alcoholic mixed drinks with my mom and the other women in our party. They never asked me for I.D. in such company. It was a night of triumph for me. I reveled in partaking in an adult evening out on the town and I felt total freedom and a sense of being grown-up. It was a mark of having made it to maturity for me.

Prom time came, but I was too shy to attend even though a nice male friend gave me an invitation. I was afraid to dance – in public. I might make a mistake – make a fool out of myself, or something. So, I stayed home.

Graduation night brought a wild party at my girlfriend Elaine's house. Friends, family, relatives, students and younger children all gathered to party the night away.

Elaine, her sidekick Susan and I got into the family Pontiac and cruised the local hot rod strip called Telegraph Road.

With six lanes going in each direction and plenty of burger joints along the way, it was the place to drag and be seen by guys. We picked up Manny (the guy from my birthday party) on the way, at his house. I had gotten pretty friendly with him the last month or two of school. He was 6'2," blond, very attractive in his hippie sort of way, Polish, and close to 200 pounds. Manny was a strong-willed Sagittarius with a mellow personality.

This night, Manny and I shared the large backseat of the Pontiac, while my two girlfriends rode up front. It did not take long before Manny and I were making-out and petting heavily. It was a night to remember. It launched a love affair with one of the greatest loves of my life. Also, I drank a fifth of whiskey and a half bottle of Mogan David sweet red wine all by myself, along with junk food and potato chips. It was one of the few times in my life I got totally, completely drunk.

I remember getting home early in the morning and collapsing on the bathroom floor. I peed all over it and my mother had to put me to bed and clean up the mess. In the morning, in the small space between my younger sister's bed and mine, I had thrown-up a bucket's worth. The day was foggy for me at best. After that night, I never drank whiskey again and I never liked potato chips.

A few days later, Manny was at my door. We continued seeing each other nearly every day. Kissing, petting and the then popular "hickies" were our daily sustenance.

My mother allowed Manny and I to put together a little space in our basement with an old couch, TV, fridge and tables so we could have a place to have time alone together. For nearly three months we petted and played and finally one night, when both Manny and I were pretty high from drinking – he was rubbing up against me and I finally decided to let him inside me.

It immediately felt wonderful. To this day I remember the exact sensation. I felt "full" in the most contented kind of way. We just lay there for a long time, with him inside me, feeling each other, before we moved. Then we two virgins experienced our first taste of sexual ecstasy. I can still recall our groans of pleasure. I will never forget the power, passion and beauty of that first time. We loved each other and that contributed to a night of magic together.

I AM LOVED

Today I rise above,
For I am Loved.
I am Loved!
Little have I noticed,
Seldom have I seen,
The Love that did surround me
And still does.
My eyes are open now.
I see and feel it all around.
I am Loved.
I am Loved and I give Love.

Unfortunately, though I remembered every detail the next day, Manny, probably because of his heavy drinking, did not. He could hardly believe we had actually – "done it." It was late summer and that night began some of the hottest love making of my life. It was 1969 (our graduation year) and "69" was very popular then. We were young and agile enough to really enjoy this and every other sexual pleasure two exploring eighteen year olds could discover.

Little did my mother know that the blankets Manny and I covered ourselves with in the basement to fend off the cold while we watched television, covered our half naked bodies. Every time one of my sisters came downstairs to throw a load in the washing machine or dryer, Manny and I were alerted by their footsteps on the stairs and pretended to hug and watch TV. If either of my sisters had thrown back the covers, they would have gotten the shock of their young lives.

Since hickies were a common pastime in the 60's, Manny and I gave each other plenty. We would suck an area three or four inches across, in a circle and cover each other's entire bodies with an outstanding array. It used to take a lot of make-up to cover the hickies that poked out around my clothing.

One day, my mother caught sight of me in the shower and declared: "Jane, we've got to get you to a doctor. You must have bad blood!" Jane was my nickname and my mother was more naïve than most teenagers of the day. Today I have a hearty laugh over the experience, but back then, I was scared and prayed she would forget what she saw and not call a doctor who would expose me. To my relief – she did forget.

Manny and I continued our relationship for a total of nearly one and a half years. Passionate sex and orgasms were plentiful for both of us. During this time I never used birth control. After all, I was only eighteen, I thought. I knew my mother had married at eighteen to my father, but she had been unable to get pregnant until she was twenty-one. I believed whole-heartedly that I also could not get pregnant until I was twenty-one – and married. I was right! (Remember – What you "firmly" believe you can make true. However, I do not advise other's to do this, as they may not have developed this ability.)

Manny and I had a continuing passion that awakened all kinds of faint memories and visions of past lives. Though my visions were rather scarce at age eighteen and I did not yet know about reincarnation, I "saw" us together in other eras and countries. My blossoming mind and emotions freely expressed the following poem during this time I spent with Manny:

DUSK AND DREAMS

It's twilight Love.
Dusk and dreams of thee.
Will you not recall the times
We Loved beneath the trees?
– In ages long past,
In lives you don't recall,
We were Lover's long before
You believe you existed at all.

Once, when Manny and I were having a particularly tender love making session, I was on top of Manny, looking into his eyes and we seemed to be transported beyond our bodies. Our eyes were locked on each other and our faces and bodies dissolved into energy. It was like hyperventilating, it was so intense. My body movement seemed to happen by itself, almost in slow motion and breathing came in simultaneous inhalations and exhalations between Manny and me.

We were transported into an ecstasy we had never encountered before. I rode Manny like a stallion I had control over. I held the reigns of our passion and rose and fell to waves of energy that danced between us. We "came" together in a burst of flames, but I did not stop. I kept going until I collapsed on top of him and could no longer move.

Manny and I felt the rapture of that love's communion for days. He later said to me: "What did you do? It was spectacular!" We had both been blessed with simultaneous full body and soul orgasms that included a taste of divine ecstasy. It was one of the many pleasures Manny and I experienced together in our exploration of sexual delights.

Only many, many years later did I realize that Manny and I had stumbled upon a Tantric Yoga (the yoga of sex which makes sex a spiritual experience) technique for three-way love making: God, Manny and I. But I prefer to accept the knowing that Manny and I had practiced this technique in another lifetime together and remembered it momentarily when we turned inward in this life and tapped into our god-selves.

Manny and I seemed to love each other with an unending passion. However, he never actually believed I had been a virgin for him. He believed the school rumors about me – that I was a "slut" and that I took money in return for sexual favors. Something I have never desired or been able to do – have sex for money – in this lifetime. I have never even had a one-night stand. Manny's erroneous beliefs eventually formed a gap between us. He thought I was too skilled at sex and I liked it too much. We had read a lot of sexual technique books together and I believe my love for him (in this and other lives) made it easy to let go and fully enjoy a variety of sexual explorations with him. Perhaps his doubts about my devotion or my virginity for him were reasons why he drank and smoked so heavily? Or maybe it was just his nature, because he was a big guy or Polish, and at the time, my understanding was that Poles tended to have a larger capacity for alcohol.

Some guys had approached me during my senior year to ask me if I was "booked" and I used to reply with a blank, confused stare. I had no idea what they were talking about. Earlier in my senior year, I made the mistake of being seen in the presence of the "wrong kind of guy." Then rumors went wild that I was a "whore" and there were many nights I cried in sadness and disbelief. At that time, nice women did not have sex until "after" high school and then only in a committed relationship. In those days, I actually cared too much about what people thought about me.

In past lives, I know I was a whore in at least a few incarnations; many women have been. But, a whore in past lifetimes was not always a bad thing to be in other eras. It was often considered sacred and an honorable profession that performed a service to society. In past lives I have been: a Japanese geisha, a Greek witch who traded sex for power, a Chinese hand-maiden, a temple priestess who performed sex for ceremonies and more in other lives. In previous lives, I learned to "pleasure a man" and give him – and myself – the ultimate satisfaction in lovemaking. We do carry over talents from other lifetimes. Several psychics have told me that I have learned a tremendous amount about love that I acquired and retained through many incarnations.

Perhaps that is why, at the present time, in this particular lifetime, I happen to love sex and have a sex drive as potent as most men's. Or, perhaps I am just too healthy right now! My doctors presently say that my natural hormone levels are exceedingly high. They doubt that I will begin menopause until I am in my sixties. I believe it is all my healthful foods, exercise, supplements and spiritual beliefs that constantly keep me looking and feeling about twenty years younger than I am.

Let's get back to Manny's heavy drinking and smoking. Manny's influence got me drinking and smoking more heavily as well. Unlike Manny who was 6'2" and close to 200 pounds, I was a little sliver of a girl, 5'3" and just about 100 pounds. These addictions took a heavy toll on me and I felt my downward tread into poorer health from these bad habits. Finally, things got so bad; I struggled for a way out. All my thinking and contemplation could only suggest that Manny and I had better break up so I could get my health back and straighten out my life. I talked to Manny and he sadly agreed. We made love one last time, and it was like an epiphany of emotions. Manny said, "There are so many kisses I have not yet placed on your body."

The night we parted, I felt as though my arm had been wrenched from my body by an accident. I lost so much – of me, in losing him. We both felt the pull, the strain. Manny and I kept seeing each other several times a week, though we had stopped our great sex. During this partial separation, Manny taught me to play a mean game of pool and darts as well. Almost immediately, after our break-up, the draft lottery began and Manny got the early number: 69! We watched the lottery together on TV that night and soon, he was on his way to a fight that was not his fight. I swore I would go to Canada if I were a man. (A somewhat prophetic statement at the time.)

Manny registered for service as a "conscientious objector" and luckily got a post away from actual fighting in Viet Nam.

Things were never the same for Manny and me again. I saw Manny a year later, when he was home on leave, but though I knew he wanted it, I could not make love to him again. So much had changed between us and I was then on the brink of destruction in my own life. Though we shared some hugs and kisses, it was not the same between us. His kisses had, in the past, been the ultimate of kisses for me. No one else's had compared. His kisses had fully satisfied me. Now they felt empty. The spark between us was gone and his lips were ordinary – very much to my surprise.

We never did make love again, nor did I ever see him again in this lifetime. I wrote this parting poem for Manny:

WINTER OF LOVE

Never again shall we meet by this tree.
It weeps for our Love as I did.
Never shall we sit as before in its shade,
Nor shall you caress me and Love me again.
For its branches are bare and cold as our Love.
It is true our tree is dead.

Years later, I tried many times to reach Manny through his mother, but she would not give me his address or any information about him. I heard somewhere that he later collected rare comic books.

At nineteen, I recognized Manny, as a powerful soulmate of mine, and one of the dearest loves of my life. Later, much later, I realized that the past is better left the past and I gave up looking for him. Now – I know – that if we had more that needed to be shared together in this lifetime, God would bring us together. Manny was the first of many, many soulmates I was yet to meet. But he, above them – was the purest love of this lifetime – for me.

FLOWERS

Flowers in their final hours,
Do not cry out when they fade.
Then why am I, when Love is ended,
So reluctant to persuade?

LOST SOUL

I am as wild as the night air.
I am as violent as the sea.
I believe I AM the sea
Breaking on the shore,
Trying to hold on to it,
Yet falling back every time.
One day I am calm and loving
To the fisherman,
Then some days, without warning,
I dash them on the rocks
And bury them within me.
How old must I be
Before I no longer care
About these things?
Will they become so small
They fade into a sea of tranquility?
Will I be lost for all eternity?

Chapter Four – Shadowlands

"Out of the night that covers me,
Black as a Pit from pole to pole,
I thank whatever gods may be
For my unconquerable soul."

William Ernest Henley
Invictus

Until now, I have mainly avoided talking about my health because I chose to focus on other aspects of my early life. Looking back over my life, I was a sickly child, constantly in doctor's offices with rashes, bruises, bumps, aches, pains and even more serious injuries. Sometimes it was because my father beat me, but sometimes I just seemed to be accident-prone. As an infant, I once cut myself up with razor blades when I crawled up to the medicine cabinet one day. Another time, I turned on a gas-stove burner on my head and scorched it. I still have a quarter-sized, round scar at the front of my head with no hair growing on it. Also, I frequently ran a collision course with kids on moving swing sets and cars on the road. I was constantly being rescued – just in the nick of time. It must have aged my mother at least ten years, protecting me from all my dangerous antics.

I remember that I hated food and was so skinny my parents tried to force-feed me. But I threw up the food or hid it in clothes drawers and closets every chance I got. My mother was constantly finding several whole or partial: hot dogs, burgers, sandwiches, bread, vegetables and even fruit in my multiple hiding places. (Obviously, another remnant from my German prison camp life – disliking food, probably because I was not used to eating much in that life. From a young age in this lifetime, I actually preferred plain bread and water to anything else!)

For most of the first dozen years of this life, I was anorexic and despised food. I had a severe rash and breaking out covering the entire back of my neck and it was often coated with salve and wrapped in old, torn sheets or flannel to keep me from scratching it. Every winter the skin between my eyes and eyebrows would also become raw, chapped, crack and bleed. I must have looked like a little monster. Not until my late thirties did I discover these rashes were connected to my intestinal parasites. While my neck cleared up by my early teens, my eyelids continued to crack and bleed in winter, until my late thirties.

As I got older, my health improved a bit, and I ate a little more. But I definitely preferred junk food and candy to my family's typical American diet of meat, potatoes and over-cooked or canned vegetables.

In second grade, I began to smoke cigarettes occasionally. Both my parents smoked. We went to the drive-in movies often. When my parents threw a cigarette butt out the window, I imitated them and smoked the butt until it went out. By age sixteen, I began to smoke regularly and began to drink alcohol occasionally.

After my father left home, when I was seventeen, I began to experience nightmares once in awhile. Not just little childhood boogieman dreams, I mean real, vivid, heart-pounding, frightening nightmares! I would wake up in a sweat, sometimes screaming. When I began to anticipate them, I would sometimes sleep with my mother, but the dreams continued and grew into terrifying episodes.

At the beginning of my eighteenth year, my real nightmares began. Movie-like dreams "inspired" by films I had seen, like *The Mask* (the voodoo version, not the Cher or Jim Carrey versions), and Fellini's *Satyricon* danced through my head some nights in disturbing patterns that caused me to wake up petrified, my heart violently pounding. Sometimes I was unable to move and other times, my body shook with earthquake-like tremors. Devils, demons, and spiders plagued my nights. But the dreams did not fade – they became worse.

During my eighteenth summer, I sought out psychiatric aid (in secret) at a free clinic in downtown Detroit. Initially, it seemed to help. My doctor encouraged me to talk about my father and my life. So I gave it my all. My new relationship with Manny at the time also helped and it lessened the nightmares. But, I was on a downhill spiral. By the following year, at the age of nineteen, my "shrink" put me on large doses of Thorazine and began analyzing me three times a week.

At that time, I had daily, pounding headaches. My daily diet was: sugar (including 6 donuts, several candy bars, cupcakes, Twinkies, and a pint of ice cream), 10 cups of coffee, junk food (refined crackers, Fritos and cheese curls, pretzels), pop, wine or mixed drinks (3-5 days a week), pizza, burgers, 2 ½ packs of cigarettes plus a weekly steak. My bad habits increased with every month that passed. I asked my psychiatrist if diet and my other habits had anything to do with my poor health and he assured me that they did not. I would have done anything at the time to get better. But my doctor said I just wasn't "spilling my guts enough." I must "dig deeper into (my) pain and thoughts," I was told. I grew worse.

The nightmares, now "day mares", had become horrifying daily ordeals. Actually, they were anxiety attacks that grew into six or eight-hour-a-day events. I would lie on my bed, sweating, and cry and scream as I watched devils and creepy, crawling spiders, jump out of my closets and come for me. I couldn't close my eyes or try to sleep. At those times, I believed that those evil spirits would enter me and take over if I did.

If I took the prescribed pills, the nightmare ended like hitting a brick wall. I would sleep a few minutes or hours and wake feeling like a Mack truck had just run over my entire body – several times over my head. I was sure that this was hell on earth. What could I possibly have done to deserve this, I thought?

I had quit my job of one year – working at a downtown Detroit bank, by the end of summer, during my nineteenth year. I couldn't think straight. I had been living in Windsor, Canada with girlfriends that summer. It was closer to my work and Manny came to visit me each weekend. We partied heavily in Canada and went to the popular Windsor Raceway each week. For this short time, I had a flare for gambling on the horses. I had good betting instincts and was particularly lucky at guessing the quinella race winners. The racetrack was a passionate six-month-long obsession with me.

By the fall, Manny was off to the military and I moved into a shared apartment with a young female university student in downtown Detroit. By then, I was speaking to my father again. I had accomplished at least some good in my therapy sessions and had learned to understand and forgive him. He had beaten me, just as his father had beaten him. But now he could no longer hurt me, so I saw him from time to time. My father was now a full professor teaching at the downtown university near my apartment. I attended his popular geography classes and was impressed with his teaching skills. He had always possessed a dashing charisma that awed the ladies. My father was fluent in twelve languages, a poet, philosopher, astrologer, and more. He actually wrote and had published two geography textbooks and one novel. They never made him any money, but writing was nonetheless one of his passions.

As autumn got underway in Detroit, I became more troubled. My hallucinations grew worse and I, more desperate. The nights were the most devastating. My whole body seemed torn apart. I half expected to see myself burst into a night demon, werewolf or some other horrific monster with all the raging of my body and mind.

WILD NIGHT

Wild Night, Wild Night!
Never have I seen such a night.
Ferocious winds, quaking trees,
Rustling and wailing of the leaves
– As turbulent as my soul.
– As insane as my thoughts.
– As heavy as this energy
Tossing within me.
Wild Night, Wild Night!

Am I wild or are you wild,
Because of me?
Wild night we howl together,
Me in you and you in me.
Did I create you,
Or did you create me?

Each day, thinking got more difficult until I could not remember what happened the day before or read one line in a book and understand it. The only "job" I could get was selling underground newspapers at the nearby university. That, and my boyfriend Sam, helped me get a meager income to pay for my tacky student housing in a dangerous downtown neighborhood.

Sam and I met on a city bus. I did not drive much or have my own car in those days. Sam took me to a five-day rock festival that was a remake of Woodstock in Michigan. It was called Goose Lake and one quarter million music loving hippies attended, me included. It was a wild experience. Music all day long, amid drinking and drugs, with loud drumming all night on the metal outhouse roofs while everyone danced like savages in the campfire lights. I refused to take any drugs and stuck with marijuana, though my boyfriend had a steady relationship with mescaline, speed, LSD, and a variety of other substances and indulged in plenty. I had a terror of taking drugs, my life was bad enough as it was with drinking three to four days a week and marijuana once or twice a week as well.

The five days of the rock concert was no picnic for me. My nightmares continued, and I had disturbing dreams of myself as a neon arrow locked in a box. Certainly not a difficult analogy to interpret, looking back. But I found it very disturbing and mystifying at the time. There was tons of junk food, living in tents, weird acquaintances and nudity throughout the rock festival. Yet, through it all, I believed it was a good time – then.

When I got back home to my mother's house (I lived there a short while between my Windsor living and downtown Detroit apartment) she was outraged. She had finally figured out I was no longer a virgin. After all, five days at a rock concert with a guy I recently met, I think the neighbors finally wised her up to the facts of my life. My mother threw me out of the house, then and there, amid screams and denouncing me: "You're not my daughter anymore!" It was then I headed downtown to get shared housing with a girl who was a university student. A month or so later, my mother forgave me and we were on speaking and visiting terms again, but I continued to live downtown so I could have my freedom and continue seeing Sam, whom she never liked.

As my hallucinations and six-hour anxiety attacks continued to increase in intensity, neither the prescribed Thorazine nor my doctor's advice gave me any relief from constant depression. In utter despair and desperation, I decided it must be time to die. I knew hell could not be any worse than my life at the time. I slept on and off for fourteen hours a night and I could not sit up comfortably for more than a few minutes without squirming and changing positions. I could not walk a block without dizzy spells and sometimes fainting. My thoughts ran rampant and I was afraid of everything.

I looked out my sunny bedroom window at the world one more time, and went to lie in bed and plot my death. As the tears flowed, I looked out at the sun and wished there was a way to live – really live – feel joy, which I had not known much of for very long. For a moment I remembered God and how happy and in love with life I had been when I had the children to play with all those seemingly many years ago. In one last effort, I whispered: "Are you there, God? Can you hear me? Help me! Save me and I'll believe in you and love you every day of my life."

I instantly felt myself uplifted and I seemed to be filled with a powerful, bright light. I heard a voice within me comforting, say: "Go to a yoga class!" I really heard it – inside of me – and I knew throughout my being that I would be all right now. I would not have to die. I knew that God was real and that somehow, I was on my way back home. I slept the most peaceful sleep I had known in many months.

For over two years I had suffered this living nightmare. It was November 1970 and I was nearly twenty. The very next day I walked over to the nearby university and right up to the exact building – to the exact place – where I *knew* there would be a sign telling me about yoga classes.

I attended the next class and was possibly the most clumsy, young, yoga student in history. Every small movement that was easy for others was painful for me. After a few awkward classes, I heard about a yoga retreat. I knew I had to attend.

It was three days long. I hated the food. It was "health food" – icky tasting but "good-for-me." It was a silent retreat and I was in agony except for the lectures! The lectures changed my life forever.

The first time I heard about reincarnation, I believed it instantly. It sounded so much more reasonable than heaven and hell. It explained why we all really are not born equal. Why was I born poor and beaten and others born rich and happy? It made sense.

The other yoga principles were beautiful and alive for me. Right then and there, I rededicated my life fully to God and to finding a way to serve God on this planet and bring others to this sense of fulfillment, love and peace. But I still had a long, long way to go.

I was high on these feelings for three days after the retreat and made all kinds of beautiful life resolutions. It was euphoria unlike any I had ever known. The first night back from the retreat, I called my psychiatrist and he walked around with me in the dead of night to try to talk me down and get me back to earth. But I was too high on God, life and my experiences at the retreat. My world seemed padded and unreal. It held no rough edges for me. Basically, I was "blissed out."

My shrink was worried – this wasn't a real world I was in. He advised me to stay away from these "yoga people" for at least a little while and get stronger before getting involved with them again. I took his advice, and concentrated on attempting to read the two yoga books I purchased at the retreat, though I had trouble thinking clearly and could not read a book at the time and understand it. But my high continued for two more days. I saw my future life spread out before me and felt and knew – the experience of God fully in my life again.

Then after the third day, I crashed. It seemed as if the bottom fell out of my world and I tumbled into darkness again. It was like seeing God and then getting cast out of heaven into hell – but it was the earth! I had much healing to do.

I moved back to my mother's house for a couple of short months over the Christmas holidays and most of January. During that time I gave up Sam, smoking cigarettes (2 ½ packs daily), my occasional pot, drinking alcohol and meat eating. On New Years Eve, I smoked my last cigarette and my last joint; I had my last drink of alcohol and ate my very last steak dinner. I arranged to move into the yoga commune near the end of January. These yoga people were all non-smoking vegetarians. I knew I had to be the same to fit in. I prepared myself mentally, emotionally and physically in the best way I was able by changing my lifestyle, diet and wardrobe.

For the first of many times in my life, I gave away most of my possessions. From my complete Beatles albums to my beloved stamp collection to my fancy dresses. Nearly everything had to go. There is much to be said about simplifying one's life. The energy it takes to obtain and maintain a lot of possessions take away from living life in the now. Dusting, caring for, working to make money for "stuff" can detract from a person seeing and focusing on the real purpose of life – to become and express one's true self fully.

Now I was stepping into a new world, and I prepared myself like a soldier going off to war. But the war was on my bad living habits and lifestyle. I had everything I truly wanted in life to gain: health, happiness and spiritual understanding. I was moving towards a way of living that would give me answers I sought to life's questions. I would cohabit with people who had the same goals I now did. It was a whole new adventure that I both feared and longed for at the same time.

The psychiatrist's methods had brought me very little relief, only more declining health and mental problems, now I was going to try what I perceived to be – God's way. I had total confidence that I would find all the answers I sought and more. I knew it would be very difficult, but I felt I had two choices: life or death, and I believed that my choice to move into the yoga commune would help me – to live!

At the end of January 1971, I moved into the yoga commune, or "ashram" as it was called, and my real work began. I was sick, paranoid, over-emotional and in constant physical pain. I had so much to learn about living well. Proper diet, exercise, yoga, meditation and wholesome living were strangers to me. Yet, I was determined to change my life for the better. God was real and alive for me again and I knew there had to be a way for me to heal completely.

The yoga commune was in another part of Detroit, an older section near a Catholic university with rolling hills and a gorgeous little meditation chapel. The commune was the Integral Yoga Institute led by Swami Satchidananda who resided mainly in New York. I felt I had found a refuge in which to heal. The ashram residents welcomed me with open arms. I shared a bedroom with Lotus, the "house mama" who was just a few years older than myself. She was a former playboy bunny who gave up her flashy life for spiritual pursuits. Lotus ran the ashram kitchen and did the shopping, cooking and cleaning.

CRYING ON THE DESERT

Driven by pain and fear and guilt,
When shall I ever rest?
At last there's a time and place for me
To collapse on my earth mother's breast.

Give me the hills – they call to me.
Heal me – Heart of man.
Show me the truth in all life's things
And tell me of "Who I AM."

Give me the courage to go on.
Let me be born again.
Let me rejoice in what is left
Of life – till the struggling end.

Now is the time to heal or die.
Now in this lick of pain.
I shall renew this life of mine
Or die – and live again!

I went from wearing expensive dresses, a Natalie Wood hairdo and layers of make up to wearing: long, flowered dresses, straight hair and sandals. My diet went from my junk foods to a mainly raw food, vegetarian diet with tons of roughage. My tortured body was in real pain then, with these drastic diet changes. My liver was throbbing day and night and I could not sleep more than two or three hours at a time – a maximum of five hours most nights.

Much of the night, I paced the square hallways that surrounded our inner, open-air courtyard. I held my string of 108 mala (prayer) beads and chanted my mantra (vibrational word(s) of power), hour after hour to take my mind off the constant pain in my body, especially in the liver area.

I knew nothing about cleansing, fasting or vitamin supplements. But Lotus, who had been named by Swamiji (3), dispensed some healing advice, took me under her wing and taught me to cook – naturally, and how to fast. Her knowledge

Footnote (3) Swamiji means: beloved swami or priest. The letters "ji" added to the end of any name means beloved in Sanskrit. Satchidananda was called Swamiji by his ashramites.

was limited, but at the time, it seemed vast to me and started me on my healing journey.

At a veritable snail's pace, I made some recognizable progress. I began doing yoga exercises or rather "postures" as they were called, deep breathing techniques and meditation as well and these greatly assisted my beginning transformation. I was nearly always depressed, but I was determined to progress and succeed. I had quit the Thorazine, along with the alcohol and smoking, at my mom's house during the Christmas holidays. (I had also given up my therapist as I felt he had done little good for me.) My new lifestyle changes and radical diet put tremendous pressure on my body and emotions. Looking back, I certainly could have died from drug withdrawal symptoms and severe diet and lifestyle changes. I feel I had to have been protected by God and my angels. Most people would not have survived my severe side effects and the intense body fluctuations that sent me soaring one minute and crashing the next. I held on with an iron will!

I paced the halls at night and in the daytime struggled through deep breathing, meditation, yoga and a full-time job working for a car insurance company. My body rebelled with extreme hyperactivity and constant agitation, but my will was stronger – I held on. I forced my body to comply, to the point of shaking, sometimes violently. When I felt I was weakening or losing control, I prayed sometimes for hours with all my might. There were times when I prayed an entire night through. I was determined to heal. I would succeed! I knew I had to. I knew I could!

Another blessing that helped to transform my life was chanting. Repetitive, mantra-like phrases, sung with a leader and response group. We sang mainly in the Hindu – Sanskrit language taught to us by Swamiji. Remembrance of my love of Latin stirred in me. I grew to love the Sanskrit chanting and eventually excelled at it and led others in the kirtan (song) chant nights. At first my voice was shaky and my pitch was off. My voice was not well appreciated by others at those times. Some listeners would have certainly preferred my silence. But in time, with the help of deep breathing and yoga, my voice became clear, smooth and steady and gained control and power enough to vibrate the room and move listeners to awe and God inspiration. My accapella voice eventually became music to others' ears and I rediscovered my deep love of singing from childhood. Adding music, my voice was magic.

Chanting also stirred spiritual memories, psychic abilities and powers within me. Sanskrit contains more letters and more sounds than the English language. Sanskrit chanting can stir up spiritual energies and uplift the entire body, unlike English words. Edgar Cayce claimed that in one of his past lives as Ra Ta, an Egyptian priest, he lived to be a thousand years old, due to the vibrations of chanting. Memories of a couple of my own past East Indian lifetimes flooded into me when I chanted, and I soon felt at home with the language and some of the East Indian customs we practiced at the ashram.

Initially, when I first moved into the yoga commune, I had difficulty understanding and accepting Eastern incarnations of God like Krishna, Radha, Rama, Buddha and other representations of the Divine. These forms of God were strangers to me and seemed foreign in every way. Jesus was my preferred expression of God. However, after months of meditation on Jesus – seeking understanding, I was granted a vision in which Jesus and Krishna merged into one for me – and I knew they were the same spirit of the one God. After that I was able to accept all world religions as equal, beautiful expressions of one Divine God represented in a multitude of forms.

These blessed experiences helped to make my physical struggles more bearable. After a month or two at the ashram, I wanted to try fasting for the first time. I managed to avoid all food up until noon at work, while only drinking water. Then I became faint. I grabbed the nearest drink I could get my hands on, a popular cola – drank half and fainted on the floor. My first fast was far from a success. Today, I tell this story to my cleansing and fasting classes for a laugh – "How not to fast." I certainly had lots to learn at the time about fasting and every other aspect of nutrition, diet, health and exercise as well.

I stayed by the side of Lotus, in our ashram kitchen, whenever I could and listened intently. I did whatever she told me to do. From her, I learned my rough beginnings of vegetarian cooking. Salad and dressings, vegetarian pizza, opma (or upmah – a rice, vegetable and fruit dish) and East Indian dishes were her specialties. Lotus thrived on handfuls of nuts, perhaps that is why her "bunny" figure quickly turned to round. Her tummy always had a four months pregnant look beneath her spunky, flashing eyes and long, brown hair.

There were two male leaders of our ashram who had lived with Swami Satchidananda in New York City and then moved to Detroit to begin an outreach yoga center. Rama and Hanuman taught most of the center's yoga and meditation classes and did the bookkeeping and paperwork. Other "ashramites" included two more local Detroit guys, myself and two or three constantly changing new women.

The first six months of my living at the ashram, I worked full-time downtown as an agent for a large car insurance company. I struggled with the work there, which went from light days to excessive work-hour days. Sometimes I did well and sometimes I was tired or "spaced-out" and barely got through some days. But I gave it my all and at the time, I did the best I was capable of. I frequently bought flowers from a downtown shop, usually weekly, to brighten my long workdays. Daisies were my favorite flower at the time. I later wrote this poem expressing my appreciation for them:

DAISIES

What is it about the simple daisy
That entices the hearts of us all?
We see them grace the fields in plenty, yet –
Who can name them common?
Like little golden suns
Surrounded by rays of white light,
They nod their heads in the breeze.
But they stand tall and firm again.
Their strength beyond more fragile blooms.
Oh, to lie and be lost in a sea
Of their divine simplicity!
To weave with them a chain
In which the fairies would delight.

This is the deciding flower
That begins a lover's troth.
For if he Loves or Loves me not,
Begins a Love that roses sent
And a bride's bouquet will continue.
Ah, humble, stouthearted daisies –
Among the rest of floraldom

You reign most sweet.
For your sunny oceans surround one
In the meadows and by streams.
You crown the hills
And deck the pathways to our homes.
But most of all, you bloom within.
A steadfast heart is but a daisy,
Bowing in the wind.

During my early days at the ashram, my older sister Trixie called one day and asked me to come and meet her new boyfriend, Scout. We took an evening drive through Edward Hines Park that wove around the extensive (more than 20 miles long) Rouge River where I had played when I was growing up. The three of us decided to take a walk in the park. Trixie's boyfriend, Scout, seemed awfully familiar to me, though I had never met him before (at least not in this lifetime). The two of them were drinking wine and I was drinking grape juice (since I no longer drank alcohol). We were all laughing and fooling around.

It was nearly dusk and for some reason, I felt in a "witchy mood" and began to pretend I was one. Scout played along, as the warlock and my sister became "the innocent." As we teased my sister, we decided it would be fun to tie her to a tree and dance around her. Scout had found some thick twine on the ground, so we proceeded to tie Trixie (gently) to a tree. She did not resist much and let out a few "helpless female" screams. Not the desperate kind, more the "oh poor little me," variety of screams. In her own way, she was playing along.

Our moods got wilder as we danced around my sister as she was bound, lightly to the tree. We murmured incantations, made up, or so they seemed and I declared that she should die before the next full moon. After a few more minutes of this, my sister was tired of this and decided to break free and run away. We gave up the game and followed her to the car.

By now it was night. Scout continued to be in a cocky mood as he drove around the curvy park road a little faster than earlier. Before long, he seemed absolutely frustrated with the slow flow of traffic and decided to pass some cars ahead of him. We were on a big curve in the road and he tried to pass no less than seven cars. The result was disastrous, a head on collision near the driver's side where Scout was. The car was completely totaled; Scout was badly injured and partially paralyzed. My sister, sitting next to him, had glass wedged in her skin near her eyes and in her knees. I was sitting by the passenger window and had thrown myself across her just before we hit and miraculously, I hardly had a scratch on me. (None of us wore seat belts; the majority of people rarely used them in those days.)

Just as the car crash had become imminent, as I was watching it happen, I immediately regretted my witchy words at the tree in the park. I silently apologized to God for my actions and begged for his help to save us: "I didn't mean it! (What I said out there in the woods.) Dear God forgive me and save us." The accident occurred just before the full moon!

I know that my prayer altered the course of the accident, and likely saved me from harm. My sister needed some glass removed near her eyes and in her knees and a few stitches but was otherwise okay. The doctor said she was lucky not to have been blinded. Scout had multiple cuts and bruises and needed many stitches. He was partially paralyzed on his entire left side for about six months and then recovered. Scout actually called me months later, at the ashram, and asked me for a date. I happily declined (he was too wild even for me) and never saw him again. My sister's and my relationship was not damaged by this occurrence and to this day she swears I saved her life by throwing myself across her when the accident happened.

Inside myself, I made a mental note to never "pretend" to harm someone again and to never play witch. I felt and knew my witch memories were an "incarnational leak" from another life when I was a witch and I believed that the consequences of such real or imagined witchcraft were dangerous and not in keeping with my spiritual beliefs and goals.

In earlier years, when I was a teenager, I had teasingly placed a "curse" on my younger sister, Loni and though I had laughed it off as a joke, she took it very seriously and cried and begged me to remove it. Loni felt it had given her bad luck. Though I felt the curse was not real, I removed it after insistent requests, and Loni claimed to feel better. She believed that her life was no longer jinxed.

To this day, I never jest about curses and rarely say or even think of bad wishes toward someone. I feel that I am a powerful woman who almost always speaks the truth; therefore there is much power in my statements. So, I must aim to make my thoughts and statements positive.

Months after the car accident, when a group of ashramites was walking the Catholic university grounds and playfully climbing some of the buildings thick, concrete ledges, someone laughingly suggested we have a mock sacrificial offering of one of us on the wall. With a terrified expression, I yelled: "No, no! If you have to sacrifice someone, let it be me!" I hoped to reverse any damage with my prayers and prevent anyone from being cursed or hurt. They were all so surprised by my reaction, that they immediately discarded the idea and I was relieved that no one mentioned it ever again.

Through these experiences, I learned strong lessons about thoughts and intentions and *words stated with power*, that I would remember my whole life. It is now my personal belief that it is wrong to hurt others in thought as well as in deed. Thoughts are things. They have an energy and we do pay a karmic debt for all wrong or unkind mental, spoken words or actions we use to perpetrate ills on others.

Living in the ashram was a monumental learning experience for me. Massive changes were underway in my body – I felt it daily. For the first few months doing yoga, especially during matsyasana or the fish pose, I had a smoky taste in my mouth (no doubt, residue from my cigarette smoking that was being purged from my body). After three months, the taste changed to a clear, delightful, fresh taste – that I called the "good throat taste."

I was the most finicky of eaters when I arrived at the ashram. Eventually I began to enjoy all kinds of foods I would not have even looked at before: strawberries, pineapple, coconut, dates, pomegranates, broccoli, asparagus, sprouts, carrots, beets, granola, yogurt, tofu, brown rice and beans made their way into my diet and I discovered a re-awakening of my taste buds. Few people know that we have 7,000 active taste buds in our mouths as children that turn into as little as 700 by the time we are in our 60s. Junk food, excessive sugars, food additives, preservatives and more, contribute to the blocking or deadening of our taste buds. Cleansing and fasting re-awaken the taste buds by removing stored poisons in the body that block our taste buds normal functioning. I did not know this in my yoga ashram days but I felt it!

The foremost body cleanse is altering the diet with better quality foods. As good food fills the body, they eventually push out poisons or toxins that have been stored in the body. Little by little, my body was transforming. Something that assisted the process for me was fasting. Cleansing (4) would have been easier and probably more beneficial but I and even Lotus had no real knowledge – yet – of the many possibilities of cleanses that could have altered my life for the better like the jet plane route to healing.

But I learned to fast! It is a healing art over thousands of years old that has been used throughout history for healing and spiritual revelation. One only needs to pick up any Bible to see fasting mentioned over and over again throughout its pages. Fasting gives the entire body a rest from constantly digesting food, which usually requires 40-60% of an average person's total body energy. The extra energy gained by fasting can assist a body to heal all kinds of health problems and diseases.

With persistence, I eventually conquered the one to three day fruit fasts. Then I did the one to three-day water fasts. Once I did a six-day water fast. I was aiming for ten days, but six days was the most I could handle living on water alone. Eventually I decided to do a grape fast. This was considered a cancer cure and was all the rage in health circles at the time. *The Grape Cure* book by Johanna Brandt was then being sold in all the health food stores. It was after all, the early 1970's. I attempted to do a two to three week grape cure, eating basically only organic grapes and drinking grape juice and spring water. I lasted only six days because the fruit sugar got me so high I could not sleep – at all.

It was a bizarre experience. By the fourth day, I could see things with my eyes opened or closed. I was so high, I could see right through my eyelids. No marijuana or hashish from my past ever got me this high. And there were claimed to be no bad side effects from a grape fast.

Besides, grapes are legal. My body blood sugar levels went nuts, however. At the time, I did not have a clue that I had terrible blood sugar problems and was severely hypoglycemic.

Footnote (4) While cleansing, one can still eat up to three meals a day and use natural remedies to purge toxins with sometimes quicker healing results than fasting on no food at all, while drinking only water. Fasting is over 4,000 years old while cleansing is less than 100 years old. However cleansing is far more beneficial for today's body types as we are loaded with artificial additives and poisons that often require specific herbs and natural remedies to be removed from the body. Steam and wet saunas also greatly enhance body cleansing.

I made a mental note, after my grape fast, to write a booklet on how to get naturally high for teenagers some day and include the details of this grape cure as one method. It was a unique experience, like none I had ever had before or since to this day.

I learned tremendous self-control physically as well as mentally from fasting. It changed my whole world of experience. All the yoga principles and techniques altered my understanding of life – physically, emotionally, mentally, vitally and spiritually – these are five bodies each human being possesses.

Yoga teaches us that every cell of the body is like a flower that can bloom and be transformed from physical to divine. We can transform ourselves one cell at time and cause the body to actually last forever. The human body can constantly be regenerated to live hundreds of years as Edgar Cayce's was in his Egyptian lifetime as the high priest Ra Ta. He claimed to live for over a thousand years due to the benefits of chanting high vibration sacred words. Numerous Old Testament figures lived hundreds of years like Methuselah who died at the ripe age of nine hundred and sixty-nine years.

Holistic health experts today claim that the human body was built to last forever and can be regenerated and live for hundreds and even thousands of years. As I worked on healing myself, I learned and experienced cycles of my own body changing. Every aspect of my five bodies was included in this complete process of transformation. I got used to experiencing depression, fear, and stepping backwards just before a big health break-through happened for me. "Calm before the storm. Storm before the transformation." Tears and sweat purged poisons from my body and prepared the way for spiritual revelations. (5)

Change is such an intimate journey within your self. There are as many ways to heal, as there are people on planet earth, I believe. Each of us has to carve out our own way. Nothing is incurable in my opinion. If you are alive – you can find a way to heal – if – you desire it enough and are willing to do the work it requires.

Footnote (5) According to medical findings, tears of sadness may contain nearly thirty different toxins that exit the body through the tear ducts. I have put many of my healing techniques and findings in the thirteen health books I've written. Cleansing information is mainly found in my books: *Your Natural Medicine Chest* and *Complete Candida Yeast Guidebook*. Fasting information is found in the two previously mentioned books and my: *For The Love Of Food* book.

ANOTHER PART OF ME
With each tear that falls
From my eyes.
A veil is lifted
From my sight.
I see my soul.
I see myself.
My raw emotions,
My raw self,
My real self,
Unfolds.
And I behold
Another part of me.
And as I see me,
I see another part
Of everybody.
Life and tears
Rip away the veils
That hide truth
From my sight.
The veils lift –
Like day comes from night.

The body is amazingly resilient, I found. I made millions of mistakes during my healing processes: I overdosed on some natural remedies; I used some remedies improperly; I agitated my body with foods I was allergic to; I cleansed poisons too fast from my body clogging my digestive tract and elimination tract; I got serious food poisoning and more – yet I survived. I would not, by the way, recommend my exact road to health to anyone. Mine was a treacherous path fraught with many dangerous and damaging pitfalls. I've had many, many near-death experiences but I believe I cannot die until I am ready, and my work for God on this planet is completed. "We create our own reality," and "What we believe we make true." (6) There is tremendous power in our beings! According to the New Testament: "If ye had enough faith, as much as a mustard seed, ye could tell that mountain to move over there."

However, I learned by my many past mistakes, gentler roads to healing that I eventually taught thousands of people through the health books I wrote and with the lectures and

Footnote (6) Huna principle #1. See First Words section at the beginning of the book.

consultations I gave and still give today.

The majority of people use far less than one percent of their personal power and most people eat, exercise, and care for their bodies and minds so poorly, that they are doing about 95-98% wrong things for themselves. The fascinating human body was created to last thousands, not dozens of years. The key is asking, listening and being willing to do what it takes to make this a reality.

While many individuals have faint desires to heal, few have the diligence required to actualize body-healing processes. The job is enormous and necessitates a complete diet, exercise and lifestyle overhaul. Every thought, word, action and habit must be scrutinized and altered for the better. It is an entire lifetime proposition that few people are fully motivated to continue every day of their lives. However, like a rolling stone, new habits gain momentum once activated. Each of us has the power to create new bodies and minds, thus creating a new world and attracting new people into our lives as we change and heal.

I presently know how to heal just about anything through the use of: good food, exercise, deep breathing, energy work, body work and therapies, fasting, cleansing, healthful living conditions, prayer, meditation, positive action, determination, positive thinking, belief or faith, forgiveness and love.

Back in my ashram days, I was still struggling, searching for answers and experimenting with methods and techniques. But I was advancing toward healing, however slowly and inadequately. "Go your way in peace, your faith has saved you." I trusted this and never lost sight of this goal of good health.

I wandered in and out of the shadows of my mind during this crucial initial healing time. I was in nearly constant physical pain from my liver – only during yoga practices and meditation was I able to rise above the pain and forget it for a time. This was my solace, my refuge, as I struggled toward the light.

When I was cleaning up my life, I began to understand some of the processes involved that affect me and my five bodies (physical, emotional, mental, vital and spiritual). As poisons exited all my bodies, memories of the times I "collected" the poisons resurfaced mentally and I experienced emotionally all the same feelings I had during those past times, such as: losing love, being hurt or beaten, binge eating to stuff down anger or pain, fear, confusion, negative emotions and more.

SOUL EPIC

Wanting to live.
Wanting to die.
Feeling ecstasy and joy
Or bitter pain and tears I cry.

Glory of heaven,
Pain of hell –
Of Life I know so little.
Love I know as well.

Forever, forever,
Will I be,
Soaring in Bliss
Or drowning in a pain filled sea?

Fiery pains come to me,
Then joys that thrill me through.
But no one will believe,
The depth in which I perceive.

No one can know
Unless they've felt it too,
Unless they've shivered in the chill of dawn
Or been through what I've been through.

Surely each of us
Must master our own fate.
Each of us has a task to do,
A burden to undertake.

Each must overcome
Trials in the road he takes.
But depth of soul
Picks the road and names the stakes.

The depth of soul determines
The joys and pains.
The depth of soul determines
The heights to be attained.

After a round of purging poisons, I usually felt an increase of vitality or vital energy and a spiritual upliftment. My aura cleared and brightened. My body felt healthier as well. Everything is connected. True healing takes place on all levels at the same time. One part cannot be hurt or healed without involving all the other parts of us or our five bodies. This revelation actually took decades for me to fully comprehend and realize. And just like the aforementioned layers of the onion skin, with each year of healing, I developed a deeper awareness of what this really meant to me, my life and the life of everything on this planet Earth.

BLISSES AND HELLS

Blisses and Hells are mine
As the universe
Flows to Oneness in my mind.

. . .

HOMECOMING

When I return to who I AM,
I'll never leave that home again.
For when I've come to rest within,
My life will have no need for sin.

Chapter Five – Resurrection

"Ah! Up from the ground sprang I
And hailed the earth with such a cry
As is not heard save from a [wo]man
Who has been dead, and lives again."

Edna St.Vincent Millay
Renascence

After struggling through six months of healing while working full time at the car insurance company downtown, Detroit, I decided it was time for a radical change. My heart was not in that work. I wanted to be at the ashram more. Living expenses were reasonable enough that I felt a part time job, closer to home, would do.

I had already begun to bake bread to sell in the ashram kitchen and was assisting Lotus in teaching some cooking classes. As a sideline business, I did crafts. People seemed to be anxious to buy the crocheted shawls I rapidly turned out – about one per week. I sold these for about twenty dollars apiece (good money in those days) to friends, family and ashram acquaintances.

This gave me more time to concentrate on my yoga practices and healing. Over the second period of six months of living at the ashram, I found other part-time work in a bookstore, candle-making and assisting with the ashram's bookkeeping. Soon I was teaching my own cooking classes and bread-baking classes, as well.

At the ashram, there were many activities going on daily for me to participate in: yoga and meditation classes, chanting nights with pot-luck suppers, visits from out-of-town ashramites and a whirlwind of all kinds of visitors and curiosity seekers to entertain and answer questions about our yoga center activities and practices.

Every month or two, other ashramites and I traveled to yoga retreats and special spiritual gatherings in the Detroit area, Chicago, New York and other cities. I attended three- five- and ten-day retreats, many of them silent retreats, with Swami Satchidananda, Dr. Bernie Seigel, Dr. Patch Adams, an enlightened Catholic/Buddhist monk named Brother David, Yogi Bhajan, Wayne Dyer, Baba Raam Dass and a host of other popular spiritual teachers. We also attended local concerts and shows of: Jesus Christ Superstar, Godspell, Laura Nyro and James Taylor.

I met and chatted with Swami Satchidananda on many occasions and he gave me the East Indian name of "Kshama", which he said means patience. And for those of you who are surprised by this, I received the name because I was impatient and my being called patience would hopefully make me patient one day. I still keep a treasured quote from Swamiji that he wrote in one of his letters to our ashram: "Keep the light burning within you. Walk like suns around the earth. You will be prophets who will lead others to peace and joy." I will always keep these words tenderly in my heart.

Swamiji demonstrated to me on several occasions that he was quite capable of reading my mind. No personal thought was hidden from him in his presence, but he respected most private thoughts and only responded to those he felt would be helpful for my or someone else's growth. Nonetheless, I developed a fear around "holy people" of having my mind read and to this day, I often find myself panicking and thinking the worst thoughts I am capable of when I suspect my mind is being read.

Despite my fears, I gained a wealth of wonderful experiences and understanding from sharing frequent time with so many revered spiritual teachers.

WAITING BE

Wait happily
Until the soul is free.
Wait hopefully
And learn and be.
Wait faithfully
And all will come to thee.

One gorgeous sunny spring day, a group of ashramites and friends including: Lotus, Gurave, Staron and I – Kshama, went to enjoy a day at a popular private school in the Detroit area with one of the most lush and colorful gardens in Michigan. The grounds spread across hundreds of acres of natural forests, rolling hills with verdant green grass and fields of wind swayed bulb flowers including: daffodils, narcissus, tulips, iris and crocus. Stately, manicured gardens surrounded a maze or labyrinth of shrubs, exotic flowers, a circled arch of cherry blossom trees, fragrant perennials, and a multitude of awe inspiring Greek statues of nearly every god and goddess imaginable. Aphrodite, Eros, Hermes, the Muses, Artemis, Apollo and more, were all gracefully poised throughout this natural expanse.

Wandering the grounds became a playful game of discovery for the group of us. We ran, skipped and danced from one gorgeous nature display to another, exuding ah's and oh's of delight at every masterpiece of sculpture or nature we found.

We were rowdy and laughing, until we came to several large open fields overflowing with newly blooming daffodils beside a cheerful lake that held – what else – graceful swans, gliding over the gentle waves. We paused at such a magnificent sight and were moved to silence. We separated to approach the lake or stopped in our tracks and drank in with our eyes, the imposing elegance of this rare sight. It is now permanently etched in my memory for all lifetimes. I will not forget the splendor of this day. It will stand out for me as one of the happiest days of this life.

I think of these scenes often as I recite the poem by William Wordsworth called: *The Daffodils*. I love it so dearly that I have committed it entirely to memory. I wish I had written it. It begins with these lines:

THE DAFFODILS

I wandered lonely as a cloud
That floats on high o'er vales and hills,
When all at once I saw a crowd,
A host, of golden daffodils;
Beside the lake, beneath the trees,
Fluttering and dancing in the breeze...

William Wordsworth

During these eventful days of ashram life, I still continued to experience pain, depressions, and trouble sleeping, as I slowly continued to heal my body and mind. But, mainly I was content knowing I was growing and progressing toward the kind of life and health I dreamed of and trusted that I would eventually achieve. I still struggled with my emotions, both in understanding and expressing them. I tended to repress much of what I felt and later through meditation, I had to sort it out and deal with my own personal consequences of that.

As I progressed, I learned to take responsibility for everything I felt. I, and I alone, created my world. I learned that my emotions were often trained responses I had to people and circumstances since childhood. While other people could trigger my emotions, it was up to me to see that they were not held responsible for my sadness, anger or pain. I could not change other people, but I could change my responses to them. I could not allow what they said or did to affect what I felt, believed, or even what I said or how I acted with them. These were new ideas for me. Childhood and adolescence had taught me to blame others for my misfortunes and problems in life. I had learned to blame my father, my mother, my schoolmates, and the world – for my troubled young life. Now, I discovered that karma – the law of "what you do comes back to you" was responsible for my tortured childhood and I was responsible for my karma. I created it in past lives and in this life with every thought I had, with everything I believed. Remember: "What you believe, you make true."

I discovered it was my job to unravel all my past faulty mental "programming" and to program new attitudes and beliefs into my own brain through: watching my thoughts and weeding out erroneous thoughts and attitudes, reading positive spiritual literature, associating with positive people; cleaning up my diet and lifestyle and elevating my body, mind and spirit to a higher level or vibratory frequency with prayer and meditation.

To do all of this required lots of work and constant daily monitoring of my thoughts, words and actions. For me, this task was horrendous. I was steeped in old, negative patterns from the past, and I fell into them over and over again, minute by minute, especially when I was tired, sick, emotionally bottled-up or in pain. Well, this was literally all of the time for me! The only time I was not struggling hopelessly to change and be positive was when I was sleeping, chanting, or meditating. As I floundered hopelessly to progress, only one course of action was clear to me: I had to step up my meditation time to successfully transform my life. At that period of ashram life, I had learned to participate in yogic meditations two to three hours a day, but this was not enough.

I had learned to sit cross-legged for many hours with my yoga practice and could often transcend physical, mental and emotional pain when doing meditation. Each of us at the yoga center had a little wooden altar covered with a pretty cloth, flowers and statues or pictures of our favorite forms of divine beings and saints like: Jesus, Mary, St. Francis, Krishna, Buddha and others. Here we sat in our free moments to contemplate the higher mysteries of life, but also to examine our thoughts, our lives, and to delve into the realms of meditation.

These meditations became an incredible journey transporting me from my worldly pains and problems into the peace, joy, serenity, and the bliss of experiencing God-inspired revelations.

WHERE BEAUTY GROWS

In a castle by the sea,
I saw things life calls beauty.
In a castle of my soul,
I found where beauty really grows.

As I entered into the silence, repeating my mantra on my mala beads, I first came to the inward door of my rambling thoughts. Any attempt to tame these was futile. I had learned to "sneak" past them by focusing ahead. These thoughts screamed and gyrated for a while until they disappeared as I ignored them. Or sometimes, I withdrew my thoughts and energy from them and refocused on my meditative goal. If these thoughts pressed too much for my attention, I looked at them, dismantled them bit-by-bit, then moved on. They had no choice but to dissolve as I proceeded ahead to the next level.

Then my body and emotions would act up with feelings of: "I'm tired. I'm bored. This is too much work. I'm hungry. I want to do something else. I don't feel like doing this. My legs hurt…" This too, I moved beyond. Then any doubts, fears, painful daily interactions with other housemates, family or friends I had – came up next to the surface to be cleared from my mind. These were cleared with reason. I took responsibility for all I felt – forgave myself and the other people involved, sometimes rethought the situations with better solutions and then – these obstacles too disappeared. I then let go of anything that bothered me, and I rose above the mind, emotions and physical discomforts.

There was no doubt or fear or pain in this next doorway. Words of God inspiration and bliss entered next: "I am with you always. It is my good pleasure to give you the kingdom," and, "Ask and you shall receive."

The truth and knowingness of these Bible scripture statements (sometimes I used the Bhagavad-Gita Gita, the Vedas, or holy scriptures from other religions) fully entered my being and with this power came understandings and revelations of life, love, truth and God. Here I saw the past, present and future in true light. Here, visions appeared to teach, guide, and bless me.

Here, at age nineteen, came some of the major answers of my life. Visions of my father – forgiveness, our past lives together, our lessons we needed to learn together – appeared with hope and healing. In one meditation, I envisioned myself as a young infant running into swings and cars, and actually trying to kill myself. The young me was trying to die to pay for my many sins in past lives – the older me – now at nineteen, kept saving the infant and saying: "You don't have to die. I've already paid for that!"

During many different meditations, I saw an array of my past incarnations as black women, several times as North American Indians, as a tortured Jewish woman in a death camp, as a nun more than once, as a shepherd, a princess, a priestess, a leper, as Japanese, as Chinese, as Hawaiian, as French, as a Mexican and more, much more. The reasons, the karma, the crimes – the forgiveness flooded over me in a procession of colors, countries, different bodies, different lifetimes. Atlantis, Egypt, Persia, Africa, Asia, Europe and the Americas unfolded before me.

With each meditation, the answers proceeded to appear. I saw and felt the times, places, people and experiences of a multitude of lifetimes. My mind and emotions then cleared. And the knowledge of infinity flooded into me. God in many forms, with many names, appeared and they all merged as one. I saw and felt and knew the purpose of this and every life. I experienced the oneness of all things connected eternally in one God, yet as diverse in form as all the matter in the universe. I felt God as neither male nor female, but as "essence" behind and within and all of everything that exists as well.

As these revelations filled me and lifted me beyond my body, I felt light and electricity surge through my being. Though I did not feel my body at all during some meditations, there were other experiences wherein I completely felt my body. Sometimes the pumping of my blood through my veins was accentuated and my heartbeat, my breathing, my very life rhythms became my sole awareness. These could become at times as loud as thunder within me. At these times, my pulse became like flowing rivers of energy surging throughout my veins and body.

When I contemplated the beauty of God as male or female, in all forms and non-forms, I made love to God and felt power move up my seven chakras (7) from the base of my spine to the top of my head. At each chakra there would be an explosion of lights, colors and energies that I can only explain as an orgasm at each chakra – yet it was more.

Footnote (7) A charka is a power point along the spine. There are seven main chakras that begin at the base of the spine, with the root chakra at the anus centering on basic needs; the second chakra at the sexual organs; the third power chakra at the navel or solar plexus, fourth at the heart exudes love; fifth at the throat affects speaking words of truth; the sixth at the third eye between the eyebrows affects spiritual vision; and the seventh chakra at the top of the head opens to constant union with the divine or God. The energy that moves up the seven chakras is the kundalini power, symbolically represented by a coiled snake.

At each progressing chakra, the voltage and power increased. No earthy sexual orgasm could ever compare, yet these experiences were like orgasms. I felt intoxicated, ecstatically in love, as I expressed all the power of my being. I adored God and wanted nothing more than to stay this way forever – locked in loving conjugal bliss with my beloved God of the universe. Forever I wanted to stay with my love. We were one, yet I was fully aware of my surroundings: the altar, the room and outside it. But I stayed there and drank the divine nectar over and over, fully intoxicated by the oneness I became with God.

Over the course of a few months, my meditation time grew to eight hours or more a day. I slept little, but still fulfilled my work and household chores. I took long walks alone or with friends on the Catholic university's rolling hills, and haunted the school's lovely outdoor meditation chapel with my constant presence.

During this time, my interactions with everyone were transformed. There was no one I did not get along with, love and understand. Even the most agitated of ashram visitors melted in my presence and had to open their hearts to the love I exuded. Now nothing could ruffle my feathers – as everything that happened dissolved into a well of love that constantly poured from me.

Now is what ultimately matters the most. I experienced the "nowness" of each moment and each moment became an infinity of expression. Like the old Popeye cartoon where Olive Oyl sticks her neck all the way around a tiny tent and looks inside to see dancing girls, elephants, fountains, and a huge royal feast – I saw and knew the immensity of each second – the eternity of "nowness". Time expanded and a moment in now lasted an entire day! A day was a lifetime. In seconds, more was seen, felt and experienced than I could write about in millions of book pages.

For two months, I lived fully in the now with the power to transform everything that happened to me and my world, to good. This divine "present" of constant bliss was a daily gift for those two months that felt like a lifetime. Each second was an hour; each hour seemed as long as a day. I was in heaven and there was nowhere to go but – here and now. I lived in the precious present.

WATER OF SOUL

Forever, Forever,
The river goes on.
I drink a bit here,
I drink a bit there,
But water – more water,
Comes up everywhere.
Oh, to bathe in it,
Dance in it,
Singing such Joy.
There's no end to the source,
No end to it now.
Can't stop the river
That's flowing now.
Oh, to stand in that waterfall,
Drenched through and through,
To rejoice in its freshness,
Drink the wet dew.
Droplets of energy,
Rains of Light;
Water, Water, Water –
Glorious, Glorious, Delight!
Like a wellspring overflowed –
Oceans, rivers, lakes and seas –
From sources never before known.
Endless, eternal, running on and on,
Like a fish in its element,
I swim along.
And dive and dissolve into
Each new wave.
Water, Water, Water –
Refreshment I crave.
Foam in my hair,
Water, Water – Everywhere.
I AM the drop I drink!
God is the only ocean
And from it all this flows.
Water of my heart and soul –
Into it I dissolve
As a wave in the ocean,
As a mermaid in the sea,
As water into water,
As me in God and God in me.

One night, during this time of total happiness and contentment, I took a walk with my friend Staron, a frequent ashram visitor. We strolled arm in arm, over to the university grounds for one of our special conversations on love. (Staron was present at the lovely gardens we visited in springtime, at the private school.) He was a couple years younger than me and was a bright spirit with a glowing aura. He was a soul of pure love with an open heart chakra. As we laughed and danced in the green fields together that night, enjoying the flowers, I climbed alone up a high, stone stairway. The stars – Staron's namesake – were twinkling in a clear, dark, cloudless sky. There was stillness in the air as I looked down from my perch and locked eyes with Staron. Everything between us and around us took on an aura of magic. I felt like we had entered a fairy tale.

We began to recite together from memory, the balcony scene of Romeo and Juliet. "Two of the fairest stars in all the heavens…having some business to entreat her eyes to twinkle in their spheres until they return…" It was as if we were transported to that actual place in Verona, Italy and I felt as if all the love ever expressed throughout all of history was filling our veins. We were both drunk on the sweetest, gentlest, most innocent, sensuous love imaginable. "My bounty is as boundless as the sea, my love as deep. The more I give to thee, the more I have. The both are infinite."

Minutes became hours that stretched, unendingly on a current of pure emotions. Never before or since have I know a love so fresh, untainted, unspoiled. True heart love filled and surrounded our entire world. We completed the balcony love scene – "Parting is such sweet sorrow, I shall say good-night until it be morrow."

We stood in silence, unwilling to end the enchantment. Then ever so gently, we caressed and hand in hand, without a word, we walked slowly back to the ashram.

Though I knew that Staron and I had shared love in other lives, and would always love each other, our consummation was to be of spirit not of body. This night was never repeated, as there were forces of change at work. This gift of love would sustain me through nights and days to come. Forever, I could access it in my heart and memories, like a concentrated food I kept ready for times of need.

O NIGHT!

O magic, magic night!
What is this stirring in the air I feel?
What breeze is it that rustles
The leaves and tree branches?
'Tis the Spirit of Life!
The spirit I most adore.
Its gentleness caresses my soul,
And I wonder what for me –
Is in store?

The winds of change were stirring. My meditations were intensifying and becoming so powerful; I was beginning to lose desire for anything but meditation.

I chatted with my dear ashram friend, Jamie, one afternoon about his latest love and wondered why he and I had not ever held a love interest for each other. Beyond anyone, even Staron, Jamie and I had a rapport with each other that was unequaled. He alone understood and accepted – all the parts of me – not just me in my blissful state, but also me before it, in confusion and pain. He loved me high or low, happy or sad. I could talk to him about anything and he to me, the same.

I brushed thoughts of us together out of my head as Jamie continued his break-up story. I consoled him sincerely and we chatted on.

In the days that followed, my meditations began to take a new direction. Those past months, I could read a line or two of the Bagavad Gita and become instantly intoxicated with love. Every line of any scripture – from the Hindu, Buddhist or Christian Bible – brought me to swooning with a divine ecstasy.

Now my meditations took on an agenda with a life altering purpose. I was being prepared for big changes in my life. I was told that soon – very soon – my whole world would be transformed. I had been given a blessing these last months and shown the powers of God in me. I had achieved these same heights in meditation in previous lives. Already I was fully capable of communing with God in complete oneness. However, this was not the purpose of my present life incarnation.

My goal, this life, was to achieve "oneness in love" within a relationship with a man.

I had already earned oneness with the divine but now – I must do it through – earthly love. This was by far, a more difficult task. Formless love was easier to attain than love of a human man with earthly faults and limitations. And I needed to achieve this love through conscious choice and under-standing. My "true love" was not to be given to me. I had to evolve through all my karmic love relationships until I had attained a consciousness worthy of a dharmic (one that assists one's life purpose) love relationship. Only then, could I main-tain an earthly love union that paralleled my love of the divine.

There was still a tremendous amount to learn before I could accept, perfect and caress fully – human love with a man. I was actually just beginning my journey of under-standing. I was given a couple weeks more to prepare myself for my upcoming explorations of love. My many hours of meditation increased as I relished and savored each hour of lovemaking with God that was still allowed to me. I felt and *knew* this precious time I reveled in – intertwined with my Beloved – was coming to a close. Soon. It was barely a day or two away now. Soon, a new journey would appear and wrench me from my beloved God's arms. Soon – it was all too soon.

ELUSIVE SPIRIT

I dance a dance that no one knows.
I dwell in places no one goes.
I am that something no one's seen.
Perhaps you've touched me
In your dreams?

SOUL SIGHT

Eyes that pierce the veils,
How many eyes will you touch
Until another pair of eyes can meet yours
And know as much?

Eyes that pierce the veils,
How many Loves eyes will you behold,
Before you cease to shy away
And touch with joy a Lover's Soul?

Eyes that pierce the veils,
When will you meet a pair of eyes that say:
You are my own and I am yours,
One Soul we are and have been and shall remain?

Eyes that pierce the veils,
Are yearning for the day to dawn,
When eyes meet eyes and Soul meets Soul,
In a warm Lover's embrace.

Chapter Six – Union

"Oh lovers!
Where are you going?
What are you looking for?
Your Beloved is right here."

Jalalu'ddin Rumi

A wedding is always a joyous occasion. It was February 1972 and I had been at the ashram just over a year. All the residents of the yoga center were invited to the wedding of our ashram friends, Peter and Lily. Lotus was a bridesmaid. This was the first wedding I had attended in some time. I was excited to share in this joyous event that stirred my heart to love and my mind to storybook images of: "they lived happily ever after." It came as small surprise to me, that I was the one to catch the bridal bouquet. I somehow knew it was mine, and that my own special day was just around the corner.

The head of our Detroit yoga center, Rama, had recently moved back to New York, and Hanuman was in charge now. Rama was sorely missed. The Detroit ashramites, like fatherless baby chicks, seemed to be a little more scattered these days. We made pilgrimages individually and in groups to visit other spiritual teachers. It seemed that someone was always off on one spiritual quest or another.

Gopala (a Sanskrit spiritual name that refers to Krishna as a child) was one guy who had been connected to the ashram since I arrived. He moved into the center several months after I did, though he frequented the place before, nearly as much as some of the residents. Gopala was my age, twenty-one and from a Jewish background with very wealthy parents. He possessed his own somewhat twisted sense of humor, yet had an endearing, playful personality and was a stable, reliable force within the ashram. Stringed instruments were his forte. He could play all of them: guitar, banjo, autoharp, dulcimer and more as well as the keyboards. He provided much of the background music for our ashram kirtan chanting nights and taught some of the yoga classes, as well.

Gopala was up in Canada at the time, in Toronto, attending his good friend Tim's wedding. The rest of us ashramites were spending much of February's cold, snowy days hovering in the kitchen, baking and keeping warm with stories of our latest guru (spiritual teacher) seeking adventures. We were all anxious to meet new spiritual teachers who could offer us additional insights into our lives, spiritual practices and our own personal searches for God realization.

I remember clearly, like it was yesterday, the details of that Sunday night. I was meditating in our bedroom when Lotus came in and informed me that Gopala was home and in the kitchen. She said that Gopala was radiant and full of high energy he received from the lady guru: Mata Eloise whom he met in Toronto. ("Mata" means mother in Sanskrit and is a term of reverence.) Lotus was bubbling over with excitement. I continued my meditation a little longer, and sought him out.

I entered the kitchen expecting to greet Gopala with a hug and have a friendly chat. But what happened next was clearly beyond my control. Looking up into Gopala's eyes, we locked eyes for what would have been seconds but extended for countless minutes. Who I saw before me was not a man. Certainly his body was present, however light rays in steady streams were pouring out of him, surrounding his body with bright, sharp, clear rays of white-yellow light that emanated from him like rays from the sun.

The words we shared were inconsequential. There was a power of increasing voltage passing between us that lifted me not only above the ordinary, above my highest of meditations, but above all earthly consciousness. I saw Gopala as the Son of God he IS, stripped of earthly form – I saw only his soul. The power, the beauty, the magnificence of who he is overwhelmed me. My knees weakened. I felt myself swimming in the divinity of Gopala. Layer upon layer of lights, colors, energies and essences surrounded us. I saw his thoughts, feelings, and expressions encircle him like a gown. I felt his spiritual radiance and it was as if I was drinking him and he was drinking me. We flowed into each other in an unending current that lifted us both above and beyond our physical bodies.

We stood outside ourselves in a vastness that stretched beyond the room, the building, the block, the city, the country, and the planet. We mingled with the universe and all that God Is – we Are! Nothing in my seemingly vast experience of God had prepared me for this. I was totally and completely in love with everything Gopala is. No earthly "falling in love" could hold a candle to the sun of such a Love as this. Union, ecstatic union, flowed between the shores of our souls. Gopala was me. I was Gopala. There was no separation.

It took every ounce of my self-control, not to kneel down before him and worship him with every fiber of my being. A zillion moments in time passed and no part of me had any inclination to divert this light display that I could taste, smell, hear, see, feel, know and – be. I loved every moment of this experience and I would have stood there until someone removed me.

Now, Gopala was speaking, and though I had been re-sponding all along, the conversation shifted in a way that required my full attention. He was clearly frightened by the entire experience. Light-bursting meditations were not daily or even occasional fare for him. He attempted to cut off the energy, but it was impossible. It continued on regardless of his wishes. He was really scared now. "I being him" fully felt his discomfort and in an effort to relieve his anxiety, I forced myself to wrap up what was to me, trivial conversation compared to what was really going on. And with all the strength of my being, I forced myself to say goodnight and quit the room.

As I left, Gopala let out a weak sigh of relief and incredulity at the experience we had just shared. He thought to himself: "I hope this doesn't mean I have to marry her!"

I proceeded to my bedroom, but thoughts of sleep were impossible. I continued to experience all the intensity and flow of energy felt while in Gopala's presence. There was no need to meditate. I was already in the presence of God! I lay on my sleeping bag on the floor all night and just watched the visions dance in my head.

BUTTERFLIES

Butterflies in streams
Fly from my soul.
Visions of colors,
Transparent delights,
On their wings
My dreams take flight.

All the questions I asked that night were answered from above. That and more were given to me. This ecstatic state lasted for three full days for me. I knew Gopala and I would marry. It was all part of the cosmic plan. I relaxed and watched it unfold before my inward eye.

Gopala, unused to ecstatic experiences, was shaken and bewildered by what he and I shared. We spent the following week talking and discussing our feelings. He felt confused by the intensity between us and suggested we drive up to Toronto the next weekend to get advice from Mata Eloise regarding our situation. No one at our Detroit ashram could help. This was a single person's ashram. There were no couples here; no one who could be relied upon to explain our situation and offer needed insights.

Friday afternoon, we took Gopala's car to Toronto. The more than four-hour trip gave us rare time alone to talk together. We arrived around nine p.m. in time to meet everyone and enjoy a light meal before retiring. Gopala had called Mata Eloise on the phone earlier that week and her ashram had been expecting us.

The Toronto ashram was almost all married couples, wed by Mata Eloise herself. They were only weeks away from moving to a piece of land they had purchased in Thunder Bay, Ontario. It was about sixty miles above Minnesota on the upper, western tip of Lake Superior.

During our two-day weekend there, we got better acquainted with the ashramites and attended a Yogi Bhajan Darshan. (8) Mata Eloise spent some time alone with Gopala and me and immediately read our feelings. She said: "You two love each other but Gopala is afraid to express it with you, Kshama. His heart chakra is not open so he resists his feelings." She pounded him lightly on the chest above the heart and said: "Be prepared for it to open more fully at any time. Stop and allow the process when this happens."

By the end of the weekend, Gopala and I were engaged. Sunday, late afternoon, we headed home for Detroit. Halfway there, Gopala felt a powerful surge of emotion and started to breathe heavily. There was a heavy pounding in his chest area, around his heart, and he could barely breathe. I helped him to steer the car off the road and held his hand as his eyes watered and spilled over. His chest throbbed so heavily he was heaving and his breath came in spasms.

As I attempted to soothe him, I urged him: "Just relax Gopala. You just have a musty heart chakra. Take it easy and you'll be alright very soon." I understood the process as I had experienced similar openings of my own chakras with dramatic energies.

"I can't breathe." He gasped.

"Breathe slow, very slow and deep," I replied comfortingly.

"My Heart! My heart feels like it – is going to – break open," Gopala weakly, groaned.

I held on to him and breathed slowly with him. After about twelve to fifteen minutes, Gopala calmed and his pulse and breathing returned to normal. We embraced and in that moment, he finally accepted within himself that we were actually engaged and he felt it was a good idea. Though Gopala had previously felt love for me, he was terrified of our level of intimacy. He felt I was beautiful and talented and desirable but any move toward a total commitment was petrifying in his mind. When his heart chakra opened, he allowed these fears to dissipate. He let go and let himself give me love and accept my love. He surrendered to the love within himself, which is never a mistake.

Footnote (8) Darshan roughly means guru's blessing – usually a lecture or chanting session with a guru (spiritual teacher).

When we arrived back at our Detroit ashram, everyone was aflutter, especially Lotus, at the news of our engagement.

The next week was even more uncomfortable than the last. Our ashram was clearly not for couples and it became evident that it would be difficult to continue living in such an unsympathetic environment. Gopala, I and many brother and sister ashramites in Detroit had taken a vow of celibacy until marriage, more than six months previously. Gopala and I had barely kissed through all of this. But all kinds of feelings were stirring and unresolved, so once again, the next weekend, we headed up to Toronto for more sage advice from Mata Eloise.

She suggested the two of us avoid playing around and just get married right away. Mata performed the ceremony that weekend and we both felt a sigh of relief. Gopala was hesitant about the traditional wedding night, so Mata suggested we take our time, sleep together a while as man and wife and wait to consummate the marriage when it felt right.

We returned to Detroit greeted by a flood of excited congratulations at our home ashram. As we were celebrating in the main satsang (chanting) room, my dear friend Jamie came up the ashram stairs. Lotus met him on the stairs with the exciting news: "Gopala and Kshama just got back from Toronto. They got married there!"

Jamie was taken aback: "No, you've got to be kidding?"

"No, it's true. Isn't it amazing," gushed Lotus.

"I'll say it's amazing alright!" sighed Jamie.

He had finally figured out, inside himself, that he and I had something special that should be shared in a relationship. Jamie had come over to visit that night in order to ask me for a date! I did not learn about this until much later on, when he himself was married.

Truly Jamie was meant to be with Kate, the woman he later married, as they had a bond that exceeded even Jamie's and mine. They had a long and happy marriage and all of us were friends for nearly fifteen years before we lost track of each other somewhere in the Midwest United States.

But now it was Gopala's and my wedding night at the Detroit ashram. We had a wedding celebration party that lasted until the early hours. Lotus had managed to set up a new bedroom for us so we could be together that night. He and I cuddled and slept without amorous intentions or actions.

A PLACE FOR EACH

Butterflies waltz by two in the light.
Moths prefer the glows of night.
Spiders dangle from a wall,
A maze of web their all-in-all.

Birds soar the air.
Fish rule the sea.
Flowers are everything –
To the honeybee.

And I – What creature might I be?
Who thrives in sunshine, dark, on land and sea?
The entire Universe is my place to be,
For I am a reflection of the Spirit in all I see.

The next day brought one of our biggest challenges – we had to tell our parents! My mother was easy-going, surprised and pleased. She had worked for Jewish bosses most of her life as a secretary/office manager and she loved the thought that I was marrying into a good Jewish family. My father was now living in Florida with his new wife (five years my senior). When I told him, he seemed pleased, but I was not concerned with his approval, or lack thereof.

Gopala's parents were another story. They had known of our engagement and heavily protested. No only son of theirs was going to marry a poor Gentile girl! Gopala had defended our engagement to them, but I wasn't certain that it was out of affection for me. It appeared to be more of a rebellious act at the time.

Now we faced his parents: Gopala's "average Joe personality" father with a peculiar sense of humor that occasionally matched his sons and his "high society" mother who had been through more operations than any twenty people had collectively. She was only a tiny thing of ninety-eight pounds, with a feisty temper. Gopala's father good-naturedly laughed off her iron grip control of him, but she definitely wore the pants in the family. I had met her once before when I had used the kitchen in her home months before with her daughter for an ashram bake sale. Gopala's mom had ended the day by screaming at us, for messing up her precious kitchen.

There was no denying, both his parents were not pleased with our situation. They had thoughts of disowning their son, but he was their only son and heir with two sisters and they could not bear to shut him out of their lives. So, they decided to accept us. They were upset not to have been invited to the wedding. When they found out it had only been a spiritual ceremony, not a legal one, they were determined to set things right with a huge wedding at their family synagogue and a very large reception at a fancy hotel.

Both Gopala and I protested. We would rather elope for the legal ceremony than be party to a stuffy ceremony that neither of us desired. After all, we were "spiritual hippies." All I wanted was a plain, gold wedding band – no diamonds please! My own divorced mother could not afford to pay for a wedding anyway. No problem, said Gopala's parents. They wanted to pay!

We settled on a small sixty people wedding ceremony at their smaller synagogue with both the family rabbis officiating and a small reception at Gopala's parents place so their friends could share in our nuptials and give gifts. Lotus was my maid of honor and Gurave, from the ashram was the best man.

Gopala's mother handled everything; I just got to help tone things down in size and opulence. My own mother found me a simple yet elegant, white, lacy dress. It was really a bit more like a fancier prom dress with a high, ruffled, little collar and puffy sleeves. I loved it. It suited me perfectly. My mother also paid for my bridal bouquet and the wedding party flowers. I chose white and yellow roses for my bouquet. Though daisies were at the time my favorite flower, Gopala had bought me a bouquet of yellow roses after our engagement and we decided the yellow rose was to be the symbol of our love. Occasionally, he would surprise me with the gift of one or more yellow roses, after we were married.

Before the ceremony, we met with one of the rabbis for a pre-wedding marital counseling session. He grilled us skillfully regarding our relationship and was not pleased with our answers. The rabbi asked us if we ever argued and we proudly declared that: "We never did." He said: "I'm sorry to hear that. You're not very likely to have a very long nor a very happy marriage." Was this prediction or prejudice? We would eventually know the truth.

While I could spend pages on the wedding itself, suffice to say it was really mainly for Gopala's parents. At twenty-one, I looked fourteen to most of the wedding guests. There was a professional photographer who took umpteen pictures. By the end of the day, both Gopala and I had given up our natural non-violent tendencies and wanted to literally strangle the photographer, as we did not have ten uninterrupted minutes away from him the entire day. After all that, most of the wedding pictures are long since buried in some trash heap somewhere. C'est la Vie!

Well, at least the families had a good show, and we were legally wed.

Lotus, who had insisted on wearing white, as my bride's maid, was delighted that many reception guests mistook her for the bride. She had trouble containing her jealously and soon after our wedding borrowed my dress for her own wedding and never returned it.

Not to be forgotten, about one week after our spiritual wedding in late March, (weeks before the legal wedding), Gopala came home to me from a Jewish holiday ceremony he shared alone with his family and relatives, and wanted to physically consummate our marriage. I was willing and ready and full of anticipation for a night of pleasure and love. I relished the commencement of a satisfying and enjoyable sex life with him.

Unfortunately, the initial act was quick, clumsy and it wreaked more of lust than love. I derived no pleasure from the initial act and silently hoped and prayed that time would improve our lovemaking as well as the bond between us.

I was headed for more disappointments. Gopala's love-making was crude, unskilled and unsatisfying for me. He rarely looked into my eyes or took the time to slowly get to know my body or my needs. He had a routine that was methodical and generally unvaried and uninnovative, and seemed determined to "get the job" done without wasting time on precious "details." Yet at that time period of my life, I was more inclined to find fault with myself. Why was I so uninspired when I was with Gopala? It was difficult for me to arouse anything close to my past passions with Manny or Sam while in Gopala's arms. As time went on, I blamed myself more and more. I thought my bad health had ruined me for good sex. Perhaps I was no longer capable of an orgasm? Time would tell.

Gopala and I planned a honeymoon with Mata Eloise's group, at their new farm in Thunder Bay, Ontario. It was an eight to ten hour drive through Lower Michigan, the Upper Peninsula and over the top of Lake Superior to this lakeside, small city in Canada. From there, it was yet another hour's drive to the farm, which was situated in a little town I will call Rotham. "God's Land" was the name Mata had given to the ashram's property.

We arrived at the farm around nine p.m. It was pitch dark and everyone had gone to bed except Adam and his wife Violet. Adam showed us a little room with candles and sparse furnishings, which included a low, wooden altar with a picture of Jesus on it and a bookshelf. We placed our own sleeping bags on the floor.

"Where is the bathroom?" we asked.

Adam told us: "The outhouse is a block from the house and too difficult for you to find at night." Then he gave us a quart jar, the type used for fruit juices with about a two and a half inch diameter opening, and said: "Use this until morning."

Gopala protested: "It's okay for me to use the jar, but what about my wife? How is she supposed to use this?"

"She'll manage," Adam replied. "The other women here have no problem using jars. Have a goodnight. We'll see you in the morning."

Though it was the middle of May, the room was quite chilly and had no heat. As there was no water, outside of a small water pitcher and one drinking glass, we did not wash up before we crawled into our double sleeping bag together. It was a poor honeymoon indeed, and I immediately wished we had gone to a motel at least for the first night.

Morning brought a cheerful reunion with the Toronto ashramites we had gotten to know and love on our several visits during our engagement and marriage.

The farmhouse was really half of a small house. The rest of the house was still lived in by two bachelor brothers named Clem and Ernie. They previously owned the land and had built into its sale to Mata Eloise's group that they had the right to stay there until they died. They were beyond sixty, a bit grizzly and unshaven and they drank a bit too much, too often. However, Clem and Ernie were friendly enough and proved to have a wealth of farming and local information.

Most of the God's Land ashramites lived in tents that spread up the side of a large, green hill. There was a big well-weathered barn, a machine shed, another large shed that had been turned into a kitchen, an outhouse, but little else in the way of buildings.

However, the gorgeous expanse of the one-mile-square farm stretched in all directions with huge hills and small magical looking mountains surrounding an array of green, gold and brown fields. The farm buildings lay in the center of a wide valley with a long, winding stream or some called it a tiny river running through it.

We spent a week there, visiting, helping with chores and discussing plans for our move there. It was impossible for us to stay at the Detroit ashram any longer, as we no longer fit into a single person's ashram. Gopala was in love with Mata and her group and I was willing to go where he wanted.

Our week-long visit was cold, damp, muddy and filled with terrible meals that consisted of wild green salads (picked off the land), soy beans cooked with bay leaves and onions, plain brown rice with tamari soy sauce, home-grown alfalfa sprouts, a few old wrinkled root vegetables (beets, carrots and potatoes) from an ancient storage cellar, and water from the small river on the property. Thank God, Gopala and I drove to the local country store a few times and splurged on some fruit, nuts, yogurt, desserts and other goodies!

There was no bathroom or shower. Bathing was done by taking a communal, all naked, steam sauna, first the women together, then the men following. The makeshift sauna shed was a quarter mile from the house. After sweating off the dirt in the sauna, that was followed by throwing a bucket of cold river water on yourself. The water had been hauled by each participant, the quarter mile plus from the riverbed.

When it was time for Gopala and me to leave the farm, I was exhausted from limited sleep, poor food and too much work, though he seemed able to handle the farm conditions better and to take them in stride. We were both in serious need of a bath and some clean clothes. We said our temporary good-byes to the ashramites, as we planned to return to the farm and live there. We packed up our car and after several hours of driving, we stopped in the afternoon, at a lovely little motel in Michigan's Upper Peninsula. It was advantageously situated on an adorable lake surrounded by acres of woods.

Here, we shared some of our happiest hours together. Gopala and I waded in the cool lake and splashed each other playfully.

FOREVER IS NOW

Crying sounds inside a seashell, soft,
Like the echo of an ocean.
Looking at the sky
Through a hole in my mirror.
I can't help but sigh
As I see it come nearer.
Sun and seagulls,
Naked – lying in the sun.
Will I ever get this moment to last?
Starfish and angels laugh.
Will you whisper in my ear?
– Toss me in the lake?
It seems now is forever.
And I'm eating waves and sun.
Splash me all around the shore.
Dive with me in the sand for fun.
Hear the echoes of that day
When for us, our world was begun.

The two of us took a long scenic walk and I felt freer and happier with him than I had in weeks. Perhaps because the pressure was off. Later, we shared a good meal at a local restaurant and spent a cozy night in a warm room. Gopala and I took our time leaving the next morning. Then we enjoyed a leisurely drive to our Detroit ashram. The day and night that we spent on the lake still remains in my memory as one of our most pleasant and romantic times together.

WELL OF SOUL

Come to me.
Drink with me,
At the well of Soul.
Dance with me.
Love with me,
If you would be whole.

THE DANCE OF SOULS

Why am I allowed to see
The souls of men and birds and trees?
The glory of manifest God
In them I see.
And I think I'd like them all
To do a dance with me.
A dance of praise and thanks,
Of Love –
With they and I entwined.

Between the hearts of me and all things,
An energy of soul does flow.
We sing and dance in each other's arms.
Ours auras as one enfold.
We soar, we sing,
We dance, we radiate.
Our beings merge as we mate.
We come together and kiss
And then we separate.

We go onward in our dance
To meet new souls and creatures, in grace,
That we may taste a bit of heaven
In all things on this earth.
For in essence we are all soul,
Created in God's likeness.
To realize this
And to dance this dance of Love,
We must all take birth.

We dance through the highs
And lows of earth.
We learn to sing and praise.
We learn to give thanks
And we learn to overcome.
Eventually we realize that
All things are possible.
When we are ready –
We experience – our rebirth!

Chapter Seven – The Farmers in the Dell

"O youth, still wounded,
Living, feeling with a woe unutterable,
Still grieving with a grief intolerable,
Still thirsting with a thirst unquenchable –
Where are we to seek?"

Thomas Wolfe
Where Are We To Seek?

It took much more than a month for Gopala and me to get our affairs in order in Detroit for our move to Canada. He had to prepare papers for our immigration. I had immigrated to Windsor a few years before, but had given up my Canadian landed immigrant status when I returned to Detroit. With married couples, it was the husband's responsibility to fulfill requirements for joint immigration into Canada. All letters and necessary legal papers had to be collected beforehand. We had to take all our belongings and papers with us to the Canadian border and present them at the moment we moved into the country.

Gopala needed medical records, letters of reference, proof of a job waiting in Canada, financial statements and more, before we were accepted into the country as landed immigrants.

In the interim, my health was failing. Our one-week farm visit had shown my weaknesses. It was imperative that I get help to boost my flagging energies. We took a whole week off from our moving preparations to visit a well-known specialized medical clinic in Ohio. Here a team of expert doctors probed, tested and questioned me regarding my fluctuating health. I had frequent headaches, dizziness, extreme fatigue, depression and rampant negative thoughts that entered my head in constant procession, and my body throbbed nearly all the time to the point of my feeling weak and faint often.

My mind and my emotions were constantly confused. Thoughts rushed together and overwhelmed me. These were unstable, often sexual and sometimes perverse in nature. It was as if my head was tuned to several radio stations at once, and the channels crossed over each other. The stations I picked up were certainly not of the highest quality. My low level of health seemed to generally allow for the lowest thoughts of people around me to settle into my mind as if they were my own. I was, at the time, adept at controlling my outer responses to these thoughts while interacting in the world – but inside of me – I was in utter confusion, helpless to these inner thoughts and feelings that controlled me. What hope could there be for my release from this "possessed" state?

At the Ohio clinic: blood, urine, skin, cell, saliva and fluid tests were given to me along with readings from various machines and apparatuses I was then unfamiliar with. They probed my body and my mind. The head of the clinic, (I'll call him Dr. Strom), was a learned man of international renown in the medical field, but he was also a master in the techniques of Silva Mind Control, as was the clinic's psychiatrist.

After examining me, the psychiatrist, named Bob, who was also quite psychic due to his training in Silva, declared to my husband: "You married her – in the state she's in?" with questioning eyes that doubted my husband's sanity.

I underwent seven full days of testing and treatments. Dr. Strom conferred with several others of the resident medical specialists – physicians, technicians and the psychiatrist, before presenting his diagnosis to my husband that I was dying. He said: "We have never seen a liver so bad in a person who is still alive. Her lungs, spleen and pancreas are also ruined," he added. Then to me he spoke openly: "Get ready to die. If you are lucky, you may have two or three months yet to live. But it is already a miracle that you are alive now. You should already be dead. It is impossible to regenerate a liver such as yours. It would take a spectacular miracle to save you, but I do not believe that is possible in your case." Dr. Strom touched my shoulder consolingly: "Prepare yourself. There is nothing we can do for you except to offer guidance and support. Take it easy, rest, take care of yourself and try to enjoy the time you have remaining with your husband."

Dr. Strom's words were unbelievable to me. In my heart, I totally could not accept them. "I have no intention of dying," I told him. "I am going to live no matter what it takes. I am going to heal myself and live a normal life."

"I understand how you feel," replied Dr. Strom, "but there is nothing that can be done for you, except to make you a little more comfortable. Make peace with your life. You have to be realistic and prepare to die."

"I intend to live," I said, "no matter what it takes!"

Dr Strom looked at me with total compassion and quit the room. I still had one more session with Dr. Bob, the psychiatrist, before being released from the clinic. Besides being an expert in his field and being able to read minds through his "mind control" studies, Dr. Bob was also a deeply religious man of notable spiritual powers and perceptions. I had several previous sessions with him and now we shared our final appointment.

Dr. Bob gave me one last spiritual exercise to do that required me to imagine myself, as I wanted to be. I managed to go deeply within, to my God center and still my raging outer mind temporarily. Then I envisioned myself as a perfected God-being who radiated pure light and love to all humankind. This love filled me completely and I felt it heal me as it poured from me unto all the peoples of the world.

At this point in my exercise, I heard a pencil drop to the ground and looked over to see Dr. Bob staring at me with his jaw dropped fully open. He looked at me with total surprise and somewhat in disbelief. He had read my exact thoughts! He sprang from the room and sought my husband. He cried: "Your wife is an amazing woman. She has the potential to become a great saint."

Dr. Bob then conferred with Dr. Strom regarding my visualization session with him and Dr. Strom now declared there was hope for me to live. My path would be treacherous, both doctors told me, but it was possible for me to succeed and heal if I fully desired it and set my mind to complete healing.

I fully believed in my own healing. Dr. Bob kindly told me that I could seek him in my mind for help at any time and he would assist me – no matter how far away I was or how troubled, he said he could hear me and would respond and send me help. I believed him with all my being and used this privilege he bestowed on me – only rarely – when in great need over the next couple of years.

Gopala and I then left the Ohio clinic and returned to our Detroit ashram to finish our moving preparations. We were armed with special supplements to help repair my damaged organs and digestive aids for me to take plus high protein foods to assist me with my low blood sugar problems that the clinic had detected during my many tests.

In Michigan, we took routine medical tests with a Detroit general practitioner for our immigration and were amused by his standard "once over" methods declaring that we *both* were in excellent medical health. We had been warned by our Thunder Bay ashram friends to obtain medical tests before coming to Thunder Bay as the immigration doctor there gave "unusually long and unnecessary 'probing' tests" to all young and attractive women whom he examined. I had no desire for such lengthy molestation.

Gopala and I arrived at the border at Sault St. Marie with our car: Gopala's Ford Maverick and a small U-Haul trailer in tow. After several hours of interviews and paperwork, we were accepted as landed immigrants into Canada. We proceeded to our God's Land ashram in Rotham near Thunder Bay in the evening of that same day. The adventure of a lifetime was about to begin!

We had purchased a large six-man tent in Detroit of exceptional quality to live in for the summer, the same as the other ashramites, on the side of a large green hill the equivalent of a quarter of a mile from the farmhouse. We arrived at the farm in the late evening of a summer day and were pleased to find that nightfall happened about eleven p.m. during the warmer months, in Thunder Bay. While it was still light, we pitched our new tent on the lower side of "tent hill" to avoid adding distance to our trek to the house and barn each day.

IN SEAS OF MOVING GRASS

On the hill,
With the trees
— In seas
Of moving grass.

By the river,
Flowing with the breeze
— In seas
Of moving grass.

On the mountain
Feeling free
— In seas
Of moving grass.

In the meadow
One with flowers and bees
— In seas
Of moving grass.

There were just under thirty people living on this land with Mata Eloise. It would take an entire book to completely express all that happened to Gopala and I on this farm. Each day was a new experience. Unlike the stable atmosphere of Swami Satchidananda's ashram in Detroit, Mata Eloise's farm seemed to have no permanent rules except that Mata was in charge and whatever she ordered was done.

The ashram owned a health food store in Thunder Bay and the men ran it and drove the hour into town each way, each day. Gopala loved doing this. The store held all kinds of cheeses, nuts, snacks and goodies which he and the other farm lads readily indulged in, while the women stayed at home and ate plain farm food just like that previously mentioned: beans, brown rice, whole grains, wild salad greens, sprouts, wrinkled root cellar veggies, sometimes plain yogurt and river water.

The women took turns cooking in the outdoor kitchen, making rolled oatmeal or millet for breakfast to be served with blackstrap molasses and/or strong flavored unrefined oil plus the other meals as previously described. The cook also had to haul water in five gallon buckets, about one block from the river to the outdoor kitchen. Each ashramite was required to eat one bowl of alfalfa and/or bean sprouts before each meal of breakfast, lunch and supper as a good health regimen. I learned to loathe sprouts and to this day, I still avoid eating them, except on rare occasions when I am served them by mistake, at friends' houses.

About once a month, we got a case of bananas so we could all get a little fruit while the land's seasonal berries were unavailable. We all fought over these bananas and stole them from the root cellar every chance we had because we were so deprived of good food variety. We were always hungry.

All of us lived mainly outdoors, in our tents and around or near the outdoor kitchen. Most of the meals were eaten outside except in rainy weather. We all wore shin-high mud boots, as it was always damp or raining and constantly muddy. I developed a permanent staph infection on both shins that lasted until after I left the farm.

Often, even in those summer months, we woke up with rainwater on the floor of our tents that had frozen to ice in the chilly nights. On sunny days, the ladies tried to dry out the sleeping bags in the sun, but often, we just slept in them damp. I think I might have frozen to death in those days if I had not had my husband to keep me warm in our double sleeping bag. In those days, my health was so bad, I seemed to retain very little body heat and would be shivering and feel freezing even on the rare days that the temperature went up to eighty degrees Fahrenheit (just about twenty-seven degrees Centigrade).

The half of the divided house we shared with the two brothers who previously owned the land, Clem and Ernie, gave us ashramites one large living room (furnished only with two long, low, home-made tables we squatted on the floor at, to eat our meals) plus three bedrooms used as sewing and work rooms and an attic for clothes and storage. Laundry was done in town, one day per week. Some of the men worked on the land and not in town, plowing fields with an ancient tractor and building an addition on to the house in preparation for the coming winter months.

Gopala's and my wedding money and presents went into the common fund to pay for our share of the land, plus a milking goat and treadle sewing machine that each couple was supposed to buy. The farm had one milking cow, several goats, a horse and quite a few chickens for eggs.

The plan for the farm was to make it a sustaining live-off-the-land refuge. Mata predicted (with the help of multiple world psychics like Nostradamus and Edgar Cayce), that in a few years, the world would shift on its axis and most of the world inhabitants would die. Our farm was to be a safe haven for wandering souls who needed a place to flee to when many of the world's lands went underwater and the global economy came crashing down.

It was the ashramites' job to make this one square mile of poorly worked land fit to nurture not only ourselves, but also others who came our way for help. We had to be self-sustaining as soon as possible.

We had a rigorous daily routine that began about six a.m. with kundalini yoga, "breath-of-fire," meditation, having Joel Goldsmith books read to us during all meals, and working ten to twelve hours on the land for those who did not work in town.

The work was especially difficult for me as I was weak and had little vitality. I was given no special considerations for my poor health except that I was given one pound of almonds per week – for protein – for my low blood sugar. Almonds were also given to one other girl at the farm who also had low blood sugar. The one morning a week I was assigned to make breakfast began at five a.m. Hauling river water was strenuous and I got calluses and backaches. I tended the chickens, daily fetched and cleaned Mata's bed chamber pot, planted and cared for the flower gardens and helped weed our large crop of root vegetables including: turnips, beets, carrots and radishes, as well as some spinach, lettuces and zucchini, daily. The other women and I picked wild salad greens, wild rose petals for jam making, rose hips (in fall) for soups and in season, a multitude of wild berries including: strawberries, raspberries, blackberries, blueberries, currants, huckleberries, gooseberries and saskatoons.

I learned to identify, pick and prepare all kinds of wild greens for eating raw, drying or cooking. We roasted cattails; steamed marsh marigolds and stinging nettles (the later tasted like cooked spinach); dried teas like: chamomile, peppermint, raspberry leaves and dozens of others and harvested lambs quarters, fiddle heads, dandelion greens, vetches, wild sorrels and flower head for salads. I learned to dig dandelion roots and chop and slow roast them for coffee. Yarrow leaves were picked and later chewed to put on cuts and small wounds. Marigold flowers were placed around the outside of the house to keep mosquitoes and other flying insects away. One benefit of the farm for me was learning to identify and utilize hundreds of wild plants, a talent that I still use to this day.

Though I did my best to shoulder my share of the heavy workloads, I was weak and dizzy often, and fainting was a normal occurrence for me. I would frequently collapse in the fields, rest awhile and begin working again as soon after as I was able.

In summer and fall months, outdoor work was plagued with flying insects that bit or stung, including: gnats, no-see-ums, mosquitoes, deer flies, horse flies, wasps, hornets, a variety of bees and more. I always had about two hundred bug bites on me at all times. The crazy deer flies tormented me and others by flying around persistently while buzzing noisily until they struck a tender spot, leaving a huge pimple-like protrusion with a trickle of blood pouring from the center. Sometimes we tried to outrun the deer flies and they could chase a person adamantly for over twenty minutes. At the end of a day outside, I looked like a leper. (This was reminiscent of one past life I "saw" at the Satchidananda ashram in my meditations wherein I was a leper.) No amount of bug spray or netting could save me or the other ashramites during a summer/fall day outside.

On the farm, there were also animals to care for; a cow and goats to milk, chickens to collect eggs from, bees to keep and collect their honey, a horse to groom and exercise, stables to clean, hay to pitch, the outhouse to shovel and compost weekly, animal manure and food garbage to compost, firewood to collect for two wood burning stoves, occasionally plain brown bread to bake and small trees to chop down for fires and building fences.

I struggled pitifully to get through each day on the farm, while Gopala enjoyed easy workdays in town at the ashram's health food store (enjoying plentiful goodies there as he worked). Our daily schedule changed all the time, sometimes daily, weekly or even hourly. Mata would send down notes from her tent perch on top of tent hill saying: "Now we'll get up an hour earlier," or "Leave everything and dig me a hole." The next day we might just fill it in. It was a test of obedience.

Our daily "sadhana" or spiritual practices at the farm,

changed frequently. We might meditate, chant and do yoga six hours a day and work eight hours at farm work, or do sadhana ten hours a day and work two to four hours on the farm. We also had a monthly twenty-four hour chanting session while fasting on water. This included an hourly rotating chant leader and the rest of us responding all day and all night. Sometimes we meditated an entire day and sometimes we worked all day. Each day became a surprise.

After a few months of farm living, weak as I was, I believed I was pregnant. After a rare trip to town and a doctor's visit, I was told I was not with child. I still felt pregnant and floundered even worse at my work. Carrying those two five-gallon buckets from the river became unbearable among other tasks for me. I maintained I knew I was pregnant and everyone said I was lazy and trying to get out of work.

The next month I was back in town for another doctor's visit. This time I was told I was two and a half months pregnant. Finally a reprieve! Gopala and I celebrated at the health food store with a small bottle of grape juice and we called our parents. Back at the farm, I got apologies for being called lazy and I was given a whole day off to rest the next day! Unfortunately, the very next day, I began to hemorrhage. I was taken into town, to the hospital and lost the baby after thirty-six hours of hard labor. I was devastated. Gopala and I had just proudly told our parents.

Gopala stood close by me during my entire miscarriage ordeal. He never left my side. I was grateful and realized then how much he really did care for me. On that rare occasion, all his smirks and jokes were left behind. His somber face – that I had never seen that way before – showed me that he had genuine love and concern for me. This event bonded us closer during this and many further trials we had yet to face together.

After the miscarriage, I was given a small vacation from farm work. My head was now more confused than ever. When I returned to work, I did what I was told, but was constantly missing sleep, in pain and mentally disorientated. I felt that if I could meditate again regularly – alone – as I had in the Detroit ashram, I could get out of this "slump," heal myself and raise my energy enough to enjoy clear thinking, more physical energy and an elevated spiritual consciousness. I was allowed by Mata to spend four hours a day doing deep breathing, in the late afternoon, in my tent or outside on sunny days.

RENEWAL

Sitting here on this green hill.
Day's work is done.
I am tired. I am weary.
I seek the warmth of the sun.

Clouds are forming,
Quickly passing,
So I lie down
In the grass.

Letting go of cares and worries,
Tiredness, aloneness, emptiness –
I give them all to the hill.
I let them go, the earth accepts them.

Caressing me in its arms,
I become one with the hill.
I let go and sink into the earth.
– My mother comforts me.

Warm, caressing, Mother Earth,
Bluest Sky,
Father Sun kissing me,
Brushing tears from my eyes.

I am a rock. I cannot move.
So firmly I lie.
Birds and creatures all around me,
Fly overhead or crawl by.

My emptiness is filled completely.
Seasons of my mind go by.
Ever changing dreams and visions,
Fill me warm with joy inside.

I need not seek worldly pleasures,
Beg for more than what's inside.
Peace within me, Peace without –
All the universe is mine.

I had learned a new breathing technique that could and should be done lying down and I attempted to do it for up to four hours a day. It was very difficult, but I persisted and mastered the chore after a couple months. Later on, I mastered using this deep breathing technique for up to eight hours a day. Little changed for me at first until it was discovered that the river water we had all been drinking was totally polluted and full of parasites. Fresh water was thereafter hauled from town until the following spring when a well was to be dug. After a change to fresh drinking water, I improved slightly and made real progress with my daily four hours of pranic, deep breathing meditations.

As I continued my breathing practices, my psychic abilities grew and I saw visions of many past lives of my own, Gopala's, and others at the farm ashram. Since my marriage to Gopala, the prison camp dreams and visions had returned to me in a regular flow. Gopala, after all, was Jewish and he had been involved with me in my last Jewish lifetime. Sometimes in good months, my prison camp recollections disappeared for a while, but during extreme conditions, which were frequent at the farm, my prison camp visions haunted me in the daytime as I lived a prison camp lifestyle again on the farm. A classic example of how past lives sift into present ones when past karmic lessons have not yet been fully learned!

For a short while, the women of the farm got to run the health food store in town and I enjoyed that immensely. I personally got to manage the store for a while as I had some past health food knowledge that I had gained at Swamiji's Detroit ashram. The drive to and from town gave two hours off from work. There were "real people" to see in town, and nuts and cheeses to sample at the store. Individually, none of us farm folk had any personal spending money. Any necessities were bought one day a week by the assigned store "purchaser." So the only way to get treats was to work in the store or receive gift packages from friends or parents.

After a little over a year or so on the farm, Mata made us sell the store so we could concentrate on farm work. She spent an entire afternoon tearing up all the nice town clothes we ashramites had and we switched to simple draw-string, denim trousers or sometimes blue jeans for the guys, long denim skirts for the gals and both wore homemade, long sleeved, bleached-white cotton shirts with a hood as a kind of farm uniform. Most of the women sewed these shirts, trousers and skirts on our old-fashioned treadle sewing machines, which I failed utterly at using.

I hated these farm uniforms! It brought back remembrances of Catholic School uniforms for me and even worse, brought up visions of German prison camp attire and living. I preferred my long flowered dresses that made me feel pretty and feminine. However, my attractive looks were proving too much of a temptation for some of the single as well as the married farm men. Mata felt this uniform had a double purpose of practicality and keeping all the women looking generic and plain – like in some Amish or Mennonite community. Months later, we had to buy new town clothes as working in town once again became a necessity required to make money to keep the farm running.

The intensity of farm work and spiritual sadhana continued to escalate. I had trouble relating to many of the women at the farm, we seemed to have little in common and they loathed my frailties and frequent health complaints. I turned to God again as a refuge from my loneliness. I barely saw Gopala in the daytime and since I did not sew, much of my work found me isolated in the fields.

During my afternoon pranic, deep breathing sessions, I discovered a disturbing past life with Violet, Adam's wife. These two were sort of like "head couple" at the farm. In my visions, I saw Violet torturing me in this past life. She was, in that life, a practitioner of the black arts who used her magic to obtain power and possessions. As I had opposed her then, she was determined to destroy me. Past Violet had imprisoned me and was having a male servant of hers torture me by sticking over 200 sharpened feathers into my body – all over – to slowly drain every drop of my blood out of my body and kill me. I watched myself die at her hands. I felt the life in my body gradually ebbing away until I drifted into unconsciousness and floated above my body. I know that I was quite upset at her, in that lifetime, for choosing to kill me. I felt betrayed by her in that life, as she had previously been a friend.

When Mata heard about this past lifetime, she "assigned" Violet and I to do special eye meditations to mend our past animosity and we also did healing energy work to remove the grudge that we had apparently carried for lifetimes. Violet and I eventually became friends, but we were never deeply close.

At one point, for several months time, we farm ashramites were required to do "Shiva Dancing," a type of fast paced spiritual dance done by couples, face to face, to intensify spiritual progress. Mata had us doing one or two hours daily, as sadhana (spiritual practice). Couples danced together and singles found an opposite or same sex partner as was available. This dancing opposite each other, looking into each other's eyes, while chanting feverishly and dancing vigorously, brought up all kinds of intense emotions between the couples. Emotions heightened and tempers flared during these dances. This was no gentle exercise that inspired loving encounters.

One troubled guy, named Loren, had been having mental and emotional problems that included crying and fear attacks from the intensity of the dancing and farm living. He "took on" the wild idea that he was a vampire and one day, during our Shiva Dancing, Loren lundged at his wife and viciously bit her deeply on the neck, drawing blood. The bite eventually left a telltale scar. This was only one of the many "crazy" episodes that occurred on the farm. The intensity of farm living easily drove some people over the edge.

Many visitors who came to stay at the farm "freaked-out," after a few hours, days or a few weeks, and had to leave. People were disturbed, frightened and even mortified by our severe spiritual practices, the extreme hard work and the poor food and living conditions.

Once, a very dark soul, a heavily bearded young man, came to visit us for our regular public chanting on Sunday evening. Most of the farm people, even those who were not psychic and myself, could see his horrible, dark aura. He had the eyes of a Charles Manson, which made him appear destined to do evil deeds and he was obviously practicing black magic arts. We were all relieved when he left that night and never returned.

Another time, a troubled young woman came to visit the farm for a day. Everyone felt sorry for her, and my friend Eva let this woman sleep on her and her husband's sleeping bag bed for a few hours before she went on her way. That began a several week long catastrophe for Eva and her husband Mark. The woman left a gift of "crabs" in their bed! Eva and Mark spent weeks shaving pubic hair, washing with special shampoos, and totally scrubbing and sanitizing their entire sleeping quarters. They were devastated by this event, but carried on with their usual kindness and loving attitudes that had always made them the most loving couple on the farm. This was not surprising as they both had uniquely open heart chakras.

Mata was always picking up strange energies and vibrations from rocks, feathers, trees and the air. She said a dead Indian haunted one pretty rock found in the river and she vibrationally "cleared" the rock and ordered the finder to throw it back into a lesser-visited, wider area of the river where no one would find it again.

One night Mata woke us all out of our beds and made us chant and meditate for hours to clean the bad energies she felt all around us. If thoughts of Jim Jones or Charles Manson come to your mind at these remarks, I must say that Mata fluctuated between divine revelations and insane ramblings. Mata actually achieved some lower "samadhis" (advanced spiritual experiences) but was by no means fully "God-realized". (Beyond earthly experiences and no longer needing to be reincarnated.) She was capable of major human mistakes as well as erroneous spiritual perceptions. Mata had developed some "siddhis" (spiritual or psychic powers) like the ability to read minds, occasionally predict the future correctly, give some spiritual experiences to followers (as she had Gopala by opening his heart chakra), and she was able to emanate some healing energies, but she had many inconsistencies in her nature and behaviors. She was as controlling as my father in her own individual way, and often just as erratic in her words and actions. (*Attaining psychic powers can drive some people crazy.*)

Though Mata would never intentionally hurt a person physically, in any way, she was not beyond overloading her "chelas" (spiritual followers) with rigid austerities of diet, exercise, work and spiritual practices. She did this "for our own good," (shades of my father!), and to supposedly help us to grow spiritually. She frequently bemoaned the fact that she felt God was forcing her to be a "hammer" on us, to hammer us into good spiritual shape.

On one day she wanted us to eat only brown rice and sprouts, days later she would give us a feast day, then she wanted us to fast. Nothing ever stayed the same. I learned to survive anything at the farm, but I suffered bitterly with many miscarriages, inconsistent sleep, thinking difficulties, low blood sugar, malnutrition and other multiple health problems as well as from the poor quality, limited food and polluted water.

During the farm years, in the early seventies, gurus and ashrams were plentiful in North America and all the "rage". There were some popular guidebooks printed yearly in a series called: *The Spiritual Community Guidebook*. These books consistently listed Mata Eloise's farm ashram as: "the strictest spiritual community in all North America."

Certainly the Ohio doctor's advice for me to take it easy was not happening at this farm. Yet perhaps the tortures of the farm were what helped me to survive and become strong? I guess I was not finished with needing reflections of my last lifetime in a prison camp, as I created more suffering beyond experiences with my father, at this farm. But the farm taught me to survive anything! I learned to milk goats and a cow, plus I saw a cow give birth to a male calf and eat the afterbirth. I developed better cooking skills, chopped down trees, planted and tended vegetable and flower gardens, hayed, drove a tractor, fed the chickens and shoveled their manure, shoveled outhouses, learned to pick wild fruit and herbs, did new crafts like making paper and baskets out of pine needles, learned decoupage, learned to ride a horse bareback, composted, companion planted, made jams, froze and canned vegetables, dried herbs, and countless other skills that have served me my entire life. Yes, it was devastatingly hard on the farm, but living in and cleaning a house with real plumbing is now relatively easy for me by comparison.

Months later, during our first year at the farm, a girlfriend of Gopala's and mine named Sara, from our Detroit ashram days, moved up to God's Land. Sara and I had a close, loving bond that helped sustain me through those struggling farm years. Several months after moving to the farm, Sara married one of the farm lads and a few years later they had a lovely little girl. Sara and I shared a natural open heart chakra communion and one day it blossomed into a once-familiar experience and I began to understand some of the meanings of one of my past spiritual experiences.

It was the day of a special farm celebration. No farm work was to be done that day, beyond necessities like animal care and food preparation. Town friends were invited to the farm for a special "darshan" (being in the presence of a "holy person") with Mata Eloise. This included blessings, chanting and a huge feast with really tasty food and lots of fruit too! Sara and I were upstairs, in the loft area, chatting before the event, and we became engrossed in our loving discourse with each other. As we gazed into each other's eyes, our eyes locked in waves of love-filled ecstasy. Our spirits rose beyond our bodies and we experienced total, overwhelming, divine love for each other. It was just like my experience with Gopala, the night I had visions that he and I would marry.

I had no idea that this experience could be repeated with someone else, and a woman yet! Sara and I only experienced a continual state of bliss for many hours rather than the three days of ecstasy I had shared with Gopala. We were lifted beyond our bodies and we both saw the reality of who we actually were – beings of God-filled light, without limits, earthly pains or cares. All the beauty that Sara is, I drank, while my own heart exploded into waves of love and ecstatic joy.

TOGETHER MAGIC

What happens to me when I am with you?
My soul seems to kiss you
And we speak not of earthly things.
Together our souls sing.
Together we take to the air
And soar likes kids on a swing.

What can be the magic when together we meet?
It is not just one soul who does this for me.
It is every soul I seem to see.
It is every wonderful You I meet.
Together, together – we merge
And our soul dreams grow complete.

What a delightful, profound and unexpected treat this experience was for me! I later found out that this experience could be repeated with anyone who opened their heart to me fully and I to them. I have been blessed with this soul-to-soul divine communion many times in my life now and it is always a treasured, luscious treat that I savor. It happened again for me, on the farm, a couple months later with a young man with an open heart chakra, named Robert who was the dearest soul. When this spiritual experience occurs between another and myself, it lets me know that I am really open, loving and connected with a person. I call it: "Seeing the God in someone."

About a month after my experience with Sara, I met a beautiful young, blond woman visitor at the farm, named Veronica. She was gentle and soft-spoken and I felt an instant rapport with her. We spoke together about our individual lives and we became open to "Seeing the God in each other." We shared this loving experience for more than an hour and I saw that she and I had been very happily married in a previous life, one wherein I was a man. I had never before experienced seeing such a lifetime. I had not known previously that I could be another sex in a past life!

I saw Veronica again after that day, only twice before she moved to another city. We always felt tender love and kindness for each other when we spoke. But neither of us wanted or needed to re-express our past life love connection sexually in this life. We had no lesbian tendencies or desire to connect in that manner. It was fully enough to express our androgynous soul love. I recognized her as a soul mate of mine. (She was one of only four women soul mates I have met this lifetime, so far, amongst dozens of male soul mates.) Edgar Cayce said each of us may meet fifty or more soul mates in our present lifetime. (9)

I also learned that it was possible for a gifted spiritual teacher to tap a devotee (spiritual student or "chela") on the forehead, heart or any other of the seven chakras and send high voltage energy into them that could awaken spiritual experiences or psychic powers. Sometimes this energy gift is temporary and sometimes it lasts hours, days, months, years or lifetimes. Mata had done this to Gopala just hours before he and I looked into each other's eyes in Detroit and he and I "Saw the God in each other." She had done it again when Gopala and I were engaged, by pounding Gopala gently over the heart. I had also personally experienced such energy gifts from Swami Satchidananda, Mataji, Yogi Bhajan and other spiritual teachers.

During my Detroit ashram days, there was a fourteen year old "kid guru" who used to "zap" his followers with a tap on the forehead and give them powerful psychic experiences, but this was rumored to be dangerous and could end up being similar to a bad drug trip. I never met this kid guru.

That first farm summer, we had many of our chanting

Footnote (9) See Kevin Todeschi's book called: *Edgar Cayce On Soul Mates* by the A.R.E. Press for information on soul mates, ISBN 0-87604-415-1 or my book: *Soulmate Realities*.

sessions in the barn loft while the house was being added on to. Just before it got bitter cold, the addition was finally completed. It included a small mudroom for boots and shoes. (We wore slippers in the house – East Indian style.) There was also a large kitchen with a deluxe woodstove, a bathroom that anticipated fixtures in the spring. (We still did the outhouse and "chamber pot thing" that first winter.) There was an upper loft that overlooked the living room, two new bedrooms and a small room down a long hallway off the living room that was for Mata Eloise

Five couples, including Gopala and me, were given one of the five bedrooms and two more couples shared the loft area. The few single women slept in the living room and the many single guys shared the large attic that had little individual cubbyhole, sleeping areas built into it.

That first year we all bathed once or twice a week by taking nude saunas, in a shed heated with a wood-burning stove – first the women all together, then when we were finished, the men would sauna together. Occasionally some couple would sauna alone or with another couple when there was time and extra wood. The sauna loosened the dirt. Then we soaped down and finished by rinsing with a bucket of stream water. In winter, instead of the river water, we just rolled naked in the snow. It was strange to bundle up so warm on the way to the sauna in winter, and after to roll in the snow. On the way back from the sauna, we could walk the quarter mile to the house in a small towel as the heat of the sauna rose in steam from our bodies and kept us marvelously warm for twenty to thirty minutes afterwards, even in below zero temperatures.

Sometime near the end of that first summer, one of the farm cooks left a bottle of unrefined salad oil outside on a hot afternoon and we all got severe oil poisoning. This is much worse than general food poisoning. We were all in spasms for hours with agonizing pain throughout our heads and bodies with vomiting unlike any other food poisoning I have ever yet encountered. I believe it was a miracle we all survived it, we were all so violently ill. After this event, all the cooks used supreme caution with all oil products, including mayonnaise and salad dressings.

The first frost that year came in September. Afterwards we gathered plant roots to dry for teas and rose hips for winter soups and for vitamin C. Fall went by very fast while we finished the haying. The trees turned brown and gold, without the customary red blazing leafed trees that would have been interspersed in my past familiar Michigan landscapes. In a few weeks, autumn was over and a long, hard, cold winter set in.

At last, there was a little time to rest more and reflect. In winter we had an easier workload. There were days to explore the surrounding frozen mountains that had turned into a fairyland of delights with glasslike icicles hanging from every tree and rock. After a new snow, everything was transported into a magical, white wonderland. Our small river became a glistening road of ice that we cracked into "ice maps." Each piece of ice carried furrows and protrusions – like valleys, hills and roads. This made each chunk of ice look like a clear glass map or a rare and precious art sculpture.

When hiking in the hills and mountains, we bundled up with two pairs each of socks and gloves with a sprinkling of cayenne red pepper in between the two layers to keep our extremities warm and prevent frostbite. Some of us wore Eddie Bauer polar jackets with many layers underneath and scarves over our noses to keep them from freezing. It could be sixty degrees below zero for two months or more in the winter. Many days were too cold to venture out and sometimes we got snowed in. We joked that we had two seasons: "winter and the month of July," as we heard from Clem and Ernie that it was possible on the farm to get a frost as late as June and as early as the end of August. We had snow or we had mud. It was rarely dry, but we did have some hot, sunny days when we sweat more and the flying insects bit more frequently.

This first year was a true test of faith – for me – and for many at the farm. I often wondered to myself why I stayed, but I knew it was because I had been convinced, by Mata, Gopala and others, that to leave was to fail. And I knew I had to succeed. No matter what happened, I wanted to grow strong, survive and heal. No matter how many mistakes I made, how many times I fainted in the fields, how many miscarriages I had: I was no quitter. I would endure. But was this farm to be my entire future? No comforts, no TV, no warmth, no enjoyments – I wondered when, if ever, my life would be – fun.

As I am breaking old chains, am I welding new ones?
As I am tying up loose ends, is there an end in sight?

THE VOICE

A small voice wanting to be heard,
Shouted out – over the valley.
And in reply, there returned,
Not even a word.
All was silence.
All was still.
Nothing stirred.

Within the Heart the voice was calling,
Crying that a prayer be heard.
And through the valley
Came a murmur.
In the pine trees thrilled a bird.
The river babbled o'er the stones.
– The voice was heard!

Chapter Eight – The Second Year

"Your eye is so wise
It keeps turning, turning
Needing to touch beauty.
It keeps turning,
Needing to find a mirror."

Hafiz

In the beginning of the second summer at the farm, a well was dug on our property that provided fresh, sweet, pure water for drinking, cooking and bathing. The water was tested and found to be of the highest quality. The well was around a hundred feet deep and rather costly. A water reservoir was purchased to hold a constant supply of water for the farm's growing needs. Finally, we had a hooked-up bathroom with one toilet and a large washbasin sink that the smaller women, like myself, could climb into and bathe in occasionally. One toilet for thirty people and guests was hardly enough, so the outhouse still had a steady stream of customers, at least in warmer weather.

By the end of the first summer, there were no children on the farm and there was one pregnant woman in the house.

The following spring, children arrived. We had one newborn baby girl plus a nine-year-old girl named Lisa and her one-year-old sister who came with her mother and her mother's boyfriend.

Early that second summer, a nearly eight-month pregnant woman named Sharon arrived at the farm from one of Mata Eloise's outreach ashrams in Calgary, Alberta. Sharon brought with her, her one-year-old plus baby girl, named Bethany. Alex, Sharon's separated husband and their five-year-old son, John, arrived together a couple weeks later.

The birth of this couple's third child was to take place on the farm. All the women and some of the men were to be allowed to witness this miracle of new life coming into the world. I shall always treasure the experience of viewing and participating in the only human birth I have been privileged to share in, thus far in this lifetime. The labor took less than six hours. Luckily, the mother and baby were both healthy as only a midwife and Mata assisted with the birth and there were no hospitals anywhere near the farm.

The excitement and love that filled that room as a new baby boy entered the world erupted in a flow of ecstatic joy and exuberance. I giggled and sighed with elation and tingled from my toes to my head. What a blessed, blessed day to thrill in! It was such a rare treat to view and even more to feel life being born! There is a purity of energy unlike any other that fills a birthing room.

Shortly after the baby's birth, the mother, Sharon, took the newborn infant son and headed east and the father, Alex, took their five-year-old John and went west, returning to the Alberta ashram.

The couple's one-year-old baby girl, Bethany, was left at the farm for all of us to care for indefinitely. Though several women were responsible for the overall daily care of baby Bethany and the other one-year-old girl whose mother was living on the farm, I took it upon myself to love and nurture Bethany at night, and every free chance I got. I became a second mother to Bethany and loved her as my own. I played with her and took her everywhere I could with me. During free time we were always together. At meals and special occasions, she was on my lap. Bethany brought tremendous joy to my life and I gave her stability and my complete love. She and I were nearly inseparable as long as we were both at the farm.

Our gorgeous farmland bordered on a huge National Forest as well as other uninhabited lands and seemed to stretch forever, even beyond the edges of our one square mile that made up God's Land. Holy Spirit Mountain was part of our land and looked down upon us every day as we entered or exited the front door of our house. One end of the mountain formed a jagged cliff that was shaped like the face of an Indian warrior. The local Indians considered this mountain to be sacred. It was sometimes shrouded in mist, which gave the mountain a mystical presence that appeared to exude spiritual power. Thousands of birch and pine trees grew all over this sacred mountain. The entire rock face held no trees at all, save one lone pine that grew out of the center of the warrior's forehead, from the third eye chakra (the sixth chakra energy center). This was an indication of spiritual vision and authority.

We ashramites often took pilgrimages up on the rocky, steep slopes of this mountain and camped individually on it for three to seven days of spiritual retreats in warmer weather. I reveled in my time on this mountain, and felt the spiritual power that emanated from its woods and mists. It was a sacred site to all who opened up their consciousness to the power of this prestigious mountain. On some nights, when the moon was full, it cast an ethereal light over the warrior face of the mountain. As I gazed upon it, I believed I could make a wish that would come true. The magic of the mountain and the moon are stuff dreams and legends are made of:

MOON

Moon, moon, moon,
Sing me a lullaby.
Moon, moon, moon,
Tell me of God tonight.
Moon, moon, moon,
Shine on, oh luminous light.
Moon, moon, moon,
Fill me with Love tonight.
Moon, moon, moon,
Take the mountain's holy glow.
Moon, moon, moon,
Bless me with it so I may grow.
Moon, moon, moon,
Cradle me in your pale light,
Until I slip into dreams
That fulfill my sighs.

Summer was everywhere now. The berries were in mid-season, the root crops were beginning their first harvest, the wild roses bloomed all over the hills and mountains and my flower gardens were alive with color. Probably for the first time since I'd come to the farm, I was feeling content and at peace with myself and my "farm world." I had little Bethany to love, Gopala and I were both on the farm, working near each other, finally, and we had grown "comfortable" together. I kept the house full of flowers and posted inspirational poems and sayings on the walls among pretty pictures that gave our crude little house a homey presence that was felt and enjoyed by everyone in our farm family.

I also posted pretty magazine pictures with related sayings that I made up myself, including:

Time is the most precious gift.
It shows more of Love than words, money or jewels.

When Love, Truth and Peace play together,
The whole world will be full of light and joy.

A journey of five thousand miles begins with one
amazing step taken in the exact direction required.

During this second summer, my older sister Trixie came for a week to visit Gopala and me at the farm. Though she was thankfully, not required to work, Trixie hated our simple farm food and made the one mile walking trek to the Rotham country store each day with our then ten-year-old Lisa. Lisa was in heaven during my sister's visit. Together they pigged out on cheese, nuts, tuna, candy, soda and desserts bought with my sister's own money. I rarely shared in these treats! My sister claimed she lost ten pounds that week. No wonder I was so skinny then and was still barely one hundred pounds!

That summer I encountered two scary snakes. One I accidentally poked while haying and I had to jump back from its attack. Another time, one violently grabbed my shovel as I was cleaning it in the stream. I think that angry snake would have killed my shovel if he had been able to. These occurrences kept me ready for anything. I never knew what to expect each farm day.

Sometimes when the farm needed extra money, the farm men were hired out to work on other farms for a few days or a few weeks. There was one very large egg farm that sometimes hired a half dozen or so of our men to shovel chicken manure for a week or so when their equipment occasionally broke down. Gopala did this job twice with other of our farm's men. He told me that the chicken manure, which smelled horribly of ammonia, was piled waist high before wall-to-wall, tiny cages that each held several chickens. There were conveyor belts that took away the eggs and brought the chickens food. The chickens spent their whole lives in these cages and never saw the sun, a barnyard, or a rooster. The poor creatures!

When the manure removal machines broke down, the men were hired to shovel it up manually. Gopala said the barn was full of huge rats. He said: "First we shovel two or three shovels full of manure, then we hit an attacking rat. Another shovel or two more and we hit another rat." The guys did this eight hours a day. The first time they were hired for three days and second time for a week. The guys showered at the egg farm before returning home, but they still smelled horribly of ammonia and reeked terribly for days after a job was completed. When the guys were asked to do this job for a third time, I finally put my foot down. This was an absolute shock to everyone at the farm, as at that time in my life, I never had strong opinions about anything.

"Gopala is not going to shovel that chicken manure again," I declared adamantly, to Mata.

"We need the money for the farm," said Mata. "If the other men do it, Gopala has to do it too." Mata and I and many others were standing outside in front of the house.

"No, Gopala will not! I will not have him smelling worse than an outhouse! The men will just have to find other work. This is ridiculous! Gopala will not do this again and the other men should not have to either! I would rather starve!" I proclaimed with a vengeance.

"We may just have to starve if the men don't do this. Who are you, Alawan (my farm ashram name), to say they should not do this job?" replied Mata.

"I told you the men are not going to do this job!" I nearly shouted at Mata. I had never spoken to her this way before. Usually I talked to her with respect and reverence.

"I do not believe it is necessary for any of our men to do

this disgusting work. I will not put up with this. NO!" I shot Mata a totally determined glace that said: don't you dare cross me on this. I took Gopala by the hand and led him into the house, to our bedroom.

That was the last anyone dared to speak to me about it. Though I occasionally overheard Mata say afterwards: "Since that arrogant Alawan won't let the men work there, the men will have to find something else to do." The men *did* get other work and they never shoveled manure at that egg farm again while I lived there!

After all I had been through and done at the farm, even I had a limit as to what I would put up with. I had never said "no" to Mata before. But I knew throughout my being that this job was beyond necessity. We have choices in life. It was time to draw the line. Remember: "We create our own reality," and "We get what we concentrate on."

Once when Mata went into one of her frequent "spiritual ecstasies," and gave her famous (to us) predictions, the voice of God supposedly poured through her and said to Gopala and I: "You are my husband. You are my wife. You will live in my heart, as long as you live _____ loving me, all the days that you walk the earth." One word neither Gopala or I heard was the word after: "as long as you live" and before: " loving me, all the days of your life." Mata and other ashramites who where standing around were convinced the muffled word was "together." I was unconvinced. If God was indeed speaking so clearly through Mata, but I missed one word – then perhaps I wasn't supposed to hear it because it wasn't true for me. "You will live in my heart as long as you live – together – loving me," haunted me, especially in later years when I doubted Gopala's and my love.

But even Mata herself was convinced that God himself had married us specially through her. She told everyone that many of the farm marriages might not last, but she was positive that Gopala's and my marriage would last forever! Mata had more faith in our marriage than I did.

My relationship with Gopala was always difficult at best. However, we were never really hostile toward each other. In the early days of our marriage, I was bothered by his constant dandruff and noticed he did not rinse all the soap out of his hair properly after washing it. So I washed it for a while and taught him to wash his own hair correctly. Also, he had a strong love of telling what I called "potty jokes." Like the time he gave his best friend in high school a birthday present he said was "a part of himself." The present was a jar of his own feces and he gave it to his friend in front of dozens of birthday party guests and Gopala was thrown out of the party by his friend's parents. There were several more "urine and feces" jokes that I had to endure the retelling of over and over again throughout our marriage.

Nothing seemed to really ruffle Gopala. His emotions were generally controlled and even dismay, sadness and upset were covered up by him with stoic joking and forced humor. He had quick-thinking faculties and could assess a situation in life and find a way to manipulate the outcome of conversations and interactions with others in his favor. He lost no time in our marriage figuring out my weak points – my mental and emotional difficulties. He controlled every conversation between us and made himself look good and made me look like the defective, complaining wife who made him suffer. In actuality, he took delight in torturing me mentally and emotionally and confusing me into thinking everything that went wrong, was all my fault. It did not take much to confuse me in those days.

Gopala kept me humble, apologetic and uncertain as to what was actually happening between us. When I got manipulated and could not understand it, I would generally get mad and scream, or else I would cry and feel defeated. Then I would go off by myself to try unsuccessfully to sort out what was happening between us. I just did not have the mental clarity to see and understand the truth in those early days of our marriage.

Our lovemaking was a boring routine for me, always the same and not very affectionate. Gopala was never a hugger and his few hugs were stiff and awkward. Sex was mechanical and clumsy and, though I always gave in to it, I could have lived without it in those farm days. I never even had one orgasm with him at the farm (or even before with him). He said it was my own fault. Here again, I figured perhaps it was. I had wrecked my own health and now I was paying. Though I had been able to orgasm nearly every time in the past, before I met Gopala, perhaps my present bad health had ruined sex for me forever?

Better to be hot or cold,
Than always be the same.
Death is when you can't recall
The difference between joy and pain.

We still had sex about two or three times a week, but it brought me no pleasure. Interestingly enough, most of the ashramites thought we had plenty of sex, all the time and many of the men were jealous. This reminds me of the old *Annie Hall* movie where the psychiatrist asks Woody Allen: "How many times a week do your girlfriend and you have sex?" Woody Allen replies: "Hardly ever, only about three times a week." The psychiatrist then asks Diane Keaton (Annie Hall), separately, how often they had sex and she says: " Oh, all the time. At least three times a week." It's all a matter of prospective!

Through all this, we were totally committed to each other in those days. I took the: "Till death do you part" section of the marriage ceremony seriously and had been raised a "good Catholic girl" who planned to make my marriage last a lifetime. Besides, I believed that if I just loved enough, I could fix anything that was wrong in our marriage. So Gopala and I found our own unique ways to battle out our problems and maintain a peaceful co-existence most of the time.

Near the end of our second summer at the farm, Mata excitedly told us ashramites that we were to be privileged with a one-week visit from "Baba" Ram Dass, who was anxious to experience our farm life. (10) Mata had been corresponding with him and invited him to our farm. He agreed it would be a wonderful adventure to visit us. Gopala and I and many other ashramites had read his very popular book, *Be Here Now*, and we had listened to his inspiring record of spiritual songs and chanting. We were thrilled to have the opportunity to meet him in person and spend time with him.

Footnote (10) Ram Dass was the spiritual name given to Richard Alpert by his East Indian guru, Neem Karoli Baba. Richard's spiritual name was Ram Dass and means: "Servant of God". Baba, meaning father in Sanskrit, is a term of reverence for a spiritual teacher and was added later. Richard was a friend of Timothy Leary and experimented with him with the psychedelic drug LSD in the 1960s. Later Richard went to Indian and experienced a spiritual transformation. He returned to the U.S.A. and began writing spiritual books and lecturing on spiritual lifestyles, yoga and meditation. Baba Ram Dass became and still is internationally well known as a spiritual teacher noted for his books, music, audiotapes and talks.

Mata's expectations were far from realistic. She hoped and confided in us women, that she and Ram Dass would fall in love and both run the farm together as spiritual heads of our God's Land refuge. I was secretly shocked by this and thought Ram Dass could have nearly any young spiritual woman he desired. Why would he want an old woman like Mata who was overweight and had to be at least sixty in my estimation, with her long flowing, gray and brown hair?

Baba Ram Dass's visit was one of the highlights of my farm life. We actually got to eat very decently for the week of his visit. There were many darshans with chanting, music and talks by Ram Dass. He played his sitar and taught us some East Indian chants including this one that became a favorite of mine:

"Radha, Radha, Radha Boro,
Radha Govinda Boro."

We were able to talk to Ram Dass regularly during his visit. The men took saunas with him and many of us were granted private interviews with him for consulting and darshan blessings. Though I was unusually shy in those days, I worked up the courage to demand his last scheduled consulting session from our group, as I was desperate for help. I confided some of my problems to Ram Dass and he declared that I was waiting to get "zapped," (be tapped on the head with spiritual power to make all my problems instantly disappear).

I admit that I was hoping for just such a miracle. Ram Dass patiently explained to me that true spirituality was a gradual unfolding process of taking three steps forward and two steps back until total enlightenment finally occurred after decades and even lifetimes of hard work (karma yoga) and meditation. He consoled me for the difficulties I faced and gave me other helpful advice that I needed and appreciated. I held his words in my heart. He later gave me a lovely, framed picture of Radha and Krishna as he knew of my love for them and he also gave me some mala (prayer) beads that I still have to this day.

While Ram Dass was a wonderful farm guest, he in no way displayed any intention of seeing Mata as other than the leader of a very bizarre and restricted ashram with rigid rules and absurd requirements for the ashram inhabitants. Though he had initially wanted to explore our ashram, it soon became evident that he had no intention of ever returning to God's Land. When his week-long visit was over, Ram Dass, gladly packed his gear and departed amidst friendly, but basically permanent good-byes.

Through rumors, we farm ashramites heard that Baba Ram Dass had been so "freaked out" by his farm visit that he immediately left us and headed to Thunder Bay for a pizza to regain his lifestyle normalcy and mental sanity. I would not be surprised if the above was true. Ram Dass was very smart never to return to God's Land.

No outsider had ever visited God's Land farm without an intense reaction that usually either awed or caused resistance and unpleasant disbelief from the visiting onlookers. Some people hated the place and some were afraid of it. Some came for a visit once, never to return. Some were inspired by the chanting and beauty of the land and came back again and again – but these were few indeed. A very few people moved into the farm from time to time, and there were always people leaving because the work was too rigorous, the food was bad and the living conditions were too poor.

One day, as I held my dear Bethany in my arms, I heard some visitors talking about a place I had never heard of before: Vancouver. My ears perked up when I first heard the strange word. "Vancouver, " I said, "where is that?"

"It's on the Western end of Canada in British Columbia, on the Pacific Ocean," replied the visitor. "It is one of the most beautiful cities in the world. It's full of flowers," the visitor added.

"I'm going to live there some day," I spoke prophetically.

"We're never going to live there," chimed in Gopala. "It's too far away."

"I said: I'm going to live there some day," I retorted. I knew it throughout my being! I, alone, was going to live in the beautiful city of Vancouver one day.

We had another hard winter at the farm that second year and my health problems became worse. I bonded closer to my little Bethany and I began to write songs as well as the poetry I wrote on occasion. Here is part of one song that became a favorite:

MELT ME LORD
I'm just an icicle hanging on a tree.
Oh, melt me Lord.
That I might fall,
Drop by drop,
Into thy rushing sea.
Oh, melt me Lord...

I was delighted when spring arrived. All winter, Bethany and I played peek-a-boo games and developed a kind of mother/daughter bond of love. She was a lovely blond haired, blue-eyed child with an endearing laugh and a strong stubborn streak similar to her father Alex's. Now, with the coming of spring, we could play outside and I could work on my flower gardens again.

As soon as the weather was warm enough, all the ashramites took turns doing three to seven day meditation retreats on Holy Spirit Mountain. My health seemed to be vastly improving over the summer, and Mata had decided that Gopala and I should take another try at having a baby. We were to take three day retreats apart and then come together for a private baby-making long weekend. I went off to Holy Spirit Mountain and Gopala retreated on another mountain to the west of it.

It was blueberry season in late summer, but I planned to fast the three days of my retreat on water with three bananas a day. I pitched my small one-man tent deep in the pines along the back of Holy Spirit Mountain in late evening of the first night. I read a little from one of my spiritual books and went to sleep early in order to get a fresh start on my treasured three days for myself – and God.

I started a regular routine on the first morning by doing an hour of Hatha Yoga (physical postures) on a large rock. Then I ate one banana, took a walk and then chanted and meditated for a couple hours. Initially, it was rather difficult to calm my mind and emotions and go within to a meditative state. Next, I spent several hours reading spiritual books and contemplated their meanings for my own life and me. Then I ate another banana and rested. I drank bottled water throughout the day as well. After resting, I took another walk, did a few hours of deep pranic breathing while lying down, ate my last banana for the day, took an evening walk and watched the sun go down from the warrior's head of Holy Spirit Mountain. I returned to my tent in the darkening light and chanted for forty minutes or so and did a final meditation. During my first nighttime meditation, I still felt like I had not gone within deeply enough. I was still restless, my mind wandered and I felt discontented. These were signs I had not yet fully entered into the silence of "now". I was not fully present and communing with my Godself.

The second day, I repeated nearly identically my same sadhana (spiritual practice) schedule. By my second nighttime meditation, I was still dissatisfied by my progress. I was not "there" yet. This would not do! I needed to be in my higher consciousness. I needed answers for my life. I had to see the truth – for me.

I was determined to stay awake all night if need be – to do whatever it took to penetrate my walls and dive within to my inner realms. I sat in a loose, comfortable, cross-legged position in the center of my short tent and stormed my inner gates. Disturbing thoughts, body complaints, and unresolved emotions all attempted to bar my way. I gently dismantled the opposing obstacles and steadily focused on finding my center within. I remembered the North American Indians' spirit quests of old, and was determined to be as resolute in my own quest for divine guidance. Also I remembered: "I am unlimited." (Huna principle, number three.)

I started to fall asleep sitting up. I shook myself awake. No! I would not allow myself to sleep until I achieved my goal of oneness! Again and again, I brushed off sleep and surged within. Finally, around the wee hours of the morning, just before dawn, I arrived at my desired destination.

Embracing the Divine, I sighed into the "Bliss of Union". I saw, felt, tasted and knew the truth and what I must do. I wanted to leave the farm with Gopala so we could lead our own lives, explore each of our weaknesses and strengths and follow God's direction from inner guidance, not Mata's or someone else's. I wanted to spread my wings and fly. It was time for me to make my own life decisions. These and other personal truths were opened before me. I saw visions of my future and destiny and wanted to rush and embrace it all.

At last, in early morning, I lay down and slept, content that I had accomplished my goal.

My dreams have wings.
Where cannot I fly?

On the third day, it was actually midday as I had slept in; I found a pile of fresh picked blueberries in the center of my tent when I returned after yoga. I knew Gopala had found my tent and left me this gift. I enjoyed this little deviation from my bananas and savored each one of the blueberries. Gopala and I were to meet tomorrow at the beginning of the fourth day and go off for our baby-making holiday. I finished the blueberries and put thoughts of him aside. I would see him soon enough.

I continued my spiritual communion for the rest of that third day. Again and again, I drank from the Divine wellspring and felt renewed in spirit, emotions, mind, body and vitality.

On the fourth morning, I went to my rock to do my yoga and Gopala met me there. I was supposed to meet him at the base of the mountain and go off with him from there. I could not. Rather than break my silence, I wrote with pen and paper for him that I could not leave my retreat now. I wanted to take a full seven days and continue my meditations. We could make a baby later.

Gopala was sorely disappointed, but he accepted my decision, as I was adamant and totally determined to stay. I continued my forth day of sadhana until just before nightfall. Then I heard some ladies calling, at the base of the mountain. Over and over they called: "Alawan, Alawan! Alawan come home, come back." Alawan was my farm name, a North American Indian name given to me by Mataji during a special celebration. It means: "singing a song of praise to God." It was given to me because of my love of singing and chanting that everyone thought I did so beautifully. Music was a passion of mine. I sang for many, many hours each day while working or playing, alone or with others. Singing and music was a big part of farm life for all of us.

I heard the ladies calling out, but I could not make out what they were saying, so I did not answer. Just at nightfall, Gopala came to my tent and told me that Mata wanted me to come down, now, and end my retreat tonight. He helped me dismantle my tent and we bundled up my few belongings and proceeded down the mountain and returned to the house.

While I was busy on Holy Spirit Mountain with my own personal vision quest, Gopala was restless and not too interested in his. He spent most of his retreat time thinking of the great sex we would have after the retreat while we were trying to make a baby. After he left me, earlier on the morning of that fourth day, he returned to the ashram.

Mataji had met Gopala upon his return. She looked at him with apparent dissatisfaction and said: "Well, that was a waste of time!" She had read his thoughts during his retreat, as she had often read all of the ashramites thoughts while we were on the farm. "There are more important things than sex, you know," Mata continued in her admonition of Gopala, as she shook her head in dismay. Then she sent a couple ladies out to look for me and tell me to return. They called out to me, but they could not find me that day. So Mata sent Gopala after me later that evening, as he knew where my tent was hidden.

When I arrived back at the ashram with Gopala, Mataji looked me square in the eyes and said: "You have led us all to believe that you are sick and weak. There is nothing at all weak about you! You are a tigress inside!" Then she added: "I want you both to prepare yourselves for a few days and then move to Winnipeg for a while. Spread your wings. Find your own way. Set up your own branch of one of my ashrams. Make some money for the farm. You will still be connected to me and after a little while, you can return and continue here. You need to go out into the world for a while."

She voiced my exact desires and the resulting guidance I found during my Holy Spirit Mountain retreat. I knew she had read my thoughts and was well aware of my entire retreat.

We prepared ourselves to leave. I wanted to take Bethany with us. Gopala said: "Don't be ridiculous. She's not our baby. Besides, we'll only be gone about six months or so. You can't uproot her for such a short time. You can see her when we get back."

I did not want to leave little Bethany behind. But I saw some wisdom in his words. "Okay," I said, "perhaps you are right. Bethany needs a stable home and we do not know how we will be living until we get jobs." I bid Bethany a tearful farewell. I did not know if she understood I was leaving for some time and that I planned to return to her. I kissed her many times and dismissed my aching heart. My dear Bethany would be safer on the farm.

Gopala and I loaded up our Ford Maverick with some meager possessions, leaving most of our belongings behind. We had spent a little over two years at the farm and it was not easy to leave a home we had grown accustomed to. With all its suffering and problems, it was still home to us. Amidst tearful farewells, we drove down the long driveway, away from our familiar God's Land. A new adventure lay ahead.

SIRENE'S SONG

My song goes on and on –
A Sirene's song.
What do I sing?
"Crash your boats upon the rocks.
Let your souls go free.
You must leave your doubts behind,
If you would see.

. . .

A SONG TO SING

The poetry of my soul
Writes itself through me.
I have a song that I must sing,
A story I must tell.
And no one knows the way to say
The words that I must use.

Each of us has a song to sing.
And we cannot find happiness
On this earth,
Until we are free enough to sing it –
Till we can express our gifts.
We have a song to sing!

Chapter Nine – The Prairies and Beyond

"Faith – is the Pierless Bridge
Supporting what We see
Unto the Scene that We do not –
Too slender for the eye…"

Emily Dickinson

Anticipation and apprehension filled us as we drove away from the farm. We headed for Thunder Bay first to pawn Gopala's banjo for traveling money. The farm had little in the way of funds to give to us for our journey and we had no personal money of our own.

We stopped for a short while at the little sunken gardens in the city, overlooking the Sleeping Giant Island. It is a famous landmark that is naturally shaped like a native Indian warrior lying on his back looking up at the heavens. It is claimed that this Indian figure protects the silver mines below it from any white man who tries to steal the silver, which is the rightful property of local Indian tribes. Indians have, for centuries, made jewelry and artifacts from that silver. In fact, no white man has ever been able to access the silver mines below the Giant, not even in modern day. Every cave and excavation site the white man has attempted to draw silver from has collapsed. Not one bit of silver has ever been extracted from this island by the Canadian government or private mining companies. The island lies off Thunder Bay's shore as a testament and a message that this is truly Indian land.

Gopala and I paused awhile in the gardens and held hands as we looked out over the Sleeping Giant. The flowers surrounding us were in full bloom, a profusion of color on this late summer morning. We meditated for a few minutes and blessed our journey. Then after one last nostalgic glance, we returned to our car and headed for Winnipeg.

Winnipeg, Manitoba is in the province next to Ontario. It was only about a day's drive away. Manitoba is a prairie province. The southern part is very flat with fields and more fields of crops, hay and wildflowers. Occasionally, there was a farmhouse and barns surrounded by clumps of trees, planted as wind breaks. It all seemed tranquil and stately as we journeyed past.

In the northern regions of Manitoba, above Winnipeg, are several huge lakes plus hundreds of little finger lakes that are a bit like those in upper Minnesota, only more plentiful. Grains, wild rice and honey are among the popular crops of Manitoba.

We arrived in Winnipeg in the late evening and found a cheap motel for the night. In a couple of days, we found a one bedroom, weekly rental. We stayed there for three weeks while we looked for jobs. Gopala found one quickly in a department store's, record department. Music was, after all, his specialty. I wanted to work in a flower shop. It had always been a dream of mine. One of the finest shops in the area had two openings for assistants. I was determined to get one of them. I had one brief interview among dozens and dozens of candidates and was painfully self-conscious that I had no clothes to wear except for the long, denim skirt and hooded white shirt that were the farm ashram "uniform." All my other clothes had been destroyed or given to the Salvation Army by Mata. I kept calling the flower shop to promote myself and my interest in flowers and due to my persistence, I landed one of the jobs there.

I was elated! I loved growing flowers and I wanted to learn to arrange them as well. My dream was to work with flowers and eventually become a floral designer. I had made a crown of flowers for my hair, for my own wedding with a hanger and twist ties. The crown had been crudely made, but it had looked quite elegant. Now I wanted to learn more.

I arrived for my first day of work at the flower shop in my farm uniform, feeling rather self-conscious and conspicuous. The head designer's brother took one long surprised look at me from head to toe and offered me one of the shop uniforms to wear. I was relieved and thankful. My shop duties were shared with three other young women and included: watering the store plants, helping to make fruit baskets, sweeping the floors many times a day (to pick up discarded flower stems), cutting and cleaning new flowers, waiting on customers, taking phone orders, and making bows for the arrangements – once I learned how.

It took about a month to learn to make professional bows, as it is an intricate process. I learned quickly, within the first month. The girl who was hired with me never did learn how to make bows in the six months that she was there. I envied the two men designers their creative flower arranging abilities and watched them every chance I had to learn new things. They told me I could not become a designer unless I attended floral design school in Toronto first. I hoped that some day I could.

My wages were $1.90 per hour, far less than my husband's pay, but I was paid weekly in cash. We decided to live on my salary and send Gopala's to the farm. Our rent was cheap and we had few expenses except for food and bare necessities. We were used to simple living, so this was no hardship for us.

Gopala and I lived easily on a budget. We had little desire for material things. I found pleasure in cooking, baking and crafts like crocheting. In a few weeks, we found a wonderful house to rent in the lovely Assiniboine Park area, near the lengthy, winding river of the same name. For extra money, I taught some natural food cooking classes in our kitchen and he taught some yoga classes at the YM/YWCA. Soon I began teaching some yoga classes, too. These classes were not too hard for me to teach, as cooking students looked at the food, not so much at me. During the yoga classes, students were told to go within and watch themselves throughout the class. This made it easier for me to overcome my shyness, as the students did not focus on me.

Winnipeg was a booming city compared to sleepy little Thunder Bay. We got to know the city quickly and made new friends easily. The German owner of the best local health food store became a staunch friend and supporter of our classes. When we were still new in Winnipeg, we had been short on grocery money and he gave us the needed goods for free until we received our first paychecks. We made friends at the local Unity and Unitarian churches as well as teaching yoga classes for them.

We also made fast friends with a very kind and warm-hearted Catholic priest named Father Ed who ran a local monastery for more than a dozen priests. He was an amazing man, very interested in yoga and chanting with Gopala and me. He attended many of our classes and weekly chant nights. He was tremendously interested in Eastern thought and religions and often said he would move into our little ashram home to study with us if he did not have such pressing responsibilities running his monastery. We were indeed setting up our own ashram. Our two-bedroom house soon held two local women student ashramites and our kirtan chanting nights were attended by more than a dozen local people.

Father Ed was a faithful and loving friend and we spent many hours talking of spiritual principles and world religions. We also sang for many hours together. Father Ed played the guitar like Gopala and he taught us many beautiful popular English songs and Latin songs, while we taught him to chant in several languages including Sanskrit, Buddhist, Hebrew and some North American Indian dialects. I will never forget the song Father Ed taught me that I loved to sing most often and I still sing today: *"Today While the Blossoms Still Cling to the Vine."*

Some of our dearest friends were a couple of chiropractors and their families. They had a clinic on the French side of town and we received regular chiropractic adjustments from them and shared many healthy meals, which I cooked in our lovely house.

Gopala soon got a promotion to manager at his record department, with a welcome raise. Every month or two, I got a ten-cent raise and was soon up to $2.20 an hour. Ha! Not a grand fortune. But, I loved it.

Christmastime at the flower store was tremendously busy as were all florist shops at that time of the year. I worked sixty hours a week in December for extra money, and because it was required of all shop staff to work overtime during holidays. The week after Christmas, I collapsed with an extended ten-day flu and virus. When I recovered, I went back to work, but I still did not feel very well.

I taught a yoga class the next week, in mid-January, and a new student came up to me and remarked on how lovely my "pink" aura was. My mouth dropped open in utter surprise. A pink aura meant that I was pregnant! I proceeded to my doctor's office that week without delay, to make sure. I found out I was two and a half months pregnant! I was relieved and excited. Hopefully, all would go well this time and Gopala and I could start our family.

Just after my March seventh birthday, I began to exper- ience extreme exhaustion and dizziness. Though I had been keeping a slower pace since Christmas and had taken a brief rest, I knew I was in trouble. One weekday morning, soon after, near the middle of March, I began to hemorrhage very badly and Gopala rushed me to the hospital.

This was very serious. I was four and a half months preg- nant and I was gushing blood. The doctor had me prepped and ready for surgery but there was no available operating room. As I lay on a gurney in the hallway, I began to loose consciousness. The nurses probed me awake; it would be more dangerous for me if I blacked out. I might go into a coma. "Stay with us. Stay with us," the nurses said over and over.

Finally, I was hauled in for surgery. They put me under anesthesia and I was finally allowed to sleep. Eventually, I drifted into a strange dream. I was flying with my arms spread out but on one side of me I clutched a beautiful little baby girl who was smiling so sweetly. She was heavy, so I could not fly very high. I kept dropping in altitude and barely missed hitting some building rooftops. An angel flew up beside me and told me: "You have to put the little girl down. You cannot carry her. She is too heavy for you. If you try to keep her, you will both be lost."

I wanted so much to hold her, to keep her with me, but I could not keep flying with her. I knew I would fall if I did, or hurt myself crashing into one of the buildings I was flying too low over. Soon I had to leave her on the rooftop and fly on without her. I was so sad. "It is not the right time," the angel continued. "Let her go." I sadly agreed and continued flying without her.

When I finally woke up in the recovery room, the dream was still vivid in my mind. It was so real. Gopala was by my side, holding my hand. I had been given nearly six pints of blood. Luckily, this was in the years before AIDS. The doctor had told Gopala I was lucky to be alive. The fetus inside me had actually died months ago around Christmastime when I had that bad flu and virus. Gopala was relieved I was awake. I was too groggy to speak for a while. When I could, I told him my dream. To me, it was a message from God and my angels. This had been a near-death experience and if I had not "let go" of the baby – inside my own consciousness – I believed that I too would have died.

This miscarriage was far more devastating for me than those I had experienced at the farm. I was much weaker and it took a lot longer for me to recuperate. I was off work for a couple weeks. I cried, alone and inconsolably when Gopala and our other housemates were at work. I had obtained a full, four-record set of the Madame Butterfly opera from the local library and I played it over and over again for weeks. The tragedy and pain in the story seemed to help me purge my own sadness. I felt like I was Madame Butterfly. Thoughts of beautiful little Bethany, left on the farm, haunted me even more than usual during this time. I felt I should not have left her behind.

Eventually, I let go of my pain as I returned to work at the flower shop. It was now April and still bitterly cold outside. Winnipeg became a city of ice and snow in winter. Like Thunder Bay, it could be sixty below and even colder, for months on end. It was a more penetrating cold that could easily cause one to freeze to death in a short period of time. It was rumored that a person could die of the cold in twenty minutes or less outside in Winnipeg winters if not properly protected. The city bus stop stalls were fully enclosed in glass and heated. If you wanted your car to start each morning, you had to get an engine block heater and plug it in every night during the winter, or your car would not start at all the next day. The radio and TV news reports regularly stated how many people were lost in snowdrifts of up to twenty feet deep, in the surrounding areas in Manitoba. Blowing snow that piled into deep drifts was a major hazard in local farming communities.

It was a dismal time of year for me to suffer such a loss. But one consolation was the lovely Assiniboine River area where we lived. This was a winter wonderland in snow. Gopala took me for walks here often to cheer me up. Spring was just around the corner.

Mata came to Winnipeg for a visit in mid-April and brought many farm ashramites with her. We set up a darshan chanting session for her at a local church and nearly one hundred local people attended. It was a great success. We had dozens of ashram guests sleeping all over our living room floor like packed sardines. It was like a large sleepover party. My spirits were lifted a bit by this visit, but I was still in a slump over my recent miscarriage. Mata had stern words for me to "buck up" and "snap out of it".

Later in the month of April, Father Ed arranged for me to do a week-long private retreat at a local Winnipeg convent. Though the resident nuns talked during their meals, I ate my meals sitting alone and kept silence as I had learned, in the eastern religious and yogic traditions. This retreat greatly boosted my spirits. Communing with God in the familiar setting of a convent like those I recalled loving in past lives, helped me to heal quickly and I had the pleasure of once again attending daily mass as I had in middle school. This helped me to realize that life was still very precious even if it was not the right time for me to have a child.

THE GOD OF LOVE

I AM the voice within the Heart of Love.
I AM the answer to every question.
I AM the Grace that pours from within – not above.
I AM the God that IS – the God of Love.

Gopala and I planned to leave Winnipeg the end of April and travel for a month before returning to the farm. We felt we had been away from the farm long enough, but we wanted and needed a vacation first. Other farm couples had gone to different cities for the winter to set up ashrams including: Saskatoon, Calgary, Banff, Guelph and Ottawa and we decided it would be great to visit them and see our families in Detroit as well as my relatives in Florida.

We said fond farewells to our many Winnipeg friends and promised to return. I knew inside myself that we would indeed return one day soon and see them all again. Gopala and I shipped our few main possessions to the farm and packed up the Ford Maverick and headed west first, to Saskatoon.

Saskatoon was bigger than Thunder Bay but a lot smaller than Winnipeg. It was a university town named after those small, round, juicy, purple, wild berries we enjoyed at the farm. Saskatoons were, obviously, most plentiful around the city of Saskatoon as well as the Saskatchewan Province. Our farm friends Adam and Violet had started their own little offshoot ashram here.

We stayed with Adam and Violet for several days enjoying their company and the local sights. Then we left for the next stop on our trek: Calgary. Before we drove fifty miles, the Ford Maverick gave up its ghost and we had to sell it for a few dollars for parts. There was no hope of fixing it. What were we to do? We decided we had to complete our trip one way or another. We returned to Saskatoon for a couple days and mailed more of our possessions back to the farm. We were going to hitchhike!

Violet and Adam thought we were very courageous and versatile in being willing to alter our plans and take our trip anyway. Gopala and I felt it was now or never, if we wanted to travel. With less than three hundred dollars in our pockets, two sleeping bags, a few clothes, a guitar and a dulcimer, we extended our thumbs and began a trip of ten thousand miles.

Being a young, attractive, conservatively dressed couple, traveling in 1975 Canada, we were given nearly instant rides whenever we stopped and began thumbing. There was one point during our trip when we were waiting for a ride at a tiny road stop, near an even tinier town. Here only one car passed by every five minutes. We were a little concerned for a few minutes, but we got a ride in the fourth car after only twenty minutes.

At one point of our journey, I grew tired of riding in cars and said to Gopala: "Wouldn't it be wonderful to be picked up by a Winnebago. We could be sitting in the back of the trailer, at the dining table, eating food and playing cards while we chatted with people and were driven down the road?" Within five minutes, much to our amazement, a Winnebago camper picked us up and we did just as I had wished for! We ate, drank fruit juice, and played cards while laughing and talking with the most delightful family, for more than one hundred miles. "Ask and you shall receive!" also "Your moment of power is now!" (Huna principle, number four.)

Our entire trip seemed blessed. The traveling was easy and we were given gifts of food and places to stay for free, in many stops along the way. In Calgary, we stayed with Alex's ashram there. He and his son John had visited the farm earlier for the birth of Alex's second son with Sharon, whose home birth both Gopala and I were privileged to see. Alex was very impressed with a thirty-two-page cookbook I had put together and mimeographed in Winnipeg. He felt I had great potential as a writer and told me that if I wanted to write a larger book, I could come and stay at his ashram anytime and write the book there, without having to worry about rent or bills of any kind. I thanked Alex kindly for his offer, but I had heard tales of Alex's strict control over his own ashramites, even stricter than Mata's I heard, and I wanted no part of an even more restricted lifestyle.

While in Calgary, we attended the famous Calgary Stampede Rodeo with wild horse and bull riders and clowns and much more, all in a popular western setting. It was an exciting diversion from our regular activities. It contributed to my ever-growing sense of freedom. After a couple days in Calgary, Gopala and I moved on to Banff and Lake Louise, both only a short distance from Calgary, about sixty miles northwest. These were resort towns and were bustling in summer months. In winter, Banff and Lake Louise were even busier with skiing and all kinds of winter sports. These lovely towns were full of tourists and Alex's Calgary ashram owned a small, but very busy and profitable restaurant in Banff. We enjoyed a few great meals in their restaurant while we took in the many beautiful sights of these two small touristy towns full of gift shops and amusements. After a few days, we were off again, this time for my dream city: Vancouver, on the Pacific Ocean.

Vancouver is a magical city. When we arrived, it was breezy, cool for late spring and full of gorgeous flowers. It was a picturesque city of around a million people (including the suburbs) with no noticeable slums! The majestic, towering mountains hover around the city like purple, snow capped sentinels guarding the beauty of this architectural masterpiece. There was so much to see here. The Manhattan-like downtown area included a five and a half mile around park, called Stanley Park, named after a local explorer. It is the largest park within a city limit in the world. This fascinating park held huge redwoods, quaint lakes and duck ponds, colorful fountains and a multitude of seemingly endless scenic trails. It also included three lovely ocean beaches, heated salt-water swimming pools, restaurants, many colorful rose and flower gardens, semi-tropical trees and shrubs including holly and bamboo, palm trees, and a multitude of wildlife from deer to foxes to raccoons.

There were also two big health food supermarkets called Lifestream Natural Foods, an outdoor/indoor public market called Granville Island with many gift shops and boat docks, a fascinating spiritual/metaphysical bookstore called Banyan Books and an array of spiritual communities that offered every kind of belief and practice including those of: Hare Krishna, Yogi Bhajan, Zen Buddhism, Krishnamurti and there were even Joel Goldsmith Infinite Way Groups.

Gopala and I attended several of the Joel Goldsmith group meetings wherein we discussed his writings. It was exciting to share his words with a whole new group of people who had a completely different perspective on his work. We made friends with a guy at one of the Lifestream stores and he provided a great place for us to stay, for free, in a house that was waiting to be rented. We also ran into one of Gopala's Hare Krishna friends from out east and joined him and his wife for a delicious feast and chanting. We spent about five wonderful days in Vancouver and then we had to move on.

It was time to backtrack our steps and head east again. The two of us by-passed the farm on our way to Michigan as the temptation might be too strong to abort the rest of our journey. We arrived at Gopala's parents' home and shared a warm reunion with them and my family as well. It was also great to visit the Detroit Integral Yoga Institute again and see many of our former housemates who still lived there. Lotus had married and moved to New York, but Gurave was still there and we spent some pleasant hours with him. Old ashram friends, Staron and Jamie had also married and moved away.

Something very amazing happened to Gopala and me while we were staying with his parents place. Perhaps what happened between us was because we were well rested and so happy to be with our families, talking, having fun and eating such good food, or perhaps it was because both Gopala and I stumbled upon some special techniques from other lifetimes that we had seemingly forgotten before. I only know that, one night; Gopala and I retired to bed early while at his parents' home.

We were feeling so happy inside; we were cuddling in our double sleeping-bag bed on the floor and discussing our day. (We refused to sleep in regular beds in those days.) I remember Gopala looking directly into my eyes, as if he was seeing me for the very first time in his life. It was as if I felt him loving me, as he had never done before. He looked at me so tenderly, as if everything that had passed between us previously was merely a mechanical dream and now was real. Gopala kissed me in a way that he had never done before, as if he was fully present and wanted to savor each moment of kissing me. He touched me and I felt electrified. As I gazed back into his eyes, I felt the waves of energy flowing between us and, suddenly, everything around me disappeared into a current of energy. Gopala, the bed, the room and everything dissolved into lights, color and an energy of spirit. Our breathing slowed to rhythmic unison. I no longer trusted my eyes that seemed to weave in and out of reality, so I closed them and surrendered to the moment.

Gopala touched me as if his touch was fire. Every movement sent my heart racing and my body was a mass of flames bursting in every direction. I responded by touching him, as I had never before been inspired to do. Soon our tongues were exploring each other as if for the first time. We were making love with every part of our beings: spirit, mind, emotions, body and vitality. It was like one, huge, on-going orgasm for me that did not begin or end. Every touch, feeling and movement fed the flames of a passion I had never dreamed could exist before. Nothing I had ever known before – at least not in this lifetime – had ever reached such heights as this. Even my precious lovemaking with Manny had not contained the intensity and longevity of this union with Gopala. At last, Gopala and I were one. I felt the burning of his touch on my body the entire night.

In the morning, over breakfast, I tenderly grasped him from behind as he was enjoying his meal, in a warm embrace of affectionate joy, and I was surprised that Gopala was surprised. For him, the night's sensations were over, but for me, my body continued to feel as if it was experiencing one, long, on-going orgasm for three full days. My body was throbbing and my heart chakra wide open for three full days of ecstasy.

NIGHT OF PASSION

Last night was magic
In your arms.
Your love filled me
To overflowing.
I felt encompassed
And at peace.
I felt at last

A satisfaction
That I never
Seem to keep.
Your love surrounded
And fulfilled me,
As all love's pleasures
Were released.

In the present moment, I am wondering why the most amazing spiritual/sexual highs of my life seem to last three days. Perhaps this mystical number holds some reason for this specific duration time? Truly, it is of little consequence. It is only my natural curiosity that seeks the answer that I know I will one day have to this question, as I believe all questions can and will eventually be answered by spirit.

After our amazing visit in Michigan, Gopala and I headed south for Florida. Somewhere in the southern states, the police picked us up. They thought I was a fourteen-year-old runaway teenager, eloping without my parents' consent. A quick check of our marriage license soon convinced the authorities to release us back on the interstate on-ramp so we could continue our trek south.

The two of us stopped at several spiritual communities along our way. One of the most interesting was Steve Gaskin's Farm in Summertown, Tennessee. We spent several days there and were amazed to see such a large farm, with hundreds of people that ran so smoothly and effectively, unlike God's Land that functioned poorly and was beyond primitive. "The Farm" was a live-off-the-land farm that was working. Working well. Mata could certainly use some lessons from Steve Gaskin. His place left an indelible impression on my mind. But was living-off-the-land in any ashram, what I really wanted in my life?

St. Augustine, Florida was a special treat for me and provided a lasting image in my mind of classic old-world charm, as Gopala and I continued our trek south. We arrived at my godmother and uncle's home in Miami and enjoyed a five-day stay with them and their three teenage daughters, my cousins. I had not seen my aunt except for once when she visited Michigan when I was around age thirteen. She was my father's sister and her family was among my French relatives who had moved from Haiti sometime during the 1960's. They all spoke four languages: primarily French, plus Spanish, English and Creole.

Gopala and I enjoyed a fantastic time with my French relatives seeing all the sights of Miami from tropical flower and parrot gardens, to beaches, to aquariums, to shows and picnics in the parks. It was a wonderful visit getting to know my relatives better. Soon, we had to say good-bye, taking with us many fond memories. My uncle drove us to a freeway on-ramp and we were on the road again.

This time we set our sights on God's Land. There were many other experiences we shared on our long hitch-hiking journey of ten thousand miles, but most of them are unimportant now, except perhaps a little story about Gopala and I getting stuck in a little town for a while that only had one restaurant – a fast food franchise. We were both complete vegetarians at the time, so we just ate French fries and some desserts. The two of us ended up getting very sick from the food for a couple days.

We were used to pure, plain, simple, nourishing food and the food additives and sugar in these foods were more than we could handle. There is something to be said about being versatile and adaptable to all situations in life. It does not do to be "too pure" – in lifestyle or diet – or so rigid or fanatical in one's living that one cannot tolerate a few poisons found in mainstream living, once in a while.

Gopala and I made our return trip north which included several tourist attractions on the way, but we were mainly intent on getting back to the farm now. He wanted to see Mata and I wanted to hold my beautiful Bethany again. We had been away nearly nine months and I missed her and wondered how much she had grown. Why had I left her behind? Would she have forgotten me?

Would that I could be with you
And hold you in my soul.
Would that I could see you,
Feel you, Know you, Love you –
We – two kindred souls.

NIGHTLIGHTS
(Fireflies)

Little sparks of light
Flickering in the night.
Fireflies –
Like bits of dreams
In my mind.

Flashing here and there,
But are you going anywhere?
They do what they must do.
The same as me or you.
And when we get there,
If we get there,
(Where is there?)
What shall we do?

Just flicker like the fireflies
And go our way.
Enjoying each bright moment,
Until we get somewhere
– Someday.

Chapter Ten – Many "Happy" Returns

"Through rising suns their radiance throw
On summer's green and winter's snow,
In such rare splendor that my heart
Would ache from scenes like these to part...
I shall not pass this way again."

Eva Rose York
I Shall Not Pass This Way Again

It was early June by the time Gopala and I returned to the farm. Summer was in full swing and most of the ashram couples, who had gone to different cities to work for the winter, had returned. My beautiful Bethany was taller and walking everywhere. She remembered me! One game of peek-a-boo and she jumped into my arms in recognition.

I hurried to plant my flower gardens and get reacquainted with the farm animals, the hills and mountains. Holy Spirit Mountain stood proud and silent as before, shrouded in mists, just less than a half a mile beyond the doorway of the house.

It took some time for me to set up our bedroom. All the possessions we had left behind on the farm had been scattered. Our luggage had been borrowed, our tent was ruined, also wall pictures, a special gift picture Bible from my mother and just about everything else had been either lost, stolen, "borrowed indefinitely," or given to the Salvation Army. Only the backpacks, musical instruments and clothes that we had carried with us on our hitchhiking trek were left to us. I was upset at this total lack of respect for our belongings and privacy. We had few possessions as it was. Others had ruined our wedding gifts during the first year we lived at the farm. Now we had much less than we arrived at the farm with. Those on the farm had already spent all the money Gopala and I had earned in Winnipeg and our meager vacation money was gone as well. At least the two of us had had a wonderful month-long trip that we could always remember.

Getting back to farm living was far from easy after our long taste of freedom in Winnipeg – in the "outside world." Getting used to the plainest of food was not so easy this time.

The large wild salad we picked and ate twice a day lost its appeal when "head man" Adam decided it was healthier not to wash it anymore and just serve it fresh from the fields for more nutrients. Watching several green worms and various bugs crawl out of your salad as you ate it certainly did lose some of the "fresh greens" appeal for me. While everyone, including Gopala, wolfed down the buggy greens, I was inspecting each leaf and wiping it on my bowl to scrape off the extra "bug protein." Okay, so we had a book in our farm library called *Future Food* that said bugs were the food of the future – high in protein, vitamins and minerals, plentiful, inexpensive or free, as well. Well as far as I was concerned, this "food" could stay in the future!

My health certainly seemed to be much better that summer – after a winter in real civilization. I actually learned to use one of the treadle sewing machines and sewed my very first dress! Not a farm uniform, a real dress that could be worn "out in the world." It was made from material I had purchased myself, in Winnipeg. Completing this project was a major accomplishment for me, as I basically disliked sewing.

In early July, we ashramites made a trip to the local Kakabeka Falls for a day of hiking and sightseeing. This is the largest waterfall in the area. It is around fifteen or twenty stories high, if I remember correctly. These Falls were a raging torrent in the spring but now in summer, most of the Falls were dry except for a seemingly small double waterfall on one side and another on the opposite end of what was, in spring, a complete curtain of water.

The daring few in our group decided to climb down the center of the dry waterfall to the bottom of the canyon. I boldly decided to go along. The going down was relatively easy; we laughed and played along the way. But the return climbing-up trek was a lot more perilous than it appeared. I found myself scrambling for hand and footholds. I got dizzy several times and once I thought I might faint – a deadly proposition. Though the fear inside me grew and my stomach churned, I continued to inch my way to the top. After an agonizing struggle, I was halfway up and realized that I could not make it the rest of the way.

I clung to the rough-hewn ledges and tried to rest my head on the edge. I was shaking, my head was spinning and I was suddenly terrified. It was still so far to the top. I panicked. I could not make it! I started to cry. A friend lowered down beside me to encourage me. I was still not reassured. My life flashed before my eyes and I thought how foolish I had been to attempt such a feat. Only a handful of the stronger ashramites had dared to attempt the climb. It seemed so easy – laughing on the way down. Now I thought: "I could die here!"

I silently prayed and mustered up my courage. No! God would not let me die here. I breathed deeply, slowly, trying to get a grip on my emotions. Slowly, slowly, my waves of dizziness passed. My friend stayed beside me, as I ever so carefully inched my way upward. When I arrived at the summit and had a hand-up over the edge, I threw myself down on the rocky ridge, clinging to the rugged plateau for a long time before I could move. Once I felt safe, I edged away from the precipice. When I was securely situated away from the falls, I looked down and wondered how I had been so foolish as to attempt such a dangerous hike. I must have temporarily lost my mind. Well, this would teach me not to be so "gung ho" in the future. How often do each of us get caught up in the "mood of the moment" and throw caution to the wind to do crazy things with others on a lark? Sometimes these stunts help us to push beyond our limits and sometimes they are just foolhardy risks that could destroy us.

Future trips to Kakabeka Falls caught me looking over the edge in incredible disbelief that I had ever attempted such a wild escapade. The mountains we have climbed in the past often look insurmountable in the present! Now I sometimes wonder how I survived any of those years at the farm.

Kakabeka Falls has a special Indian legend like so many of the local sights around the Thunder Bay area. It is said that an Indian princess named Kakabeka was captured by an enemy tribe and forced to lead them on an attack against her own father's tribe. She deceived the enemy and led them all over the Falls in their canoes, to their deaths. She sacrificed herself to save her people, so they named the Falls after her, in her honor.

My recent fright at the Falls made this story seem very real. It was a long, perilous drop to the bottom of the Falls. I certainly would not want to try it in a canoe!

Later that summer, around early August, some of the ashramites entered some plants and homemade products in the local county fair. I entered a large quilt I had crocheted along with some of my garden flowers including my pansies, marigolds and a begonia. Others entered rose petal jam, some lacework, sunflowers and various other plants and handicrafts. I was thrilled to win first prize for each of my three flower entries and an honorable mention for my quilt. My flowers were spectacular as I used a ton of composted manure on them so they were huge and their colors were bright. I had never before entered or attended a county fair before. It was certainly a highlight of farm living.

All that summer, my inner discontent grew. I had tried to hide it. But it wasn't working. Ever since Gopala and I had returned from Winnipeg, I felt I wanted to leave the farm. This was not how I wanted to spend my life. I wanted to take little Bethany and go back to Winnipeg with Gopala.

Each day I grew more and more unhappy with the farm and with Mata. A house on Tent Hill had been completed for her that summer, so she could be away from the "house energies." Mata interacted less with our work schedule and held more darshans. She kept blessing me in particular at these chanting and meditation sessions and saying God had special work for me to do. But I was disenchanted and frankly bored with life on the farm and of her guidance of me, and all of us. I wanted to run my own life. I gently broached the subject of leaving the farm to Gopala a couple of times and he would have no part of it. He wanted to stay on the farm forever. He said he was "happy here."

In mid-August, I saw my chance. I suggested to Gopala that we go to Winnipeg again, just for a few months, to make more money for the farm and to see our Winnipeg friends and teach a few classes. At my frequent urging, Gopala finally agreed and we prepared to leave by the end of August.

I took great care to take every possession of ours that I wanted to see again from the farm. There was only one final issue to discuss with Gopala. I wanted to take Bethany with us. Her own birth mother certainly did not want her. I did with all my heart. When I told him how much I wanted Bethany with us, and that I wanted us to adopt her, he flew into a rage and adamantly refused her: "She's not our baby!" he nearly shouted in a rare angry mood.

"I don't care," I said. "I love her and she needs me."

"No she doesn't," he retorted. "She has a home at the farm. She's not coming with us and that's absolutely final!"

All my tears and pleading were of no avail. The only way I could take Bethany would be to leave Gopala. I was not willing to lose my husband. I knew that if I left Bethany now, I might never see her again. But it was Gopala or Bethany – so I let go of her again. I regretted this decision for years to come – but I felt I had to let her go at the time. A part of me felt sad and defeated. I was tired of farm life and all the struggles that farm living entailed. I was sick of the rain, the mud, the bugs, the hard work, the lousy food, the lack of privacy, and so much more. I could not face another winter on the farm; indeed I felt that I could never put up with this life in hell again.

ON AUTUMN ROADS

Feeling now
Like a yellow rose
On autumn roads,
That unfolds in splendor
Before my inward eye.
Only kisses
Of wind and stars
Meet me
Before the winter breaks
And sets me free
To sleep away.
I cannot face the blasts again!

The icy chill
Would freeze this heart
To stone. And I,
Now withering fast,
Like a yellow rose
On autumn roads –
Will sleep again
And waken not
Until springtime seeks me,
Begs me,
Yes – entreats me –
Bloom again!

Gopala and I had, as you may recall, chosen the yellow rose during our engagement and wedding, as our flower. It symbolized our love, which was in dire need of rejuvenation at this time. The rigors of farm life had created a severe test of our love over our nearly three and a half years together as man and wife.

In Gopala's mind, we were only going away for about six months or less, one last time, to make money and say good-bye to our Winnipeg friends. In my mind and heart, I planned to never return to God's Land. I was totally determined in this and I would not be changing my mind! We bid a second tearful farewell to our farm friends and we departed in an old Buick Gopala's father had recently purchased for us.

I was especially glad to leave then because Mata had decided that everyone (except the children) on the farm was going to do a complete forty-day fast on only water, just like Jesus did, beginning in September. The purpose of this fast was to "purify everyone" so the farm folk would finally "get their act together" and make God's Land a real, sustainable live-off-the-land farm. She was now talking about getting rid of the tractor and plowing with horses. "Would Mata's insanities never end?" I thought. This was, to me, the final straw! This information was a complete reassurance for me that it was time to leave God's Land forever. I certainly had absolutely no intention of further starving myself on water alone for forty days. They say there is a fine line between genius and insanity and I felt that Mata had crossed it – more than once.

She was a very strong-willed woman who possessed many spiritual powers and energies that she could use for good, but also for her own ego purposes. Her overall intentions may have been positive however she misused her spiritual abilities to control others. It is so easy to go a little astray on the spiritual path and eventually – go very much astray and lead others into dangerous pitfalls.

Rasputin was a similar personality. Initially, he prayed and developed spiritual powers to do healing and good works, but power does corrupt and he eventually became a distorted monster who manipulated people and eventually led the powerful leaders of Russia – to destruction. If you recall his story, it took enough poison to kill a dozen men to murder him and end his twisted control of the Czar Nicolas's family.

Jim Jones was another powerful spiritual leader who began his career by helping people in the U.S. and eventually, partially due to drug abuse as well as distorted ideals, poisoned hundreds of his religious followers, and himself, in the jungles of Guyana, South America in the late twentieth century.

Nearly two months after we left the farm, we heard that more than fifteen people had attempted the forty-day water fast with Mata. In the second week of the fast, one man actually died. Later that same week, another unstable man was carted away to a mental institution as he went berserk and was now certifiably crazy. We got the news from our good friends, Jack and Lydia, when they passed though Winnipeg in late October and stayed with Gopala and me. They had actually completed the forty-day water fast! Lydia showed me how the skin on her arms just hung loosely, like an old woman's. She had lost so much weight and muscle tone. They were still young, in their twenties, yet they both aged prematurely from the fast, had a number of gray hairs (they had not had any previously) and they looked many years older. After their visit, I was even more thankful to have left the farm.

When Gopala and I left the farm in August, we headed for Winnipeg as before, and this time we found a very cheap little house nearer the main part of town. It was the perfect place. Now we could live inexpensively and save money – not for the farm, but for our own life together, I thought. The tiny square house was actually more of a shanty. It had a higher roof in the front of the house that slanted back to just barely six feet tall in the back. It was an old, old cottage or shed-like structure built just before the turn of the twentieth century with a white-washed front and tarred shingle sides and back, a white picket fence and two plum trees in the back yard. The inside of the shanty held two tiny bedrooms, a small living room, bathroom and a quaint kitchen with an old-fashioned, embossed, tin ceiling and tin walls, painted white. There was also a tiny one-quarter basement like those common in the Winnipeg area. It was more like a root cellar than a basement, quite damp and mainly for storage.

The house was situated on a lovely street appropriately named: Home Street. It sat among a beautiful row of houses that were all more handsome and luxurious than ours.

As soon as we moved in, I planted a row of hothouse marigold plants along the front and sides of the house since it was far too late in the season to plant from seeds. After we were situated in our modest little house, we found marijuana seeds and leaves stuck in cubbyholes in the walls and basement (which we discarded) and Gopala and I realized this house had some strange "vibrations" leftover from the previous renters.

Once again, we set out to get jobs. Gopala was able to get his old job back at the record department. I did not want to go back to the flower shop, as I wanted to make more money this time. I got a job at a fancy jewelry chain store, the best in the city. The pay was slightly better than the flower shop. In my first two weeks at the store, I sold an unprecedented amount of jewelry boxes, comb and brush sets, glassware and other jewelry store gifts. I did not work in the actual jewelry section, rather in the accessory part of the store. My boss was very impressed with me. He was disappointed when I suddenly received a second job offer for more money at an office supply/book store and left his jewelry store behind. My boss called me a couple days later to match my new wages and get me back, but I was more interested in selling books and office supplies. Jewelry was not a passion of mine at the time, but I did love reading and was excited to be around books all the time so I stayed with the office/bookstore.

Gopala and I got some yoga and cooking classes going right away as well. He was having second thoughts now about our leaving the farm. He missed our farm friends and felt it was too soon after our return for us to leave the farm again. I decided it was time to tell him the truth. I told him I was done with the farm and all it entailed. I was tired of starving and working so hard and I had no intention of ever going back there. Gopala could not believe his ears and tried to talk me out of my decision. I was immovable. He was beside himself with dismay. Why did I want to ruin his life?

"I want us to have a life," I told him, "a life of our own."

Over the weeks that followed he reminded me frequently that I was ruining his life. We were meant to live at the farm our whole lives, he felt. He wanted to go back. Finally one day his upset fanned to anger and he began to yell and scream at me over his discontent.

"I want to go back to the farm," shouted Gopala. "I don't want to live in Winnipeg or anywhere else. We belong at the farm."

"I am never going back to that farm," I replied. "I'm sick of that place. I want a real life."

"We had a real life at the farm," continued Gopala. "All our friends are there."

"We have friends in Winnipeg too and we can always make new friends," I said, defending our present life.

"Well I intend to go back to the farm," declared Gopala adamantly.

"Then you are going without me," I yelled back. "I am staying in Winnipeg."

"No you are not!" yelled Gopala.

"Yes I am!" I shouted in return and I threw a book in Gopala's direction that hit the wall about a foot away from him.

"I'm going back and you're going back with me!" He was really furious now. I had never seen him this angry ever before. He grabbed my arms and started to shake me. He had never hurt me before. Neither of us had ever struck the other. Now he grabbed my head in his hands and looked me right in the eyes. "We are going back," he insisted.

"No! Never!" I declared. Gopala's hands were around my throat now. He was still shaking me and was grabbing me tighter around the neck. I was choking, gasping for air. He continued to squeeze my throat. I was getting dizzy, beginning to black out. But I was now furious. I was not scared; I was livid with anger at his attack on me. I had to do something quick, or I would not be going anywhere.

I reached my hands up to pull his hands from my throat but I was not strong enough. I could not budge him. I mustered up all my inner resources and began to claw at his hands and face with my fingernails. I was making my mark now, he was bleeding.

After many deep gashes from my fingernails, Gopala released me and howled in pain. I pushed him away from me and gasped for breath. I was horrified! My own husband had tried to kill me! I choked and tried to get my breath. I was panting now. He finally realized what he had done to me and he was looking at me like a repentant criminal.

I would have none of his apologies. I looked Gopala square in the eyes with a vicious look and told him: "If you ever, ever lay one finger on me again, – I'll make sure you regret it for the rest of your life," I stammered, between pants. "I will hire six men to beat you within an inch of your life. No one is going to hurt me ever again. You know my father beat me and no one, – especially not you, will ever hurt me again!" I staggered to pick up the discarded book from the floor and smacked him along side of his head, hard! "You just try to touch me again. I won't kill you, but I'll make sure you are nearly dead and live to suffer a long time!" I growled at him.

Gopala was humbled now and begging my forgiveness. He did not understand what had come over him. He blamed the "bad vibes" in the house for making him attack me.

I would have no part of his excuses either. "You can go back to the farm yourself if you want to go, but I am NEVER going back!" I continued, gaining strength. "And if you stay, don't you ever, EVER mention going back to that farm to me again!" I slammed and barricaded our bedroom door, as it had no lock, and left him to sleep on the couch, a small, covered single mattress on the floor.

Gopala never laid so much as a finger on me again in anger. Any further thoughts he may have had regarding returning to the farm, he kept to himself. He acted contrite and was especially nice to me in the weeks that followed. I forgave him completely. To not do so would mean we had to say good-bye. I could not live with him without fully trusting him again, but it was a several weeks before I let him make love to me.

PEOPLE WHO LOVE

Love is not something
You make for a day.
You don't pull it out
And then put it away.
Love is forever.
Once made it never dies.
Love keeps on going
Through truth, hate or lies.
You can cover love up
And pretend not to see,
But love will find ways
To escape and run free.
While love is eternal
And always the same,
It sometimes looks different
Or has different names.

Whether love of a lover,
A sister or mother,
Or love of a friend,
Or a father or brother.
We need love to give
And we need love to take.
The more you share,
The more love you make.

We settled into our lives in Winnipeg and were constantly visited by farm people and Alex's Calgary ashram folks. Our spare bedroom was a constant haven for visitors. We had little real time to ourselves. Another drawback of our little house was the mice that appeared as soon as the cool weather pushed them inside. There were only a few, but they could be rather annoying, jumping over us as we slept in our double sleeping bag on the floor. One night I woke up as a broom slammed down between my legs. A mouse had run up my legs and Gopala tried to smash him. The next day, I made sure Gopala bought mousetraps and that was the first and last time I woke up with a mouse (or a broom) between my legs.

I did very well at the office supply store and within six weeks they offered me a raise and a promotion to manager. This pleased me and stirred my confidence but I realized that my heart was not in office supplies. I wanted to work with flowers again. We had saved up a little money by now and we discussed the possibility of my going to floral design school at the end of October for the three weeks the program lasted.

Soon, I enrolled in the school and quit working at the office supply store. I headed for Toronto with a farm friend and Gopala stayed in Winnipeg to continue working. In Toronto, I lived with a Winnipeg girlfriend's parents while I attended school six full days a week. I loved being in design school. It was delicious to be surrounded by flowers and be able to arrange them myself. I made friends with a lovely blond, Dutch girl there and we became best friends during our three weeks of classes. I learned to make corsages, wedding bouquets, table arrangements, funeral bouquets, casket sprays and more. It was all over too soon. I graduated the top of my class and was now a qualified floral designer.

When I returned to Winnipeg, later in November, I went to the trendiest street in town, Osborne Street, and got a job at a little shop there as one of their main designers. My beginning work was just average, but I didn't care. I was still learning and I was improving rapidly. The owner was pleased with my progress and I loved floral work. It was actually very hard work. The wires, sprays and flower greens cut and stained my hands but the resulting beauty made it all worthwhile. I had the run of the shop most of the time and thoroughly enjoyed each day there. The owner was often out of the shop purchasing, so I was able to create new designs and explore my own ideas.

While I was away at school in Toronto, Gopala had all kinds of farm visitors to keep him company. When I returned home to find our house full of guests and my new bicycle broken by them, that was the last straw. There would be no more houseguests, I declared! Luckily, he had also been spending more and more time with our chiropractic friends on the French side of town, as well. He wanted us to go down to a special four-day seminar at Life Chiropractic College in Atlanta, Georgia, with our friends near the end of November to see if he was really interested in attending Chiropractic College himself. I was more than glad to see Gopala getting interested in something other than the farm and gladly agreed to go with him and our friends.

Three couples, including us, flew down to Atlanta and had the time of our lives. It was a long plane ride, and Gopala brought his musical instruments along. We had the whole plane singing and even chanting with us and they loved it. When we arrived at the college, we attended a number of seminars there and also took in the sights of the city. Someone booked Gopala and me as entertainment for the school's Saturday evening party and we performed several musical numbers that were the hits of the night, for around a thousand people. Unfortunately, the airlines lost our luggage on the way down and I had to buy a new dress for the event – one positive side effect of the loss. On the return flight home, we once again had the plane singing and the stewardesses begged us to fly more often as they had had one of their most enjoyable flights. Once again, amazingly, the airlines lost our luggage on the way home as well. They delivered it to our house several days later. Was this a bad omen?

Gopala made up his mind rather quickly to attend Chiropractic College. The only difficult decision was deciding which college. There were many. Only one in Canada, in Ontario, but there were plenty in the United States. I wanted us to go to the school in Chicago, a booming city only four hours from our parents' houses. Gopala wanted to go to Atlanta; he didn't like Chicago. I did not want to go to Atlanta because I did not like being treated like a "silly little wife." In Atlanta, people had asked me: "What will you do, sugar, when your husband goes to school? Will you stay home and have a baby?" Humph! It was more than I could bear. So we compromised and settled on Palmer College of Chiropractic in

Davenport, Iowa, two and a half to three hours southwest of Chicago, about eight hours away from our families in Detroit.

Our chiropractic friends urged us not to wait. College tuition was going up every yearly quarter at all the Chiropractic schools. The longer we waited to decide, the more it would cost. When Gopala's parents learned that Gopala wanted to go to Chiropractic College – and not return to the farm – they were more than overjoyed and anxious to help us out financially.

Gopala enrolled at Palmer College for the next quarter beginning in January of 1976. That was barely six weeks away and there was plenty to do in preparation. One of the chiropractic couples who had gone to Atlanta with us had been planning a December wedding and I was going to do their wedding flowers! It was a small nighttime wedding to be held in the Winnipeg flower conservatory. The bride wore turquoise and white, and I used gardenias and white roses for the wedding bouquet and corsages. Gopala became the wedding photographer, as he was good with a camera.

The wedding occurred during the height of a violent rainstorm and the bride was more than a little anxious this might be a bad omen. But the couple had gone to Chiropractic College together for several years and, as of today, I know they are still married and have two lovely sons together.

Gopala and I quickly made our arrangements to leave Winnipeg and we were not sure when or if we might return as the Chiropractic College took three to four years to complete. Luckily, Gopala had attended several years of University before we met, so he had his pre-requisite studies completed.

We quit our jobs a couple weeks before Christmas so we would have time to spend with our friends and say our proper good-byes. Father Ed was one dear friend that we had not taken time to look up when we returned to Winnipeg at the end of August. Now we sought him out and were more than dismayed to find out he was in the Winnipeg Hospital and dying of cancer! We were shocked and so sorry we had waited so long to contact him. He was such a dear man and one of the kindest, sweetest men I have ever known. We just had to visit him before our departure.

It was such a surprise to see Father Ed lying in bed, looking so thin and frail. He had lost a tremendous amount of weight and it was obvious that he had only a very short time left here on this earth. He made a weak smile when he saw us and I know he was pleased to get a chance to say good-bye. Our humble bouquet of flowers seemed like such an insignificant offering to one such as him who was now so close to heaven. We sang him one last song, as he was tired and we blessed him. He thanked us with his eyes and then he closed them to sleep as we crept away. My heart was aching for him. He was a dear, dear man of exceptional qualities. His gentle spirit would be missed on earth.

Father Ed's death greatly affected me. We were kindred spirits. I could not help but think that his death was a necessary step in his spiritual unfoldment. I remembered how much he had wanted to live with Gopala and I, and study Eastern religions. He had not been able to, because of his pressing duties at his monastery. Now, when I heard of his death, just before our departure, I felt sure he would be reborn into an East Asian family so he could study the Eastern religions he loved so much and so strongly wanted to explore. Gopala and I blessed his soul on its journey and often sang Father Ed's favorite song in memory of him: *Today*.

After a joyous Christmas celebration with our Winnipeg friends, we loaded up the Buick and a small U-Haul and once again we were on the road. On New Year's Day we passed over the Canadian/U.S. border. I could feel the difference in the air between the two countries. There was what I perceived to be like an invisible gray veil that seemed to lift as we slipped over the border. It was a veil that I would get to witness dozens and dozens of times yet in this lifetime. Late that night we arrived in Davenport, Iowa. It was another town, another adventure. Who could know where we would finally end up?

Months later, we heard from our Winnipeg friends that our little shanty house had been condemned and torn down after our departure. How appropriate that no one else would live in it after we were gone. I decided that it was to be our last impoverished living space. We were going to live like normal people now, in a real North American world with modern housing, work and entertainments. It was time to leave prison camp nightmares behind and create a new and happier world. I was ready to make big changes and I expected a better life.

Rise up. Rise up – To your own truth within.
Heaven is your destiny, If you let it in.

DÉJÀ VU

I'm sure I know you.
Have we not met before?
It must have been somewhere.
I'm sure I know you!
No, we have not met before.
– At least not in this life.
And yet I look into your eyes
And know you,
Know you well.
As if I've known you all my life.
We smile and our souls touch in love.
We say hello (there's no good-bye).
And then we continue on,
Each to his own way.
– On to meet new souls.
And perhaps if it is meant,
We'll meet again some day.

Chapter Eleven – Revelations

"If we are to understand our innate urges and dispositions
We must seek out our soul and learn of its experiences.
Only then can we completely understand why we are
The way we are, and why our life is the way it is."

John Van Auken
Past Lives and Present Relationships

Crossing the Canadian border into the United States was more than a change of location. It was an even greater change for me than for Gopala. From Winnipeg to Davenport Iowa was less than a thousand miles, yet it was a million miles in consciousness to me.

My entire world was about to shift in a totally different direction – forever. I would never again be the Alawan of God's Land, the submissive wife, the shy and fearful young woman who struggled to do as she was told. I was about to be reborn. Little did I know or understand the energies in me that were about to be released. I was only seeking a better way to live. I was tired of suffering and I wanted to be free and enjoy my life. I had never really "lived" before. My entire existence had been pain, suffering, striving, and forcing myself to put one foot in front of the other to overcome my past. Certainly there had to be more fulfilling days ahead?

I knew throughout my being that my past hells could not only be overcome, but I believed I could be happy, actually happy and experience joy in life. I knew that my past painful experiences could be the "manure" that made me into a glorious flower. I believed that the past nurtured a new and better me in the present.

Now I was ready to move ahead, and discover my new world and freedom. No more father or Mata or any restriction outside myself beyond natural human boundaries and legal laws that allowed for "the pursuit of happiness." What lay ahead was far beyond my dreams and expectations. Yet, I was just about to begin a new life. One about which I still had very much to learn. But I was willing and ready. Whatever lay ahead – high or low – I knew I had to march on. I wanted to take whatever steps were required.

"I'm free! I'm free! My God I'm free," I thought to myself as Gopala and I drove over the Canadian/U.S. border. But even freedom has a price. I would pay it. No matter what it took, I would do anything to be free.

We reached our destination late at night on New Year's Day, 1976. We were staying with Roy, the brother of our Chiropractic friend in Winnipeg. Roy lived in a large trailer park on the outskirts of Davenport, Iowa, on the mighty Mississippi River.

There it was again – the river. My life was always flowing with the river. There was the Rouge River near where I grew up in the Detroit suburbs and in God's Land, there was a stream of a river, but Davenport held one of the largest and most majestic rivers in the world, the Mississippi. Where would this river lead me?

Gopala and I spent two weeks living with Roy in his trailer. Luckily, his wife was out of town visiting relatives, so we were not really in anyone's way. Roy tried to convince us to buy our own trailer to live in. He said we could sell it for more than we paid for it when we left. I was unconvinced. The trailer was very cold in winter. Every wind seemed to rock it. Later I found out it was hot in summer, too. The sun beat down on the metal roof and sides and nearly baked the trailer. When it rained, you heard every pellet of rain clinking on the roof. No, I told Gopala, a trailer was not for us.

We searched the city for an appropriate home. Finally I found a one-bedroom rental, top floor of a house, near a park, on a high hill, overlooking the mighty Mississippi. The "energy" felt good in this house. I liked it and Gopala had to admit, it was perfect and only $150 per month. It was one mile from Palmer College, a good walk or easy bike ride. It was in a beautiful neighborhood with an even larger hill, up above it on one side that gave a breathtaking view of the river. It was such an amazing green, grassy hill, the kind you love to roll down, laughing.

Here the two of us set up housekeeping. Actually, I did. Gopala was helpless with household chores or at least he pretended to be. He seemed incapable of wielding a hammer. I pounded nails and placed pictures on the walls and hung the curtains. I had sewed simple, long, dark blue curtains from inexpensive remnant material and made bright, multi-colored throw pillows with an old *White* sewing machine he had bought for me one Christmas in Winnipeg. I found an old, small mattress for a couch and we rolled our customary sleeping bags on the carpeted floor until I actually found us a real bed. Gopala was skeptical, but I decided it was time we got up off the floor and slept in a real bed – like normal people. I also bought a card table and chairs for a dinette set. Then I shopped at thrift stores for dishes and knick-knacks to make our house a home.

In the meantime, Gopala explored the school and prepared for his classes that began just about a week after we moved to our own place, in late January. I found myself a part-time job in a bank. After all, I had worked in a bank in downtown Detroit for over a year after high school. I had experience.

We settled into school life. I joined the chiropractic wives' clubs and made many new friends. In Iowa, I went back to using my birth name of Jeanne and Gopala went back to using his real name, Aaron. Soon it was study, study for him and we spent very little time together.

Soon, I began to observe other school couples and realized that Gopala and I were very different. I did all the cooking, all the dishes, the laundry and the cleaning and he only took care of the car. I noticed other couples shared household responsibilities. What disturbed me even more was that, since our marriage, after a shower or at night, Gopala would just drop his dirty clothes on the floor wherever he was and just leave them there until I picked them up and put them in the clothes hamper. Other wives did not have husbands who did this. Why should I pick up after him? Not only his clothes, but books, instruments, projects, anything he did, was dropped where he left it and I cleaned up everything.

I attempted discussing this situation with Gopala one day. He saw no reason to change things in our lives. Why did I want to stir things up and change them? He had important schoolwork to do. I should be a supportive wife. I let it go another week and talked to him again. This time I was determined and I was upset. "Okay," he said, "I'll make an effort to change." He did not.

Now I was really upset and absolutely adamant. "Gopala," I declared, "Your dirty clothes and projects will stay where you leave them. I will not wash any clothes of yours that are not placed in the dirty clothes hamper. If you run out of clothes, it will be your own fault."

He ignored me. His dirty clothes piled up on the floor, around the bedroom and all over the house, but I did not touch them. Eventually he had no clean clothes, and began wearing the dirty, wrinkled ones for a while until they were too disgusting. Then he got upset and said: "Alawan, you have to wash these! You are my wife. It's your job to take care of me!"

"No," I refused. "Put your dirty clothes in the hamper or wash and iron them yourself," I insisted.

Gopala made one attempt at washing and after turning the wash blue and shrinking a couple of items in the dryer, he left everything in a big ball until it was overly wrinkled. He finally had to give in! He reluctantly conceded defeat and learned to use a clothes hamper. I was triumphant! Finally, no more dirty underwear on the floor. However, it is hard work training a man who does not want to learn new things!

My other ideas about marriage also began to change. Gopala never cooked or washed a dish. I told him he had to do the dishes once in a while if he planned to eat my cooking, so he kept saying he wasn't hungry, and told me just to cook enough for myself. Then he ate my food and left me the dishes anyway. We got into a shouting match over this, but even that way of resolving our differences had to change.

At the farm and in Winnipeg, we had argued often. I eventually had to yell before he listened and he eventually submitted while acting like a poor tormented husband who had a bitchy wife. Everyone had felt so sorry for poor Gopala, but he acted the noble husband who was determined to suffer through even though I was so much trouble to live with.

Now I finally saw through his ruse. I was the bad guy and he was the long-suffering husband. No more, I thought. Yelling did not get his dirty clothes off the floor, psychology did. Now I was determined to do as many others of my women friends did and use my mental capacities to get what I wanted. I would not yell again! I was steadfast in my resolve. Once I made up my mind – I kept true to it. Now when I wanted him to learn or do something around the house, I asked him. If he did not comply, I ignored him or refused to do the task myself and let the unfinished task get in his way.

Gopala was more than a little upset at this turn of events. How could I ignore him, walk off and leave things undone? Didn't I love him anymore?

"If you really loved me, you would help keep me in line," declared Gopala one day in cold February. "You never yell at me anymore. Don't you love me anymore?"

"Of course I love you, Gopala," I replied, "but I don't want to yell anymore. I'm tired of being a 'bitch.' I want to talk about things, not yell. I'm tired of being the heavy and trying to keep you in line."

"You don't love me anymore," he moaned.

I was beginning to wonder if he was right. He kept saying it over and over and I began to ask myself if I still did love him? What did we actually share – except a history at the farm and Detroit ashram? What did we have in common? The answer was always the same. We shared a past in spiritual communes and now we shared a love of music. Sometimes, we had sung together up to six hours a day. Always, even now, we sang our spiritual and popular songs at least an hour or two a day.

Before we left Winnipeg, we had been invited to sing and entertain at the Winnipeg Folk Festival in early autumn of that year. This was a major event in Manitoba that brought thousands of attendees and music lovers. Gopala had rejected the offer as he said it would have been "too egotistical" for us to perform there. I had never been able to forgive him for refusing this offer. I had begged him to accept it and allow us to sing, but he had been immovable. In my mind and heart – singing loving songs of God was not egotistical. Did not God love all songs sung in his/her honor? I believed that God did.

No, I could not forgive him for ruining our chances of singing publicly along with a major chance to become recognized folk singers in Canada. He had, I felt, destroyed any chance we had for name and fame in singing careers. Though I was shy in public, I was not shy when I sang. I opened my heart then and sang for God. Perhaps to Gopala, it was egotistical, but to me it was like the meaning of my American Indian spiritual name, Alawan: "singing a song of praise to God."

He continued now, to say I did not love him. If I did, I would yell at him, like his mother always had. Yelling was a sign of love to Gopala. But I was not going to yell any more and continue to be someone I no longer wished to be.

I wanted a gentler life, a kinder way of interacting. I wanted to lovingly discuss what was best for both of us. We became divided then. He wanted everything between us to stay the same as it always had been. I wanted change. Where could we go from here?

While he was studying day and night, I was increasingly bored. Three days of bank work a week, cooking and household chores and crafts, my women's clubs and the free babysitting I did weekly, still left me with time on my hands. I was used to working constantly at the farm, now I had little to do in comparison.

I read every good book I could get my hands on and now I began to read, *The Magic of Findhorn*, by Peter and Eileen Cady. Little did I know that this book would change my life and my beliefs forever. I believe that we each draw to us what we need, when we need it. This book provided new ideas and vital keys to important life changes for me.

Since we had come to Davenport, Iowa, (which is part of the Quad-Cities) about two months previously, I had been getting regular Chiropractic adjustments, free of charge, at the Palmer clinic about twice a week or so. (They were free for student's spouses.) These adjustments were changing me. I was healthier than I had ever been before. My menstrual cycle was regular for the first time in my life and I had more energy and was mentally and emotionally happier than I had ever been.

In "Palmertown," chiropractic was the ultimate health care. There were many miracle stories floating around about how chiropractic had saved lives, healed people of diseases and made people's lives so much better, in general.

I started to see a very popular and energetic student doctor at the clinic who had over two hundred patients. Most student doctors had only thirty or forty. This doctor's name was Jesse, and he had a remarkable experience with chiropractic care that had changed his whole life. He had been in a serious car accident many years previously and had gone blind. When he was adjusted by a chiropractor a few years later, he miraculously regained his sight. Jesse became a faithful supporter and believer in chiropractors and of course decided he had to "be" one and was now at Palmer College completing his final year of schooling.

Jesse was an attractive, powerful man who had a black belt in martial arts and he practiced Zen Buddhism. He had the spiritual strength and power of ten men with exuberance and determination unequaled at Palmer clinic. Unfortunately for him, he misused his power and was a womanizer, though he had a loving wife and children.

Despite his notorious reputation, Dr. Jesse, as he was called, was helping me tremendously with my health. My energy kept rising and my consciousness was expanding. I could see my life – my past and present – in better perspective and I was now looking at everything in life with new eyes. It is similar to living your life at the base of a mountain and suddenly being at the top and viewing everything you have known your whole life through a totally new perspective. This is one that allows you to see a higher truth.

With these new eyes, I now viewed my life and my marriage. I was not happy with what I saw. While I was changing rapidly, Gopala resisted change and kept pulling me back to old states of consciousness that I wanted to move beyond. But I was committed to him for life. Had I not taken him "until death do us part?" I believed I could change anything with my own love and determination. I would change our relationship. It would become a higher-level relationship of two God-loving beings who would do great things in the world. I would love enough for the both of us. My love was strong enough to change everything. I fully believed this – at the time.

I told myself this would be so as I buried myself in the book *The Magic of Findhorn*. It came as an earthshaking moment for me when I got to one chapter that shook me to my very roots. My ties to my own beliefs were uprooted in a single day of shattering realization.

About halfway through the book, Peter, the book's hero, pursues another man's wife, a woman with four children no less. He approaches her and tells her she is supposed to be "his" wife and she should leave her husband and go with him to start a new life. She of course, thinks he is stark raving mad. This woman rejects him and he continues to pursue her until he finally convinces her to leave her husband. She, Eileen, loses everything: her husband, her children and her old life.

But together, the two of them establish the Findhorn Community and their miraculous gardens eventually produce forty-pound cabbages and fertile, lush gardens that become known throughout the world. These gardens produced huge vegetables and magnificent flowers that were mainly grown in sand and poor soils in Scotland. But with help of the fairy folk and nature spirits, these gardens flourished and now live in history. This is a true story.

My tremendous shock was the fact that this woman left her husband for a better life. She did not stay "until death do ye part." If it was okay for her to get a divorce and leave, maybe it was okay for me, too? This new thought-seed had become firmly planted in my mind, a mind that had heretofore never conceived of this possibility. The winds of change were blowing again. How would this affect my life and all I was to do and be?

March was in full swing. Gopala brought me his traditional gift of yellow roses for my March seventh birthday and I was working on a beautiful new wall hanging about four feet long and three feet across on red velvet. It was a blue and gold velvet peacock with real peacock feathers and beaded wings. I bought long, dark blue tassels to hang from the four edges of the wall hanging. It was a lush, rich work of art that I took great pride in. I loved peacocks. They reminded me of my mother's dreams before I was born.

At the end of March, we would celebrate our fourth wedding anniversary. We always counted our spiritual wedding date as the real one, not the legal date of the Jewish wedding we had a little over a month later, in May.

My discontent in our marriage was growing by late March. Gopala was persistent now in his constant claims that I did not love him because I kept changing. I was quieter now and would not argue with him at all anymore. I tried talking with him about our problems, but he refused to talk and kept saying things had to stay the same. When talking failed, I went around him and proceeded as I thought best. My beliefs were shifting and I was opening to the possibility of a marital separation. He was not getting my messages. I honestly told him what I wanted and he was hanging on to the past, a past I no longer wanted nor believed in. It has been said that a man marries a woman hoping that she won't change and a woman marries a man hoping that he will. Gopala and I were becoming a living example of this statement.

> When your body and mind
> Become a well traveled road by me,
> Will I become tired of the scenery?

How could I make him see? How could I get him to accept our altering lives and our transforming relationship? Perhaps if we separated for a while, he would finally get my messages? What would it take to shake him and wake him up?

My chiropractic adjustments were still making an impact on me. As I was adjusted and worked on and especially right afterwards, fresh thoughts and new ideas were surfacing from deep within my psyche. Previously untapped parts of my mind seemed to be opening up. More than five years before, I had been so seriously ill, I was hallucinating. At that time, I had lost most of my memory and could not even read a book. Over the last five years, I had regained many of my mental abilities. Now I could clearly remember yesterday and today, read books and though my thinking had often been muddled over these past five years, my mental capacities were constantly increasing and growing beyond my earlier limitations.

Over five years, I had seen many different people's auras but I also had watched my own diseased liver's aura change from black to dark gray, to smoky gray, to dirty gray, sickly yellow, yellow green, pale green, light green and finally to a bright, rich, deep, verdant, grass green. My liver was now quite healthy. Often, in the past, I had felt like I was "lost" inside my liver, as if I was drowning in it and the health problems it created for my entire body. Now I peeked my head outside of this lower energy state and felt as if I was standing above it, free from its pull that kept me confused, depressed, disorientated and unable to interact with others in a stable, confident manner.

I could see clearly enough now to look back over my marriage and see that I was more than half asleep through it. The poor farm food, polluted water and hard work may have helped to toughen me so I could survive, but they also handicapped me, at the time, so I could never quite think clearly. I could not see all of Gopala's games and mistreatments of me – until very recently. He had been "getting away with murder" – of my true beingness – for years. Now I was back! Or more correctly, I was awakening to a brand new "me." I was becoming reborn as my real self and I now insisted on being free.

As I received each consecutive adjustment, the thoughts and energies in my brain were expanding. It was like climbing to the top of that mountain and finally – decisively seeing things as they really were for the first time. In the past, my mind was like a many-roomed house that had been so large and so much work to keep up, that I had to throw dust covers on the furniture and close up many of the rooms of my brain. Back then, I had to limit my thinking to the immediate present, as there was not enough energy to comprehend other thoughts and memories.

In my pre-ashram days of depression and hallucinations, I could barely remember today, let alone yesterday. At that time, I could barely access and utilize any of my mental faculties. Now the gears of my mind felt like they were turning, turning. I felt spirals and waves of energy flowing into my head and I felt thoughts re-awakening that had not stirred for five years or more. Plus new understandings were blooming in my consciousness and exploding with epiphany-like revelations.

I remembered my past: my childhood, my father, my schooling, my dark days and my early ashram days. I remembered what I liked and did not like. My own beliefs, hopes and dreams flooded into me like rivers into the ocean of my own thoughts and beingness. My many-roomed house became alive as I opened corridors and rooms and tore off dust covers from the furniture. I felt like I was – myself – as if for the first time in my life.

All the things, people and places that held me back dissolved now into my past. Not my father, Mata, Gopala or anyone could take away – my thoughts – my own beingness. At last, I was more myself than I had ever been!

LOVING PLACES

I'm loving places
And wondering why I do?
I look up on the hill
And see the grass and trees and school.
They remind me of the places
That I've been before
And yet –
They're all so far apart,
In distance great.
I feel them all
And love them all the same.

The sky's there too.
Of course it's blue.
The same sky over me
That's over you.
Wherever YOU might be.

I Love them all –
The Places.
And I visit them right now,
Recalling memories more alive
And people I have loved,
More than perhaps,
Someone I see now every day.

I Love the Places.
And I want each one – Forever.
With me they will stay.
The places, the things, the people –
I Love them all!
They all exist for me today.
And I find it strange,
That there's nothing I don't Love.
Beauty is everywhere.
Even in pain, I see no hell.
Just the beauty of a flower unfolding –
The beauty of labor before birth.

I Love the times.
I Love the spaces.
I Love the people.
I Love the places.
Born again am I in each new thing I see!
And in each experience that happens to me.
It is the Love of it all, I perceive.
I sit here drifting –
Looking at the grass and trees and school.
I'm loving places
And wondering why I do?

Gopala and I continued to drift apart. He kept to his study books and classes and I did my job, household chores, baby-sitting and reading book after book. I wanted a TV set. I had not been around a television set on a regular basis since I left my mother's house to move into Satchidananda's ashram in Detroit over five years previously. Now I was bored and I wanted one. I talked to Gopala about it and he was furious. He would not have one of those "unspiritual idiot machines" in our house. His response infuriated me and we had one of the nastiest verbal fights of our marriage. It blew over in a couple days, but my discontent was even more of a division between us now. I felt trapped in the past with him and I wanted to move ahead to a new future.

A day or two later, I went to the Palmer Clinic for my bi-weekly adjustment. Dr. Jesse began working on me. I had to tell him what was changing inside me and how I was mentally, emotionally and physically growing. Jesse and I already shared a closeness of spirit that only two souls steeped in Eastern cultures and energies could share. His Zen Buddhist practices and my East Indian yogic practices created a common ground for us that allowed for a "friendship of spirit." Jesse was touched and excited for me that I was progressing both physically and spiritually from the chiropractic care he was giving me. He was also dismayed for me regarding my relationship dilemma. He cautioned me to move slowly so as not to make a hasty change in my marriage that could create an unbreachable gap that would destroy an otherwise good marriage.

I touched Jesse's arm in thanks and for the first time in the more than six weeks that he had been giving me chiropractic adjustments, we gazed deeply into each other's eyes. What occurred between the two of us next, was beyond my comprehension. It went far beyond "Seeing the God in each other."

Jesse and I did not merge into each other's souls, as I was accustomed to have happen when two heart chakras opened together and the God within flowed between two people. I actually opened up and "fell into him." He was like a vast ocean without beginning or end and I felt like a tiny ship lost at sea. I was drowning in the infinity of ocean that was Jesse. I placed my hand on his heart and he jumped back as if electrified. The current seemed to scorch him and he gasped: "what did you do!" My touch was like a shock wave that tore him asunder.

Jesse reached for my hand and pulled me to him. He drank my bewildered eyes and plunged into me for a kiss that melted both of us into one. I did not feel my body – or his. I only felt swirling seas of energy like ocean waves dissolving me into a vast current that stretched into infinity. I knew Jesse as I had never before known anyone. He was part of me, not momentarily, but I saw that we had always know each other and been one.

I had known Jesse and loved him life after life after life. More than a dozen lifetimes that he and I had shared together flooded my memory with one past incarnation in particular surrounding us both. Our last lifetime together, which I saw in flowing images, unfolded in detailed sequence within my inward sight. My very breath was sucked out of me. I hung in suspended animation. The intensity, the joy, the love, the pain, the tragedy of it all danced in visions unlike any I had envisioned with others or seen on my own. Jesse and I had a bond of love that stretched beyond a few lifetimes. We were actually part of each other.

What was happening? Now I was undone! What I was doing with Jesse suddenly felt like infidelity and I was a married woman who took her marriage vows seriously. But this was not a sexual tryst; this was a mutual soul orgasm that had occurred for Jesse and me – all by itself. How could I blame myself for this? Nevertheless, I pulled away from Jesse's arms and struggled to regain my worldly bearings. I needed to return to Earth, get a grip on this life's realities. I could not allow myself the luxury of abandoning my present life's responsibilities for a few moments of soul bliss that I did not even understand. Yet I felt totally, completely in love with Jesse. What was I doing? How could I have allowed this? As I broke free from Jesse's arms, I looked once more into the ocean of his eyes and fled the room.

I walked the mile home in a daze. My world was no longer ordinary. I was changed and how could I ever return to what I was? Did I even want to return to it?

When I saw Gopala that night, I was an ocean away from him and I could not bridge the gap. I went to bed early saying that I needed to rest; I was especially tired. But I was processing, still struggling to comprehend the waves of energy that still ignited me and kept me awake all night.

The next day, Gopala left early and I was relieved that I did not have to face him and explain my distance from him. What would I do? I felt filled with Jesse from inside and there was now no more room for Gopala. It was as if I was lifted beyond myself, up to that mountaintop again. I could see my past, my present and possible futures.

I realized that I no longer truly was in love with Gopala. Although I felt a kind of love for him in my heart, I fully knew that this kind of love was not enough for me. My time with him was through. There was nothing I could or would do to change this. I saw that we had accomplished what we had needed to share and do together. Our time was over. (Later in life, I also came to know that if we had truly been one together, Jesse's energy would never have been able to come between the two of us.)

Though I had no assurance or understanding that Jesse was my destiny, I knew that the soul love that he and I shared had been a catalyst in raising me to my highest self so I could move beyond my present rut with Gopala. I knew that Gopala could not go with me, where I needed to go in this life. My consciousness was expanded and I saw and knew the truth that had to be. Jesse's one kiss still burned within me, yet it was not just his kiss – it was the kiss of the infinite, my divine lover that had kissed me through him. I felt kissed by the entire planet – all things in and beyond my world.

KISSING
Kissing the wind.
Kissing the dusk.
Kissing, kissing, kissing,
Everything I touch.
Does this seem so hard to do?
The kisses return to me
And I am buried in Love.
One kiss begets a thousand.
I give them all to you.
Kissing, kissing, kissing,
You, You, You!

Gopala came home that night and sensed my separation from him. We had already been distanced from each other by my previous changing attitudes and now he suddenly knew that this was serious. He wanted to hold me close, just hold me, like he never usually did. As I mentioned before – he was not a hugger. I obliged him and held him close, but I could not feel him. There was an ocean between us.

He felt this too and noted: "I know you are here holding me, but I can't feel you. It's like you are not even here, you are gone and there is nothing left between us."

He was so right. I was lost to him. I knew what we had was totally over. I tried to hold him closer. I wanted to comfort and reassure him but I could not give him what I no longer had to share.

"Gopala," I said, "we cannot go on together anymore. Things have changed between us and have been changing since we left the farm. I believe we need to separate for a while." I paused and the silence was heavy in the air. I felt his mind cloud over and heard him involuntarily gulp. He seemed to be searching for a solution, a way to dissolve this situation that was an unwanted nightmare to him.

"You and I need space," I continued gently, "to make needed improvements in our relationship. Things cannot go on the same way they have been in the past for us." I wanted to soften the blow with the possibility of separation, though I knew in my heart this was an unlikely possibility. In that moment, I felt our relationship, our marriage, was essentially over.

"Why not?" declared Gopala. "Why can't things stay the way they are?" He was uncharacteristically sobbing now. He almost never cried. Almost nothing ever seemed to move him to emotion (except my miscarriages). "I love you. You're my wife." Again, he made an unusual declaration of love. He rarely said I love you.

"I don't want anything to change between us," he added. "I want things to be the way they used to be."

"Things can never be as they were for us," I whispered to him. My voice was cracking now and I let go of some silent tears. "Life is about growth and change," I continued softly, "and I am changing. I cannot live with you in the same way as we did before. We have some relationship problems that have to be fixed. I don't think we can fix them while we are together. We'll just keep handling these problems in the same old ways that don't work for me anymore. We need to separate and alter the bad habits we have in relating to each other."

Gopala looked at me in sad disbelief. But he realized that this change was inevitable for us. "Okay," he relented. "We can live separately for a little while," he continued as he held me closer to him.

"It doesn't have to be forever," I continued. "We just have to work on how we interact and learn to treat each other differently." This was actually a tall order. Could we do it? I did not really know inside myself in that moment. But I was suddenly willing to try.

I told him that I would find a new place to live and I looked around for a couple days. Then it struck me. Why should I be the one to move out? I had found our apartment, pounded every nail, hung every picture, made curtains and pillows and purchased everything we used together. Gopala should be the one to start over. Let him put together his own place, I thought. I told these thoughts to him and it took a week longer for him to move. But he did and I sighed a sigh of relief. I was careful to divide our belongings evenly between us. I helped him pack and encouragingly sent him on his way.

At last I was free to be myself and I intended to be true to who I really was from now on in my life. This was another tall order that could not instantly be fulfilled.

Expressions seeking release – I will never have peace till they cease. Yet they will not – Till I can express who I AM.

YOU

You are more to me
Than you can see.
The real you – the you I Love,
Not the things
You have accomplished
Or things you have said or done,
But desires
Of your heart and soul.
The beauty – the Love –
That you are.
That seeking, trusting, open soul
That Knows,
That Sees,
That Loves,
That Feels.
The warmth of you I see,
In all its glory – set free.
Your body and mind
Are beautiful to see,
But your soul,
– Your Soul,
Set me on fire
With Love and Desire!

Chapter Twelve – Being of Light

"They will come back.
Come back again.
As long as the red earth rolls.
He never wasted a leaf or tree.
Do you think He would squander souls?"

Rudyard Kipling

After Gopala had moved out and been gone a couple days, I finally felt strong enough to see Dr. Jesse again. I had to see if I had "dreamed" what happened between us. I doubted the meanings of my experience with Jesse. Had I just created an excuse to end my stagnant marriage? Had I been too vulnerable, too open to allowing a separation between us? Also, if we really had a good relationship that was balanced and working, would it have even been possible for Jesse's energy to come between us? I did not think so. Happily married couples did not part so easily – or did they? I had no experience along these lines, only conjecture.

Dr. Jesse met me at the clinic door with a bashful look and eyes that darted around but did not gaze into mine. He worked on me in silence as what could be said in words about our previous experience? I broke our silence, as he completed my adjustment and told him my husband and I had separated.

"No, no," Jesse protested. "This isn't right. You need to go back to your husband."

"I can't," I replied. "This had to happen between us. I do not believe this has anything to do with you. Our experience together just made it more obvious to me that my marriage was not right to begin with. My husband and I have been drifting apart for some time. I believe this needed to happen."

It was already coming between Jesse and I as we spoke – the energy was mounting between us. We could both feel it. It was enormous. Jesse did not try to kiss me again but it was as if he already had.

"What is happening," he said. "This all feels so surreal. It feels like we've done this before. – Spoken like this, known each other before."

"We have," I told him. "I've seen it." I proceeded to tell him of the past lives we had shared that I had viewed during our last visit.

"That's incredible," replied Jesse. He believed in past lives, but like most people, men in particular, he had no conscious awareness of them. "I don't understand why this is so power-ful?" he said. We're not even touching each other. The room feels like it is electrically charged and I feel plugged into you."

"I feel the same," I admitted.

It was as if we were both continuing something we had started a long, long time ago.

"You need to go home to your husband," Jesse finally squeezed out.

"I can never go back to him," I said. "Something new is in motion in my life. The past is dead and I can only move forward."

"I can't do this!" Jesse blurted out.

"You don't have to do anything," I replied. "My life is my decision. I don't expect anything from you." I could see his tortured look and made it easy for him. "I'll see you next time," I said as I walked to the door and exited without a backward glance.

As I walked home in my flowing white dress, I thought nothing more needed to happen between Jesse and I, but I was wrong. Awakening energies surrounded me now and I could not shake the powerful flow of energy that connected me to Jesse.

I went home to meditate, but it felt like I was already in a deep state of meditation. I felt high, elated, transported to a state I had never encountered before. Night after night – I was in ecstasy. Day after day – I floated on a cloud I could not come down from, no matter what occurred in my everyday life. I was like a woman constantly "stoned." I can only compare it slightly to my state of deep meditation for two months that occurred at the Detroit Integral Yoga Institute.

The big difference was, I was not even trying to meditate many hours a day. The meditation seemed to be happening as I walked around, worked at the bank, taught classes, babysat and played with the children or when I was alone. It was happening all by itself. At night, I could only sleep two hours, total. The rest of the time I lay awake watching the pictures in my head. Vision after vision danced before my eyes. I was lifted to a place beyond earthly realities, yet I was still functioning on the earth. Poem after poem flooded out of me, night after night. In the past, I had written a poem or two every few months. Now I might write several in a night, even a half dozen or more.

One dark night after midnight, I woke from my two-hour "nap" and in the pitch dark, I wrote *The River Daughter* poem at the beginning of this book. I did not "think" it. It just "wrote itself" through me. I just watched the process in my head – which was exploding with light – while I scribbled out this poem in the dark. In the morning, I read it and only changed one word. It happened as you can now read it.

When I worked at the bank, now five days a week, especially at the outside teller window, I found out that I could easily read people's energy as they drove up to my window. If they were happy or sad, I could feel that, and I especially sent extra loving energy to those who were unhappy, tired or upset. One day a group of teenagers, high on drugs, drove up and I felt a contact high as they drove up, even before I saw them. Once a loving, simple man, looked up at me with an open heart to which I responded in kind and he ran home to get me a special book on Jesus he felt he had to share with me.

Each day, I felt so free, so alive. When I closed my eyes, I could see the light inside my body, even in the dark, I was like a walking sun.

Walk like a star.
How beautiful you are.
The light of God flows in you,
And fills you like a star.

I went to Palmer College nearly daily. Though I rarely saw Jesse except in the clinic, I could feel him. When I was within a block or two of him, I felt his energy and I saw a white line of current, like a string or cord of white light that stretched from my heart to his. If I followed that line of energy, I walked right up to him. What did this mean? Why was I, literally, so attached to him? Jesse had a wife and children, He would not be leaving them, I knew, not that he was so faithful or perfect in his marital love. Though I sensed that he and I had been brought together for a purpose, I felt that now was not a time for us to be together. My physical body still required healing but I was not sick. I floated on and in this current of energy that carried me through each day and night.

Gopala and I saw each other every few days and he was desolate. I felt for him, but could not really reach him with my energy. I tried to console him but he was not able to be consoled. Nothing changed between us. He kept saying things needed to be the same as before and I kept saying they had to change. He wanted sex and I wanted us to date and talk about our lives, perhaps get counseling. Gopala was not interested.

One night, Gopala came over in a determined mood and said he was not leaving until things were back the way they had been. I told him things would never be the same – just as I had been saying to him continually. Things had to be different. I was different. He refused to leave, so I called the police. We were legally separated; so one word from my lawyer and the police removed Gopala from my house. He was told not to come near me without my permission. He refused to talk to me after that, go on dates or get counseling. He unyieldingly demanded that we get back together and be as we were before. That was impossible. At one point, Gopala even offered me a new television set as a bribe for getting back together. That could never be a solution for us.

So every week or two, then it was every month or so, Gopala would just call me and say: "Can we get back together now?"

I would reply: "No, we need to talk about things."

"I can't," he replied. "We need to get back together."

"No," I repeated, and he would hang up. It was like a broken record with him. We had the same circle of conversation – the same request, the same reply.

In the meantime, my exalted state continued. I was "high" twenty-four hours a day and continued to sleep only two hours a night for about three months or more. I did not understand how my body could take this. I seemed to be healthy enough at the time, through all of this. I felt free now, in a way I had never felt before. I felt like handcuffs had been removed from my wrists and I had been let out of jail. Often I danced around my living room like one who had just been freed from exile. I felt free!

My marriage had been a jail of sorts, full of limitations. I had grown through it and because of it, but Gopala's and my time together was finished now. I knew this throughout my being. While I had been open to reconciliation with him initially, he had been unwilling to even attempt the changes that would make this coming back together a possibility. By his refusal to work on our marriage, I knew that it was completely over.

I continued to see Dr. Jesse in the clinic, about twice a week, as usual. He was about to graduate in June, which was now barely six weeks away. He and I continued to have powerful conversations and energy connections that drove us both to distraction, yet we continued seeing each other, but only in the clinic or when we ran into each other on Palmer campus.

My mother and sister Trixie came to Davenport for a few days to visit me when they found out that Gopala and I were separated – to console me, but I did not need consoling. I did enjoy their visit though. They brought me a lovely new dress and we had a great time together.

In the interim, my "highs" and poetry continued. I saw myself as I had never before seen myself in this life except for a brief time in childhood when I had sat by the Rouge River and believed that I could dive in and separate my body cells and then fly up into the heavens.

I was having frequent feelings and knowings of myself as a being of light – a nature goddess of earth and the heavens, throughout this time of awakening that began with my cosmic kiss with Jesse. (Was this the magical kiss of Prince Charming?

It had released me from a past spell.) I was not entirely sure what all this ecstatic energy and the nature goddess memories meant for me. I only knew that I believed I was now and had been such a goddess. I was reliving right now, what seemed to be a portion of a lifetime when I was a goddess of nature who commanded and nurtured the earth. At that time, my body was made of light and stars. This poem and many others like it came though at this time:

VISION OF MY SOUL

I see myself a free spirit.
I stand with long hair flowing down,
Crowning my head and caressing my body.
– Naked I stand,
With a glowing white light
From my inner being to clothe me.
In my forehead is a bright star –
Radiant – it is the light of my being,
Impossible to look upon
With eyes not of the soul.
Wings spreading from my shoulders,
Are huge transparencies of delicacy,
Of colors so vibrant –
No earthly rainbow has yet known their hues.
I dance upon the earth,
Yet my feet touch it not.
I AM not of the earth –
Yet here I AM.
My song is the wind.
I laugh with the rivers,
Soar with the birds.
"O my soul doth magnify the Lord!"
For I AM an expression
– Of that Perfection –
That is the truth of my being.
The Love I know I AM –
Free Spirit – Being of Light!

It would take many more years of my life before I more fully understood these visions of myself as a star creature /nature goddess. Nearly two decades later, I experienced more fully, this unusual lifetime that I barely tapped into in childhood and now I saw it again, as my married life with Gopala was ending and my new single life was beginning.

As long as Jesse was in town, I had no desire to date. Our occasional meetings in the chiropractic clinic for adjustments and conversations seemed to sustain me. But both Jesse and I were far from content with the limitations of our relationship. Jesse was constantly amazed by the energy that flowed between us. "How did I do it?" he wanted to know. I did not know either, where the energy came from or why it was so powerful. This voltage was and is the most intense energy I have, to date, ever felt in this lifetime. Jesse was more than just a soul mate; perhaps he was a twin soul? In those days, I believed we had many soul mates and a few special twin souls that it was possible to meet in a lifetime. Perhaps he was a twin soul?

As Jesse and I spent time together in the clinic, there were a few times when we lost control and could not resist touching each other beyond the adjustment. Our touches were electrified – always. A mere holding of hands or placing my hand on his heart was supercharged with a voltage that shook both of us to our roots. We were both confused. Jesse was a powerful man and not incapable of indiscretions in his personal life. He had amazing intelligence and quickly grasped every detail of life around him. Yet, his eyes were glazed over with a veil only I seemed to see. Somewhere, inside himself, he was lost, separated from his real self. He did not really know or understand his true nature in God – or the universe, if you prefer. His earthly senses meant more to him than his spiritual ones. He had cosmic abilities without cosmic understanding.

Jesse's increasing energies and heightened physical talents were not circulating with God or Infinite/Innate Intelligence. The powerful current of energy that flooded Jesse's body had nowhere higher to go and I could see by looking into his eyes, that his own power – was driving him mad. Already there were distortions in his aura that signaled dangerous roads ahead of him. No wonder he had to dissipate the voltage he carried with frequent marital "indiscretions."

Jesse and I had never had sex, yet I heard it rumored that he had been as enthusiastic in his extra curricular "bedroom studies" as he had been with his astonishing patient load that was more than six times that of the average Palmer student. One day everything changed for us.

Now, it is time to relate Jesse's and my most recent lifetime that I had seen the first time we kissed. What surprised me most about our last life together was that it was more than familiar to me already in this lifetime. Jesse had, in our last life, been a British naval officer and I had been the daughter of a prominent Japanese government official. We had a lengthy and intense affair and he left me never to return. I had a child by him and pined for him secretly in my heart. I continued my life in Japan rather quietly and became dedicated to my work. I remained unmarried and took care of my child.

Shades of Madame Butterfly! Was this lifetime with Jesse why, during my last miscarriage in Winnipeg, I had played this Japanese story opera over and over again? I believe it is! Also, I had just that year, completed reading Pearl S. Buck's book entitled: *The Hidden Flower* about a Japanese woman who marries an American naval officer and comes to America with him only to be neglected and mistreated terribly, so she leaves him to return to Japan with her prominent Japanese suitor who marries her. Before they leave the U.S., she gives birth to the American's son and gives him up for adoption.

All this happened before I even met Jesse. I had even written a poem about the story from the woman's perspective, not my own, which I rarely do in my poetry.

JEWEL

Oh Jewel,
Oh hidden flower.
Joy Blossom
Born out of soul's Love.
Are you growing even now?
Or are you waiting
Still above?

I am waiting,
Ever watchful.
Are these signs that I receive,

Messages that you
Are blooming,
Hidden flower,
Just conceived?

Many things
I think to do,
Wanting and
Not wanting you.
Yet accepting
What must be.
Little Jewel I love thee.

Dear God –
Whatever I must do,
That I will do.
Oh my God,
I trust you.
Whatever must be,
Must be.

There were just too many coincidences here. The first day that Jesse and I had kissed in his office had brought on a parade of past lives we shared. I had not previously envisioned so many lifetimes that I had spent with one man before. But this Japanese lifetime was the most recent incarnation for Jesse and I together and the most detailed and relevant to what we two presently shared.

One day in June, Jesse actually called me on the phone and wanted to come to my house. He could no longer contain himself. He wanted to see me and be alone with me. I consented, not knowing what the outcome might be. But I trusted my own inner sensing and guidance. I would see what was possible. When he arrived, we talked and as always with him, I found myself saying things that surprised even me. My psychic premonitions prompted me to tell him things about himself that amazed him. I seemed to know all about him.

I was like an oracle telling him who he was now and what areas of his life he needed to work on and improve. As I read his aura, I warned him regarding his blocked energies that could affect his mind precariously in the future. Apparently, I was so correct in most of my information, he assumed I must have also been right regarding my future predictions as well.

This gift of "reading people" has grown in my life and I use it today during nutrition consultations and when giving past life readings. I can see the past in this and other lives and the past and present health of an individual including major organ problems and diseases. Also, I can see and recommend a specific path of healing for someone and as a nutritional intuitive, I suggest particular foods, a diet outline, natural supplements, exercise, cleansing, and special healing aids for each person I counsel.

Now Jesse and I were through with talking. He gazed into my eyes and I saw something that had not been there previously. His eyes were full of lust – plain, brazen lust. It was a hollow kind of look. He reached for me and pulled me to him. I felt intense longing for him, but it was not the same feeling as before in the clinic. Now he appeared quite sick. His eyes no longer fed mine with energy. I tried to get him on track – to focus on his heart love – not his loins' lust.

"Look at me with your soul Jesse," I said to him. "Open your heart, as you did before." Jesse lifted me to the floor and wrapped his arms around me. He wanted me desperately. His hands touched me with fire but it was an empty feeling of outward lust without emotion. His heart was blocked, his spirit caged. It was as if he was fighting himself. He gazed at me with utter confusion. He seemed to be searching, or rather groping, for answers – for understanding.

"Look at me with your heart, Jesse. See my soul," I continued. "You have done it before. You know how."

But he did not appear to know how, now. He was unable to comply.

> I asked you if you loved me.
> Your trembling lips said no.
> Your fearful eyes said I cannot.
> Your poorly hidden heart,
> Said yes I do – With all my soul.

I did not know how to help him. I only knew I could not make love to him while he was in this powerless, confused state. Neither of us really understood what flowed between us so intensely. However I knew I could not betray myself and give in to something that had become a distorted energy in Jesse. It would be totally wrong – for me – and him to merge our bodies in this way, without Jesse being his real self.

Perhaps it was because only part of him wanted me or perhaps giving in completely to the power that moved between us terrified him, as it was a new experience that threatened to take him over. Jesse wanted, yet resisted the real power we shared. This nullified the purity of spirit between us. Nothing could happen between us now, I knew.

Part of me wanted to make love to him anyway. I saw the real him. I was fully present. But, no! He was not! I knew I could not be with him in such a way. He was unconscious of what was really important between us. It would be a lie to my soul to make love to him while he viewed our act with mere lust. I wanted him so in my heart. I had to let go of my desires. I could not deceive myself; I was far too honest for this.

I kissed Jesse ever so gently and looked deeply into his pained eyes. "We cannot do this," I told him lovingly. "I cannot have so small a part of you. Only when you can open yourself to me in heart and spirit can this be possible." I knew it would not happen now. Perhaps it would not happen ever in this lifetime. Jesse remained silent. But his eyes spoke volumes of emotions to me.

> Never before have I met a soul
> As deep and determined as mine.
> For you my love, I'd wait forever.
> If it takes eternity.
> If it takes all time.

We embraced. He got up to leave and shot a longing, bewildered glance my way. As I stood at the top of the staircase watching him leave, he stopped and stood at the bottom for a long time, staring up at me. I flashed to our last lifetime. He was once again the dashing naval officer gazing up at his beloved Japanese doll. A part of him never wanted to leave me. Another part of him had to. Jesse looked up at me for what felt like a million moments in time. Then he turned and was gone.

WANTING YOU

You've left me burning again…
Unsatisfied – wanting more.
More than you can give me now,
Because you can't surrender yet –
Surrender to the Love you have for me.
The Love you can't believe in.
The Love you don't understand.
Because it doesn't make sense to you.
 – It breaks all the rules
You've tried so hard to believe in.
Your principles of right and wrong,
Those laws and rules of mind,
That allow no room for the expression
Of that infinite soul Love within you.
And I want to cry. I want to die.
Pained, as I am – wanting you, wanting you.

Jesse and I saw each other only a couple more times in the clinic before he left to start his practice in New England. The energy between us was still powerful. I continued to see the white cord of light energy that connected my heart to his when I walked the Palmer School campus. Despite the power between us, it was controlled when we were in each other's presence. Perhaps the energy between us was more pure in the clinic because the power and love Jesse held for chiropractic poured out there in a steady flow of undistorted energy. We could connect there to our higher selves because of the untainted healing force in him, which was unlike his mangled love energies.

YOU POSSESS THE KEY

Your chains are big and heavy,
Too strongly welded for me.
I can never break them.
I can never set you free.

You alone are master
Of your soul beloved by me.

Only you can break the chains.
Only you possess the key.

Will truth ever win you over?
Will the truth you ever see?
Oh yes, you will have freedom.
You want it as much as me.

But I think perhaps the distance
Between our souls is wide indeed.
Perhaps we'll not Love till heaven comes,
And both of us are freed.

During those last couple of clinic visits with Jesse, he looked at me with a kind of helpless resignation and I, understanding the difficulty of his situation, did not try to stir up any of our energies. After all, Jesse had a family to think about. Though there was an immensity of power between us, it was distorted and how could Jesse leave his present situation for something neither of us understood? There was no time or means for Jesse and I to explore the energies between us. Also, both of us knew the unlikelihood we had of making a relationship between us succeed under such horrendous conditions.

Perhaps, if Jesse had really been consciously connected to his spiritual side, we could have been able to access, together, the meaning of our joint power. Then we could have both proceeded with our lives – knowing and understanding – what was really going on between us.

Under that stiff exterior of you,
There is a sensitivity
That is divine.

I felt that he was greatly handicapped by his inability to access his spiritual side properly. I was concerned that he might eventually go crazy from the energy blockages within him. He had so much power that he did not really know what to do with it. I now believe that if we both had been more conscious, our ending could have been less painful.

But we were not.

So this is Love!
The Joy of it – the Pain.
I do believe I'm going to go insane.

And I must trust that all that happened between us was right in its own way. We did eventually choose the high road, based on what limited information we had regarding our connection. I have no regrets, only natural curiosity, to this day, to find out why we were so powerfully connected. What did (or does) it all mean? I fully believe that someday I will have answers to these questions.

You're gone again.
You've left me waiting,
Wishing,
Hoping…

After Jesse left town, at the end of June, my overall energy levels decreased to normal. For the approximately three months since Jesse and I had first kissed, I had only slept two hours a night and I lived in a high energy world wherein I was enjoying all the benefits of a high meditative state without even having to meditate. I had visions, wrote poetry, and had loving connections with everyone around me – even Gopala – though I could not give him the relationship he truly wanted.

Now my life returned to everyday living with all the ups and downs a normal life contains. I worked in the bank five days a week, I babysat, I hung out with my friends and women's clubs, I taught some cooking and nutrition classes, I sat in on some Palmer classes and life went on.

Once Jesse left town, it took me a few weeks to fully let go and say good-bye inside myself to him. I wrote an entire poetry book dedicated to Jesse.

QUESTION

Your Love was as deep as the deepest sea.
– My love like a boundless sky.
I Loved you for what you had to be.
And yet you would have crushed
My dreams and me.
And my love would have only
Burdened – Why?

This was the first time in my life I had written a book of
poems for anyone. Despite the flood of emotions I had felt
for Manny and Gopala for years, my poetry was limited to a
few simple poems for each. Now my heart seemed rent in two
over a man I had never even made love to. – At least not
physically and not in this lifetime. But Jesse and I had made
love – in our hearts and souls. It had happened without our
ever trying to. It had happened all by itself.

Unspoken Love,
Untasted Love,
You are a curse.
Never to have met you,
Or to meet and live without you,
– Which is worse?

So now I grieved. Even the grieving seemed to be happening as a matter of course. It came from deep inside me. On the
surface – in my conscious mind – I knew I had no call to
mourn Jesse. On a physical level we had shared almost nothing. But, inside myself, I was a torrent of emotions. It was as if
I had been torn in half. I felt as if someone had reached into
my body and ripped my heart from my chest. If my pain had
been visible, my heart would have bleed, soaked my clothing,
and run into rivers on the floor...

THE TEMPEST

The river flows in blood tonight.
And I cannot help but fight
– The flow of it.
Pain comes in swirling seas of storm.
Hurricane tempest surrounds me
And enfolds me in its deadly arms.
With each new wave
I go under again and again,
Swallowing salty sea.
And how I wish the waves
Would drown me.
– But no – I must go on.
Oh, the pain of Knowing Love
And never tasting the glory of it!

Slowly, slowly, the waves of my pain subsided into an everyday life. Eventually my flood of tears dried up. I lifted my head and surveyed my new world. I was single, attractive, an excellent cook and craftswoman, and now – I was beginning to feel a bit lonely. I had only been living alone a short while, but I did not really like it. I liked having someone to cook for and care for. I wanted a chance at a real life with a real man who could love me for who I actually was – scars and stars. Inside myself, I knew I still had a tremendous amount to learn about life, health, love and relationships. So it was time to get on with my life. It was time to begin dating again.

IN LOVE

For all I know,
I may be just –
In Love with Love!

MY LOVE

Today I light a candle in my head.
— A way to see things.
Pictures range themselves around my bed.
I choose to see this one:
I am loving souls too deeply.
Being younger than I am, I show myself too quickly.
Yet I am old enough to shun games of strangeness
And I loathe coy words.
But to give my love so freely, is too be misunderstood.
For I offer not my body as a way to get to know me.
Rather offer I — my heart and soul
And bid you take these first.
My body will come willingly enough,
Thereafter — For one man alone.
Joyously I shall be yours,
If you but see ME first and know me.
Take me as I Am.
Can you kiss my soul before you take me to you?
Can you hold me in your heart
And drink my eyes till drunk?
Oh! — To dance with you in heaven!
There's a taste I crave for wildly!
Oh, to satisfy this hunger —
All my life I've followed Love — Blindly!
I never cared if I fell or burned myself in trying.
Is there not a soul like mine,
That seeks the Love for which I'm dying?
Oh, languish my heart and soul and body!
Die for Love if you must and will!
But I will never settle
For a Love that's less than I can give.
Rather would I die of wanting,
Than in a shallow pool of love.
A love that binds and possesses,
But never sees and never frees you.
Give me oceans for my Love
And give me lakes to fill!
Are you true enough to find me?
Seek me in your Heart Beloved.
Run to me with open Soul.
I am waiting. I am waiting still.

Chapter Thirteen – "Palmertown"

"True worth is in being, not seeming, –
In doing, each day that goes by,
Some little good – not in dreaming
Of great things to do by and by."

Alice Cary
Nobility

"Palmertown" as the area was nicknamed, was actually part of four small cities: Davenport and Bettendorf in Iowa and Moline and Rock Island on the opposite, east side of the Mississippi River in Illinois. The four cities and the surrounding areas were called the Quad-Cities. It had been called the Tri-Cities in the past and occasionally it was called the Quint-Cities, but officially, it was the Quad-Cities, U.S.A. It was a combined city of approximately a hundred thousand people back in the 1970s and has grown considerably since then. Ronald Reagan had an early start as a radio announcer at one of the local radio stations here, decades before.

Here, lives revolved around the muddy Mississippi River. It was vast and pulsing with the lifeblood of the Quad-Cities. Most of the year, the local news included how many residents had been drowned or washed away, weekly, by the river.

An opposite change from Winnipeg where winter news reported how many locals were lost weekly in snow drifts.

The mighty river was breathtaking, but dangerous. It was expansive, swift and deep. The currents were too powerful for even some of the best swimmers. Locals preferred small, distant lakes or pools for swimming, or the rural abandoned rock quarries that had filled up with water. The younger Quad-City residents and especially the Palmer students and families often went "skinny dipping" at the quarries. An occasional raid by the police sent dozens of people scampering naked back to their cars to escape a fine for "swimming in an undesignated area." But still, the quarries kept busy with a steady flow of uninhibited enthusiasts.

A second favorite local haunt was Wild Cat's Den. It was a park full of caves to explore, a great day trip. Another was Lake George, popular with boaters. It only allowed non-power boats like canoes, rowboats, paddleboats and small sailboats. It was quiet, serene and idyllic with acres of green trees lining the abundant shores of this pleasant lake of moderate size.

A few weeks after Gopala and I had separated, I had exchanged my part-time job at the bank, doing check processing for five-days a week full time work as a bank teller. The bank was downtown Davenport, several blocks down the hill from Palmer College. I waited on lots of Palmer students there. My bicycle was my main form of transportation for work or play. Gopala had taken the car, and I took the few hundred dollars extra cash in our bank account instead.

One day, a beautiful blonde-haired man came into the bank to do business and his aura was radiant. He looked like a Viking god and I determined that I was going to get to know this man. The fact that he was married did not deter me. I knew he was a great soul and I would have been glad just to talk to him occasionally. In a few weeks, I met him again at a church I attended and eventually became close friends with him and his lovely blonde wife, who looked every inch, the "Viking's" soul mate.

My thoughts were now turning to dating, and soon I had a couple dates with one of Gopala's school friends – Derek. All of Gopala's friends had been quite impressed with me before our separation. They thought I was gorgeous and a great cook, too. But Derek mysteriously disappeared after a couple of dates and I noticed that none of the other Palmer men seemed interested in me though they had seemed to be when I was married. In fact, I had few dates at all that first year of Gopala's and my separation. It took several years before I found out that Gopala had spread the word to all of Palmertown that I was "frigid." He did not want anyone else interested in me as he was determined to win me back for himself at some point down the road of our lives.

That first year of being "single," I kept myself busy organizing some cooking and nutrition classes at my place a few times a month and sitting in on some Palmer nutrition classes during my lunch hours or after work, which started early and ended by 3:30 p.m.

Also, I became a beloved babysitter to several small children from two young families in particular. The parents were "Palmer People" and I took care of three-year-old Bryan and his baby sister Anita, one or two afternoons or evenings a week, plus I watched four-year-old little Rosey once or twice a week as well, to help the parents out. I never accepted a dollar for babysitting. I loved the children and they helped fill the hole in my heart over losing little Bethany and not having any children of my own. I played games with the children, took them to the park and beaches, read them stories, taught them to write and say their letters and basically just enjoyed being with them.

At the time, I also baked eight to twelve loaves of bread a week and freely gave them to these families and other friends, keeping only two loaves a week for myself. I was still used to long farm hours of working and I had lots of energy and time that I needed to put into giving to others. This kept me basically happy. My biggest unfulfilled longing was singing. I never really missed Gopala when he moved out, but I missed our singing together every single day. After hours of shared singing to nothing but singing on my own – I hungered to sing with others.

One amazing thing about the Quad-Cities that pleased and excited me was that here, in the middle of the prairies, the Quad-Cities held the largest and best collection of Haitian Art in the United States. Imagine – the bright, colorful, bold colors of my birthplace, Haiti, were plentifully displayed at the small local art gallery! It was my first real adult taste of the riches of my heritage. I spent many happy hours drinking images of the ravishing lushness in bold reds, bright greens, yellows, purples and blues portrayed especially in garden, jungle and ocean scenes that are common in Haitian art.

On Sunday mornings, I took the church bus to a local new age church in Bettendorf. I became good friends with the Palmer student who drove the bus, Reid, and we used to chat for hours about life, love and God just like too kindred spirits. This huge, cathedral-like church had been a former Catholic Carmelite Nunnery where the actual Von Trapp family singers, of *Sound of Music* fame, had performed during World War II. It had been purchased and was now maintained by a local new age church group and I delighted in spending my Sunday mornings there for church services and staying for the social hour afterwards. The church was beautiful and spacious, set atop a high hill overlooking a spectacular view of the Mississippi River and much of the surrounding areas. I had many friends among the church members and quite a few were Palmer families.

I was still very shy and withdrawn during this time, far from who I am today. I had a lot of trouble expressing my feelings and myself. Primarily, I did not understand them and even when I did know my own feelings, I was often unable to express them in words. Often, I had to slowly pull bits of my emotions out of myself and piece them together. I mulled over my feelings and worked hard to uncover them and interpret what they really meant to me. It sometimes took contemplation and meditation for me to see what was really going on inside me and it took great effort to overcome my timidity and express those feelings about something or someone.

Since I still had some health problems, I ventured into a holistic medical doctor's office at one point for a check-up and some tests. He was actually amazed by my level of good health, he said. The doctor checked my nutrient and salt levels among other things and asked me if I was eating meat three times a day. He said my protein levels were off the charts.

I proudly informed him that I had been a pure vegetarian for over five years and that my high protein came from eating beans. He was astounded! The doctor was also impressed with my nearly non-existent sodium levels and was surprised to learn that I ate plenty of sea salt and tamari soy sauce – all I wanted. Few people realize that eating plenty of complex carbohydrates like brown rice, beans and vegetables allows a person to enjoy higher salt consumption without the resulting high sodium levels in the body. Plus I avoided fast foods and most pre-packaged foods like chips, dips, soups and frozen entrees that contain extremely high amounts of salt.

All my other tests came back normal or above average, so as far as my general health was concerned, I was okay. But I knew I still had lots of work left to do on myself before I actually achieved excellent health. Most doctors' tests do not show up a health problem until a condition is quite severe. At home, I continued my own regime of good diet, fasting and taking supplements to continue the healing of my liver and pancreas as I still had problems breaking down fats and I had low blood sugar attacks from time to time plus some occasional depressions and memory problems.

Summer soon turned into fall and though I was working full-time, my pay was low, withholding taxes high, and I barely seemed able to pay for rent, food and a few personal items. I was just scrapping by. So, I was delighted when the minister at my church and his wife invited me to live at the church in some of the old nun's chambers that were plentiful – for free – in exchange for doing cleaning work around the place. There were already several Palmer guys living at the church who did maintenance and repair work and the lovely blonde "Viking-like" couple – Andrew and Laura, whom I had first met at the bank, had just recently moved into the church as well.

Well, this was all the encouragement I needed to say yes! I would have three, tiny, private rooms with my own staircase located just above the chapel. In fact, there was a large, hidden window in my little living room that opened up to overlook the church sanctuary area. Perhaps sick nuns had peeked through it in the past when they were ill, to be part of the church services below. I, as a former past-life nun, certainly felt at home on these premises. There was also one large commercial kitchen shared by the guys, myself and Andrew and Laura, who had their own larger quarters in another part of the church rooms.

This new living arrangement was like an answer to a prayer. I moved in the beginning of October, long before the weather cooled. At first I was responsible for cleaning the kids' bathroom in the basement that belonged to the pre-school that was held there. It was a five-day-a-week commitment that took about an hour and was far from easy as the little kids often missed their aim in this five-stall bathroom and it required diligence and a subdued nose to get through the job each night, after my bank work. Luckily for me, in a couple months, I was given an easier cleaning job I could do once a weekend for several hours, instead.

Once I had been fully installed – living at the church, a few weeks later, I actually met a local man (not a Palmer student who had heard the rumors spread by my husband), and began dating him. He became important to this story for two major reasons I will soon unravel. His name was Seth and he was recovering from a troubled marriage just as I was. Like attracts like. Seth presently lived at home with his mother as his ex-wife got the house and he was working a so-so job until he could get on his feet again.

Seth put me on a pedestal right away, which should have worried me right then and there, but I was elated to find a "spiritual man" who had similar interests, to talk to. It is an unfortunate fact of life that a person who puts you on a pedestal – above them – eventually tears you down; throws you to the ground and later attempts to trample you.

No one likes to feel beneath someone else – even when they, themselves, place you above.

In the second week of our dating, I had a vision of us in a past life together. We were in an ancient temple I am not presently familiar with. It could have been Babylonian or Middle Eastern, but it was definitely B.C. – long before the time of Jesus. In my vision, Seth and I were in the inner sanctuary of the temple. He was a high priest with a tall, black, almost conical shaped, headpiece on his head and he wore loose, black, flowing pants, bound tightly at the waist and ankles. Past Seth's chest was bare except for a huge, round, bronze medallion approximately six to eight inches in diameter he wore around his neck, that appeared to be hammered in a slightly curved back fashion. He also wore a long, flowing, open black jacket (like a robe) that hung nearly to his knees. His look was stern, commanding, exacting and a little cruel.

I, a priestess at the temple, was kneeling reverently at Seth's feet in light lavender robes with an open veil, all of a gossamer-like material. I was in a subservient position and he was ordering me to do something. I could tell that I displeased him but I dared not disobey him. It was obvious that I was afraid of him as I trembled slightly and had a look of almost respectful terror in the recesses of my eyes. I did not look up into his eyes from my kneeling position.

This detailed vision should have been a clue to me, or a bad omen, to beware of, if I had been paying attention. Past life relationships tend to continue where they left off, and I usually received visions of the best and the worst possible most recent past life events between others and myself. I "see" these images very clearly, like transparent images superimposed over whatever I am looking at in the physical world with my eyes. I seldom hear accompanying words, but I receive "knowings" that impart to me what the visual scenes mean and these help me to determine "when" – in what specific past lifetime (or alternate reality if you prefer), these scenes took place. I generally tend to heal and move on from these other lifetime situations, but those I encounter in this life rarely seem to recognize, resolve and move beyond our shared pasts.

What proved even more interesting than my vision was a discussion I had with Seth, no less than one week after I saw this past life. I had not told Seth anything about my powerful vision as I was generally more inclined to keep most of my visions to myself in those days, unless I felt very comfortable or safe telling them to someone, lest they think I was crazy.

Seth and I were sitting in my little living room, and he was telling me about his life. For some reason, he wanted to tell me about a Halloween party costume he made for himself one year. It was the first time he had ever made his own. Imagine my surprise when he described the exact same outfit I had seen him in, in that B.C. lifetime! How could he have so precisely duplicated what I had seen only a week earlier? Seth had no conscious recollection of the lifetime I mentioned. He said he had a wild idea for a costume that he "dreamed up." But he also said he loved it, and felt very comfortable in it, and wished he had a reason to wear it for more than just a Halloween party!

Interestingly enough, most of us are attracted to things from our past lives and these can show up as favorite: colors, gems, flowers, food, places, people and a multitude of other things as "incarnational leaks." You'd be surprised how much each of us does vaguely or seemingly unrelatedly remember of the many details of our own past lives. We receive constant clues. A lot of what we think is "just our imagination" or is just an idea, whimsy or daydream, may have significant roots in our actual past lives. If you have a great love of Paris and the French language or if you are drawn to the Roaring 20's – you may have been there and enjoyed that scene a lifetime or more ago. Here is one of my poems of a past life of mine in Persia:

REMEMBRANCE

Memories of loving you,
In a garden full of blooms.
Far beneath the Persian skies,
That twinkle like a thousand eyes.
The fountain plays upon the stone
And close beside the peacocks roam.
The lotus and the jasmine scent
The air with fragrant magnificence.
The full moon sheds a luminous glow,
Creating shadows down below.
As on our silken cot we lie,
Eating pomegranates and sipping nectared wine.
Every so often you reach for me;
You touch me and sigh.
There can be no better heaven
Than in your arms tonight.

Seth's costume revelation really floored me. I had never had this kind of validation before of one of my visions. While I was excited about the match up, I should have been concerned about that lifetime's implications in this life instead. I was soon to find out.

We enjoyed an intimate relationship that appeared to be heading in a good direction. Our sex was reasonably satisfying, though nothing to write poems about. He seemed especially thankful and happy to be with me until one day, he landed his dream job. He became a well-paid counselor at a downtown public clinic and within a few days of celebrating his success, he dumped me. He was moving up in the world and had just landed a job of prestige and power. Seth no longer needed a "subservient" commoner like me – one whom he must have vaguely remembered from that past life as one of many women (priestesses) under his dominion.

Seth now had his "super job", and his praise and appreciation of me now instantly turned to displeasure and censure.

I, who he at first seemed to adore, could now do nothing right. He was now in a powerful position and I was just a lowly bank worker. What in the world had changed between us? I could not piece it all together and understand at the time. Remember, my understanding and emotions were a bit primitive then. I had trouble accessing and expressing all my feelings. Seth brushed me off like an insignificant underling – a fly buzzing too close to his wealth of food.

If this alone was not shocking enough for me – finding out a week later that I was one and a half months pregnant with his child was a cutting blow for me. Seth "gallantly" agreed to pay for half of my abortion. What a horrible plan! I had never even considered such a nasty course in my life. I who love children – intentionally abort my own child? It was unthinkable! But after considerable thought, I had to agree it was the right course of action. To parent a child to such a terrible man was too tragic to endure, and what if I had another miscarriage anyway? That was too painful to consider!

Finally, I agreed to the abortion and a girlfriend took me to a special clinic for the operation. I was very relieved to find that the intense pain lasted a mere twenty minutes as opposed to the many hours of labor (up to forty-eight in the past) I had been accustomed to enduring with miscarriages. It almost made me wish that all my past miscarriages had been abortions. While emotionally still very traumatic, abortions were physically – by far – much less painful!

The day after my abortion, I marched into Seth's newly decorated clinic office, slapped him across the face, shoved the contents of his desk onto the floor and marched right out again. I was proud of myself that I finally had the guts to stand up to him. Seth dared not oppose me at his precious new job site. Though I still suffered mentally, emotionally, and physically from my loss of him and the baby, I knew I had done the right things for myself.

I had always been totally opposed to abortion in the past (just as I had always been morally opposed to divorce), but now I realized that everything on earth had a right place and a right time. This was it for me. I knew I had made the best decision for my own health and most likely prevented another miscarriage as well. And I was glad that never saw Seth again after that day in his office.

To cheer myself up, a week later, I got my ears pierced

and bought some earrings. I attempted to put the abortion and Seth out of my mind and emotions, but I was still quite distraught about the entire situation. We had sex only a handful of times and it had been okay but not great, now I truly wondered if I still liked sex. Had I lost all enthusiastic desire for it?

Living at the church was at least a high point in my life. I had the friendship of Andrew and Laura, the minister and his wife, and the several guys who lived there (plus my many other Palmer friends). All the church residents (except the minister and his wife) shared a communal kitchen and enjoyed each other's friendship and conversation over meals. Shortly after my miscarriage, a male friend of Andrew's, named Pablo, moved into the church to share the men's wing of rooms. Pablo, nick-named "Taco," was short, dark, Mexican, from Colorado, cute but a bit rough edged and very sexy in a macho sort of way. He was thin, muscular and agile and had thick, black, combed back hair. Pablo was also well mannered and friendly, and soon we were exchanging frequent conversation.

In the meantime, I was still attempting to come to terms with my abortion and my struggling concerns regarding sex. Would I ever enjoy it again? One night, I had reached a low point and I bought myself a bottle of wine. I had not drunk any alcohol since New Year's Eve at my mother's house, at age nineteen, before moving into the ashram. Now, eight years later, I was twenty-seven. The pain of everything in my life seemed more than I could bear. That night I got rip snorting drunk in the communal kitchen. In my state of frustration and alcohol-induced lack of inhibitions, I made a pass at Pablo who politely refused to take advantage of me and promptly helped me get upstairs to my bed. I was sorely disappointed that I could not bury my sorrows in sex as well as wine. Even if I did not like sex all that much – I had to try. Pablo nobly never mentioned that night to anyone, including me, again.

A couple weeks later, when I was house sitting at Andrew and Laura's church apartments, Pablo came for a visit to watch their TV with me. We had a wonderful conversation and I soon forgot about anything amorous happening between us. Pablo however, had not forgotten. After we chatted and watched a movie, he made his move to kiss me. Now that I was not drunk and in charge of my senses, he felt it was the right time to get close to me. He had been just as interested in me as I had been in him all along.

I found myself totally surprised by Pablo's advances as well as by his kisses. His lips set me on fire with deep, sensuous, lingering kisses that drank my mouth and awakened latent passions from the hidden recesses of my body and soul. We joined in very physical, all-consuming passion that included heart and soul. Pablo stirred feelings in me I had thought were long dead. How could I be so aroused? Firework energies exploded in me at every touch, every kiss, and every deep glance of his that poured into my eyes. We made love over and over again that night – more times than I could count, and each time brought earthquake-like orgasms that flooded my entire being with total satisfaction that filled all the empty, hungry places in me. I was alive again! I felt the throws of love and I gave even pleasure to him whom I desired with every part of me to fulfill as he had fulfilled me.

I took Pablo in hand and tasted his magnificence. I was hungry and starving to enjoy all of love's pleasures that I had so long been denied. I wanted him more than I had ever wanted anyone, since Manny, so many years ago. Pablo and I traversed each other's bodies as we would a virtual Garden of Eden we hoped to inhabit after probing its secrets. With childlike enthusiasm that exuded from our naturally playful personalities, we had to engage every amusement in our playgrounds. We spent all night and most of the next day in each other's arms, not wanting to let go of the nourishment we gave to each other. It was as if we had both been starving, and finally found a feast that provided every titillating food imaginable. Intermittently, we nibbled and then devoured each savory morsel set before us. We explored each other's bodies to discover every hidden treasure they could hold.

That erotic night brought forth months of renewed pleasures that Pablo and I shared in secret and hid from the other church dwellers. We thought it best to keep our sizzling affair to ourselves. Not that others did not sense our heat together. But they got no clue from Pablo and I that the flaming passion that passed back and forth between us in playful verbal banter was being consummated physically.

My experiences with Pablo taught me that chemistry is all-important between two people for great sex. He and I had fiery chemistry, and I realized that Gopala and I did not. Did Pablo and I share past lives? Most definitely! We were lovers many times in past lives, including one we lived as North

American Indians; but most importantly, Pablo had been my beloved son in a precious past lifetime. Pablo brought me alive sexually again and I have never let any man (since Gopala) convince me that I am not a sexually vital woman capable of incredible heights of passion. Mutual chemistry is now usually immediately recognizable to me; however, I have found that sometimes it might go unnoticed – or untapped – for a period of time, until a good opportunity opens up to share romance and enthusiastic love making with someone.

Pablo was attending a local college in Davenport to get needed extra credits and courses to enter Palmer College of Chiropractic. Our hot affair lasted about four or five months until he finished his chiropractic school requirements, then Pablo wanted to visit his family for several months before attending Palmer. Until he left, Pablo and I enjoyed a near idyllic relationship, which included dating away from our church friends. We went dancing and to local clubs as well as to movies over the winter months that we were together.

It was still cold and snowy when it came time for Pablo to leave. He held me tenderly one last time and told me that he loved me. I savored his declaration and confessed my love to him as well, though I knew our love relationship could not last a lifetime. We had different roads to travel, but I treasured all the beauty, warmth and caring that Pablo had so generously given to me.

Now it was impossible to be sad at Pablo's departure, because I felt that our love continued on in spirit. We parted in love, honesty and kindness and letting go of a love like this was not truly an ending in my mind. Our love lived on.

THE SNOW

The snow –
How warm it feels
Because I'm cozy inside,
Wrapped snug with thoughts of you.
Did you have to go
Before I could feel you – this deep?
The white earths like heaven.
Seeing it moves me to Love.
Could I be any gladder
If the sky was blue?

For summer isn't missed
In the joy of the first snow.
And Loving cannot be sad
If it never ended with your leaving.
Snow around me some more!
Make this day a blanket
Of warmth and Love and thoughts of you.
Make the winter a song
Of ice and snow and gray days.
And make my world
Forever be this new.
Snow flurries –
In my mind, about you.

While Pablo and I were together, early in our relationship, I decided I had to take safety precautions to avoid another unwanted pregnancy. A couple weeks into our affair, I headed for the local free clinic and arranged to get an I.U.D. I had a copper seven intrauterine device implanted in me by a Dr. Savage. It was more painful than I had expected and caused me many problems. In less than six weeks, it actually fell out and ripped my insides as it did. Luckily my relatively healthy body mainly repaired itself. I refused to return to that clinic or to Dr. Savage who had put it in incorrectly and obviously had a cruel side. Later I learned that Dr. Savage hated women – a surprising attitude for a free-clinic gynecologist? I wondered why he had even been allowed to practice medicine with his nasty, cavalier methods and attitudes.

A few months earlier (when I was with Pablo), just before Christmas, I began to tire of my bank job. The money was not good and I had to find transportation from Bettendorf to Davenport five days a week to keep up the job. I had decided to leave the bank in the New Year, trusting that I would find another job closer to home quickly.

After Christmas, I quit the bank and searched the want ads. I finally found what I considered to be the perfect job for me working as a waitress in a nearby Bettendorf restaurant. I was sorely disappointed when I arrived at the restaurant to find it overrun with applicants. I did not stand a chance. I walked outside and stared into the January cold and wondered: "Oh God, what am I supposed to do now? How will I be able to support myself?"

My eyes misted over with tears, but I would not let myself cry. Somehow I knew God would help me. I turned within myself and said a silent prayer. Then I looked up to gaze at the frosty sun, and my clearing eyes caught a sign that appeared to be bathed in white light. It stood out among dozens of other business signs in the distance, about a half mile beyond the restaurant I stood in front of. It was the sign of a Holiday Inn. Throughout my being, I knew this was actually a message from God. This was one of the first of thousands of times I was to see white light around a place or business I was meant to enter and directed to by angels or God-guidance.

I walked the chilly, easy half-mile to the Holiday Inn, marched up to the front desk and asked for a job. The lady behind the counter was amazed. The ad for new help was not going to appear in the papers until tomorrow. I convinced her the job was meant for me! I landed an easy, comfortable job working at the front desk full-time with a varied schedule of some evenings and weekend day times. The job was perfect for me.

While Pablo and I were together, we often met in the Holiday Inn lounge for drinks and to watch the free floor show. I drank a little then, two or three nights a week. I continued my job at the hotel even after Pablo went back to Colorado. The Inn offered several diversions including weekly entertainers, a restaurant and a multitude of varied guests that offered interesting profiles for character studies. There were a few famous actors that passed through, lots of businessmen, tourists, Palmer student parents, locals having a tryst and more. There was always something going on at the hotel. When it was slow, later at night, before my three to eleven o'clock shift ended, I got a chance to catch up on my reading.

The Inn's lounge acts were mostly average singers and groups from all over the U.S., but occasionally, some of them were good. I got to know all the many employees and the local regulars who hung out in the lounge a few nights a week or more. Soon I was partying with the best of them. I even smoked a few cigarettes now and then – not more than five or six a week – just for fun.

One night, I was sitting at the bar with a girlfriend who also worked the front desk, and we drank a little more than necessary. I asked a long-time lounge "regular" for a dance and when he burst into laughter at my request, I took offense.

My Marguerita ended up in his face and I ran off with him in hot pursuit. For some reason, I hung on to my drinking glass and when I threw open the ladies' room door to escape, the glass shattered into my hand and ripped open my thumb. My blood splattered across the bathroom floor, mirror and stalls in a fascinating display reminiscent of an eccentric artist's new masterpiece.

The lounge regular whistled when he saw the artistry of blood. He had no intention of harming me, he only wanted to playfully teach me a lesson and he had not intended to insult me when I asked for the dance. He had been laughing totally at something else. Now he rushed to my aid. I was too drunk to be more than shocked at the blood portrait I had created. I actually laughed. He helped me wrap up my wound and my girlfriend drove me to the hospital. I did not feel a thing. I laughed throughout the stitching up of my wound.

Thirty-eight stitches later, I now had a lifelong scar that would never let me forget the folly of drunken escapades. In the future, I kept my occasional drinking to a reasonable limit, and my emotions in check, after this episode that left me with a constant visual reminder that drinking was not a necessity for my life. This happened just weeks after Pablo had left town, and may have been my way of escaping the fact that I did miss him more than I was willing to admit.

Throughout my time of living at the church, I experienced relatively good health. Like everyone else, I had some bad days and some very good days. I was basically happy though I really wanted a long-term relationship. I had the knowing that one day soon – I would take the thirty-two-page cook booklet I had mimeographed in Winnipeg and make it into a real, full-length cookbook. When I told others of my plan, they laughed at me. They said that everybody wanted to write a book but almost nobody did it. They felt I would fare no better.

My mother even went so far as to insult me by saying: "You're a nothing and a nobody. You can't write a book." She'd had her own frustrating experiences with publishing. My mother wrote a delightful array of children's stories that my siblings and I had grown up treasuring. Mom had absolutely no success with publishing them. Also, my father's two geography textbooks and one novel that had been published – never made a dime. My mother slaved over the typing of those books with carbon copies on a manual typewriter, for years.

But I was determined to write my book. No one could dissuade me from my dreams of writing, because I "knew". I knew I was destined to write great books and I always believed it was meant to be. Something inside myself was unshakable in this knowledge. It was only a question as to when I should start my first great book. It was soon. I knew. I could feel it! Soon, I would begin my first great book and eventually it would sell over a million copies. Of this I was certain. However long it took, it would happen. It was my destiny!

While it was still cold, I flew up to Winnipeg for a short visit with my dear friends there. They knew about my break-up with Gopala and many of them rallied 'round to comfort and support me. Before an evening party one night, I was lying on a floor mattress sofa with cushions, with my beloved friend Ronnie, and talking about any and everything. Ronnie had a fully opened heart chakra and we shared a wealth of heart love that few people have ever experienced. Just talking with Ronnie was a heart-to-heart love fest. I had missed him the most of my Winnipeg friends.

Ronnie was in turmoil now about his life's direction. He was such a sensitive soul; easily hurt by the harsh world a-round him. He had previously had a live-in relationship with a woman for several years and had a very difficult time ending it. It took him over a year to work up the courage and strength to ask his girlfriend to leave his house. She responded with a tem-per tantrum, grabbed a razor and slashed her own wrists, right in front of him. He had been horrified. Though Ronnie had rushed her to the hospital and saved the woman's life, he had been so shaken by the experience, he had not dated a woman since. Now he wondered if he was gay. I doubted this possi-bility. I knew Ronnie, and how overly sensitive he was. He had once taught a yoga class in a prison and had been attacked, and he had never been able to teach yoga again. It seemed that every time he had a bad experience with anything, he rejected whatever he was doing when the bad experience occurred.

Ronnie had been a regular at our chanting nights in Winnipeg. At first his voice was shaky and crude, and people preferred him not to sing at all. Then his voice blossomed into one of the most melodious voices I had ever heard. Ronnie had a gift. His music was like angels' singing and he had taught himself to play anything on the guitar that he heard. He was becoming a good folk singer in Winnipeg, and the East as well.

Now Ronnie and I lay wrapped around each other on his mattress sofa, discussing his dilemma – was he or wasn't he gay? In our loving discourse, we were cuddling like very close friends and soon began to caress each other. Our conversation changed to fondling and soon we were in the midst of foreplay. Before we progressed very far, another male friend of ours arrived early for the party and had let himself in with the spare key. He caught us in the act and wanted to join us. Certainly, I would have said no to any such plan, but this was a spontaneous moment and Bob blended into our caresses as easily as if we had all been lovers before. In minutes, we were all intertwined. I was sandwiched between two men I loved and cared for and there was no jealously or possessiveness.

The feeling of being touched, held and fondled by two loving men at the same time was extraordinary. I had never felt such an enfolding of love from all directions. I kissed and stroked them both. I savored this rare experience that was unlikely to occur again for me. Both men set me on fire with four hands touching and caressing my entire body. We never fully undressed. It was more fun to explore through opened clothing and indulge in what would have been forbidden love to me if I had allowed myself to think about it. But I did not. This felt far too wonderful to walk away from. Ronnie and Bob's hands seemed to touch all of me at once. Gently and firmly, they slowly brought me to an earth shattering orgasm that burst like fireworks throughout my entire body.

I was pleased to bring them equal pleasure, though they never entered inside me; my touch brought them similar satisfaction. It had not felt right, for me, to have actual intercourse with either or both of them. However, we all experienced something new that evening that we would all treasure in our hearts and memories. This taste of shared love was a healing balm for me, and I suspect them as well. Later, after the three of us had finished our love-play and put our clothing in order, other guests arrived and we had one terrific party. No one suspected what had transpired between Ronnie, Bob and me. But, if they had been looking closely, they might have seen a little extra sparkle in our glances at each other.

All too soon, my visit was over. I did not see my Winnipeg friends for more than another year. Later, Ronnie did come down to Iowa once for a visit. He brought his male lover with him when he came and I had another boyfriend at the time. Ronnie decided that he did prefer men later on. As far as I know, he is still a member of the gay community. We eventually lost touch but I will never forget Ronnie's open heart and the love he always exuded, and I know he continues to exude, to this day.

Throughout my church residence, I saved money to buy a car. In the spring, I finally managed to buy an old, standard transmission Dodge Colt. I drove so seldom and here I was getting a car with a clutch! It was hilarious to watch me attempt to maneuver it the first month or so. I had trouble slowing to a stop and was always confused by the footwork required. I remember one passenger who had to disembark as I was rolling, or rather attempting to roll, to a stop. I was determined to learn and eventually I mastered the clutch and became a rather good driver – for short distances that is. Then I felt truly free. I got out on the highway and felt like I could go anywhere. I was finally in control. No one else had to take me anywhere. This car was like a rite of passage for me. Finally, finally, I was free. I felt a new part of my life open up before me. Now, I felt free!

The entire time I lived at the church and even before, I had an ongoing friendship with Reid, the Palmer student who drove the church bus on Sundays. We two kindred spirits had the liveliest conversations about health, life, love, and truth, God and just about everything imaginable. He was a handsome, fiery Aries (the ram in astrology) and with my own Venus and Mars in Aries, we had a real spirit, mind and heart connection that allowed for unlimited gusto.

> Would that I could Love you,
> Freely, deeply, in my soul.
> Would that I could see you,
> Know you, hold you.
> Would that our Love could enfold us,
> We – two kindred souls.

Reid and I were as comfortable with each other as brother and sister, yet there was a romantic spark between us, a natural love chemistry that was unmistakable. I know that Reid felt it too. It was impossible for anyone not to see the rapport we shared, the easy way each of us complimented the other in looks, manners, habits, interests and conversation.

At first, I was content just to be friends with Reid and see him when our schedules allowed, but eventually I wanted more. It came as more than a surprise to me, many months after Reid and I had been sharing time together, that Reid chose to get seriously involved with a girlfriend of mine to whom I had introduced him to just a short time previously. She was plain-looking and boyish but smart, a Palmer student like Reid and she was skilled in leatherwork. Nancy was not at all Reid's type, but he courted her and they soon became an item together. I grieved inside myself but kept a steady hold on my outer emotions and congratulated Reid and Nancy on their love. But inside myself, my heart wept:

WORDS COME EASY

Now the words come easy.
Is it only longing
Makes me write
My heart in words?
Is losing love
My inspiration?
Are my pen and ink,
My memories of you?
You are gone but,
My thoughts run on.
It could never be more
Than it was.
But – it was enough.
It was what it was.
And it was Love,
And it was learning,
And it was sharing,
On the way.
And there are some regrets
This time,
Though less was lost
Than all I gained.
And now I write.
The words come easy.
Could it be, when Love is near,
No words are needed?
But when Love's gone,
Words are the memories
That carry on.

Reid was very good looking, all man, smart, but always struggling to get by and make enough extra money to get himself through school. Nancy had plenty of money as she produced a steady flow of it from her leatherwork. She made key chains, checkbook covers, wallets, leather journals, belts, purses and more. Now, as Reid and Nancy were a couple, Reid no longer had to worry about money; Nancy taught him leatherwork and now he had a steady, comfortable income as well.

In the two years that Reid and Nancy had remaining at Palmer College, the three of us hung out together much of the time. While Nancy and Reid slept together, I had Reid's earnest friendship as well as his genuine affection. Once Reid even admitted to me that Nancy's talents were the reason he was with her. She was "going somewhere" and he was going with her. Reid also disclosed to me, on more than one occasion, that I had his heart while Nancy only had his body. I was bewildered and sometimes forlorn that I had not been enough for Reid – not talented enough, not smart enough and not able to generate money enough.

When I looked at Reid beside my friend Nancy, I could easily see that they were not right for each other. They did not fit together. Their auras did not complement each other and flow together as one. Within a year, they got married, Nancy had a baby girl and they asked me to be the godmother. I was flattered, but felt I had lost the real prize in losing Reid. My scrapbooks still hold many pictures of the three of us all together.

Eventually, about another year later, Reid and Nancy and their baby left Palmertown to start their own chiropractic clinic in the Southeastern United States. We kept in touch by writing often. Before two more years passed, the inevitable happened, Reid and Nancy divorced and Reid continued his own separate chiropractic clinic. He no longer needed Nancy.

By then, I had written my first book and was enjoying my first taste of success. I talked to Reid on the telephone and he confessed that he had always loved me, but had not felt I was talented enough and I was not "going anywhere." Now, he said he wished he had followed his heart. He was alone now and finally realized that what he and I had shared had indeed been real love. But it was too little, too late. He had his Southern practice and my new book had set me on a course all my own. Missed opportunities in life do not always present themselves a second time. Only rarely do we get to return to a road (in one lifetime) that we had once forsaken. Now was not to be one of those times.

DEDICATED TO MY LOVE

So much more I wanted to say to you,
Before you left.
– And now you are gone.
So much was left – unsaid, unshared.
You seldom told me – you cared.
But I saw it in your eyes,
Amid the truth and lies.
There was a something special
– We had.
It could have been an always Love.
Feelings for you will go on,
When others are long forgotten.
You took without giving,
Yet you gave more than I've ever had.
You held without touching.
You kissed without knowing.
I loved you and I needed you too.
I know we only touched for moments
When our roads crossed.
But they were moments of forever.
My song of you goes on.

One thing Reid's rejection did for me was to spur me on to accomplish significant things in my own life. I had not been talented enough to please him, and I was not taking any further chances at losing future loves because I was just a good cook with a pretty face. If men wanted a talented woman, then that is what I would be. I was more determined than ever to succeed in my life and become a well-rounded and desirable woman. If men wanted me to be ambitious too, well I was not going to disappoint them in the future.

Little did I realize at the time that Reid was the exception when it came to men. Most men wanted a woman they could feel superior to, not equal to. My experience with Reid led me to a path that may have hurt, more than it helped me, in my desire to be appealing to the opposite sex. But at the time, I was only beginning to discover who "I" really was. I had so much yet to discover about who I was and what I wanted in my life. My own personality was far from being fully formed. I still had a tremendous amount to learn!

LET IT BE

Perhaps I never knew you.
Perhaps I only saw in you
What I wished and needed to see.
But if that makes me happy – Let it be.

RIVER OF SOUL

As I hold you in my soul,
And kiss you, touch you
– Love flows.
We ride the river of soul
– Together.
You call me a vision!
You beg for love tonight.
I say no – because,
I've seen too many nights like this.
In the morning you will wake
And think me but a pleasant dream.
Don't you care to seek me out
In daylight's brightness?
Am I something you fear
To touch but once?
You fear the rightness?
Will I always be a vision
Only sought for one kiss?
Will there ever be a prince
That sees me as his own?
Will there ever be a Love
To quench my soul?
Will there ever be someone who knows?
– Who really knows?

Chapter Fourteen – The Church on the Hill

"When the weather kills your crop,
Keep-a-goin'!
Though 'tis work to reach the top,
Keep-a-goin'…
When it looks like all is up,
Keep-a-goin'!
Drain the sweetness from the cup,
Keep-a-goin'!

Frank L. Stanton
Keep-a-Goin'

    The freshness of spring was in every clean-scented breeze that blew through the sunny windows of my apartment in the church. Inside myself, I felt my new book surging, growing – yearning to be born. It was only a matter of months now. Soon I would begin to write. My inner voice reassured me that the right day to put pen to paper was approaching. I planned to write the book in long hand before typing it. My creative flow seemed to be released more easily through handwriting. I continued with my job and classes and with life each day, knowing that the perfect day to begin would present itself, unmistakably, to me.

I loved living in the church and got along very well with everyone there. One of my favorite pastimes was to sit on the church roof for hours at a time, throughout the warm weather. In the daytime, the sun shone down gloriously on the city below our church hill and the mighty Mississippi River flowed as if it was in harmony with everything around it. At night, the twinkling city lights cast a glowing multi-colored light display on the dark and dreamy river. Everything for miles appeared to be lit with millions of flickering candles reflecting the bright stars in the sky. It was a magnificent city and an enchanted river. I felt the magic of the river pervading everything around it. My eyes loved to drink in these scenes and I never tired of gazing, hour after hour, out over the city and the river that wove through it and all the lives of its inhabitants.

Love flows between the shores of our souls.

As spring was turning everything to green, I decided it would be a great idea to plant a flower and vegetable garden at the church, in its huge backyard. The yard was full of trees and shrubbery but it was totally lacking in blossoms of any kind. I used my own money and purchased quite a few flats of plants and bags of fertile soil. I planted all along the edges of the long stairway that led to the sunken backyard and all around the fir trees and several of the larger trees as well. I bordered everything I could with flowers and colorful plants.

There was a huge, barren, built-in, concrete garden planter about ten feet across and five feet wide, in the center of the courtyard with a pretty concrete birdbath in the center. This garden area had been full of only dirt for the two years that the new age church had owned the property. Now, I filled it with vegetables and flowers for a cornucopia display that mimicked the pilgrim's Thanksgiving harvest. The yard soon became a visual delight that Sunday churchgoers reveled in. Now everyone enjoyed strolling the grounds, looking at the multi-colored flowers and enjoying their scents. Even the butterflies flocked to the churchyard now.

Little yellow butterfly, thank you for just fluttering by.

Besides providing the outdoor flowers, since before Christmas, I had been arranging flowers for Sunday services, inside as well. Occasionally, I did live flower arrangements, but mostly I did plastic and silk flower arranging to save money and be able to reuse the flowers. The church gave me a small fund to purchase flowers for the services, but I also spent quite a bit of my own money on these flowers. I built up quite a stock of dried, silk and plastic flowers for making all kinds of floral arrangements.

Every Sunday, the church had a soloist perform a song or two for the congregation. I was awed by the singers and truly missed performing regularly as I had in the past with Gopala. One Sunday, the regular soloist was going to be out of town and I got the chance to sing for a couple of church services. It was for me, one of the thrills of my young life. Unfortunately, I did such a good job and was praised so heavily, that the regular soloist made sure not to miss another service for many, many months afterwards.

Soon the whole church was bustling with excitement because Andrew and Laura had a new baby boy. He was the first baby to live in the church and it was wonderful to play with him and baby-sit occasionally. Baby Ivan had beautiful blonde hair and blue eyes just like his parents. His mother Laura had swollen fingers for a while after the birth and often removed her diamond engagement ring in the kitchen. It was not surprising that one day; the ring disappeared and was lost. Laura was resigned to its loss after a bit of vague searching about the kitchen. But I knew where it was. It was in our huge communal trashcan in the corner near the sink. We let a week's worth of garbage pile up before it was hauled outside, usually by one of the guys, because it was so heavy. Laura and Andrew were all for buying another ring rather than going after it by picking through a week's worth of smelly, decaying garbage that was sure to be infested with all kinds of bugs and bacteria.

I was undaunted! After nearly two and a half years of living on a farm, shoveling outhouses, chicken manure and all manner of debris, I was certainly not frightened by one load of putrid trash. I poured out the entire contents of the garbage and spent over an hour picking through the foulest of rancid foods and decaying fruits and vegetables. Finally, at the very bottom of the bag, amidst cups of liquid slime and putrid food remnants – I found it. I washed it off and handed it to Laura, who placed it on her finger with thanks and relief. I was the only one living in the church crazy enough to inspect the garbage; no one else there would do it. To me, it was nothing at all difficult. Not even dirty diapers fazed me in the least. I had changed enough of them to have had three children of my own by now. Laura was very appreciative of what I had done, but I brushed off any reward because it was easy for me to do. I was just thankful that I was no longer on the farm doing even dirtier jobs there, daily, rather than once in a blue moon as I did presently.

For me, sharing my feelings, interacting with friends and in relationships, was far harder than facing any amount of physical garbage in my life. I still had a great deal to learn. I tried to make friends with the church secretary, but it soon became evident that she and I were from different worlds. She was an ex-model who was still bulimic. Raina treated men like objects and she brought a new man home to sleep with her in her church apartments every weekend. She played with them a few days, and then tossed them aside. Soon she had a local reputation for "lovin' and leavin' um." Raina was little better than a prostitute and her lack of people skills and men problems soon got her thrown out of the church completely.

I decided to stick to my friendships with Palmer wives and other church ladies like Laura and Nancy. I seemed to get along even better with men. I understood and related to them well and their company filled some empty places in me left by my separation from Gopala. I almost never saw Gopala. He took care to avoid me in person and I was mainly involved in my Bettendorf church life now and I seldom visited Palmer except when I taught some classes there. Gopala still called me every month or two to ask if we could get back together. As usual, I answered no and he hung up.

Pablo was still away in Colorado and Reid was with Nancy, so I turned my thoughts to dating other men. I met a couple of guys at the Holiday Inn and dated them, but I knew that they were not really right for me. I enjoyed their company, but I kept shopping. The right guy for me had to be out there.

Around mid-summer (1977), I felt the writing urge overtake me. The very next day I woke up knowing: "Today is the day!" I sat down at my typewriter and began to type up, double-spaced, with carbon copies – my new book. It had begun!

(Remember, computers were not yet widely available. Only a few prosperous businesses had access to them at this time.) In a paper notebook, I wrote out over a dozen titles for my new book and settled on: *For the Love of Food*. This was a "Complete Vegetarian, Natural Foods Cookbook." I had been gathering recipes for six years and I knew my original thirty-two-page booklet would grow enormously over the next months. Who knew how long it would take to complete it?

From the moment I began to labor on my book, I consistently worked a minimum of fifteen up to twenty hours a week on the book throughout the summer and into the fall. Writing this book was an amazing experience. It was one that would change my entire life. I had the discipline, desire and inspiration to proceed even on days when I was tired or not as motivated. I persisted, even when it took me hours to get into the flow of my work, through dry periods and when I felt blocked. I still plunged ahead and broke through any resistance I felt in my mind or emotions – just like I had learned at the farm – nothing stopped me. At no point during this time did I put the book aside, even for one week.

This was a project I was wholly dedicated to until completion. I loved and thrived on the writing process. It came naturally to me. I believe it is in my blood. I was born to be a writer in this lifetime. Here, as I typed my collected recipes and hand wrote new pages and typed them, I found a new kind of fulfillment I would savor all my life.

In the meantime, I continued my desk-clerk job at the Holiday Inn and I taught a yoga class at the church one night a week. I began to teach cooking and bread-baking classes for the Iowa Community College as well, and these classes were highly successful. I only taught a few summer classes, but in the fall my classes multiplied. I developed quite a following of students and admirers, and I was happy knowing that I was helping many people to take an active part in improving their diet and health.

One summer night, I went to a popular Quad-Cities Illinois nightclub: the *Rock Island Brewing Company* (R.I.B.C.) with a girlfriend, Sally, who worked at the church. This hot nightspot had the best music in the area. The cream of the crop of Chicago clubs came here to the Quad-Cities to play. This place was a music Mecca for anyone who loved the best of popular music groups.

My church friend and I sat at a table enjoying the rhythmic sounds, while I surveyed the dance floor and tables for interesting male prospects. Eventually, my eyes caught sight of a terrific dancer on the floor. He was handsome in a John Travolta/*Saturday Night Fever* kind of way and I noticed he was alone, and rarely danced unless asked by one of the bolder females.

I myself was one of those bolder females. More than six months previously, I had first ventured timidly into the R.I.B.C. and kept to myself, nervously sipping drinks and wishing I could dance. But that rarely happened. I noticed most of the guys did not dance at all and many wanted you to ask them. I had never asked a stranger to dance before.

Back then, I had finally mustered up the courage to ask someone to dance and when he said no – I was devastated. Then I thought about this feeling of failure for a long time. I thought – imagine how a guy would feel if he got rejected after asking a woman to dance – perhaps just as dejected as I had felt. I decided I was going to master this "asking a guy to dance" thing. I would watch, take notes, and observe what worked, and what did not. I was determined to keep asking guys to dance until it no longer hurt to have them say no.

I spent many nights at the *Rock Island Brewing Company* studying the situation. I noticed that no guy liked to dance within the first twenty to thirty minutes after entering the place. He initially wanted a relaxing drink and perhaps a smoke too. One could never ask a guy to dance right after he got a fresh drink or had just lit up a new cigarette. Do not ask when he is deep in conversation, has just danced, or if he looked ruffled in any way. It was especially the right time to ask him if he was casting longing looks at the dance floor.

Armed with this vital research, I proceeded to experiment. I got several dances and rejections. Each rejection cut like a knife. I made up my mind to never say no to dancing with any sincere guy who asked me as long as he was not drunk, disrespectful or obnoxious. If a guy had the guts to ask me, he deserved at least one dance. I was going to build up "good dance karma."

It took many weeks of trial and error to master this "dancing/rejection" thing. After a few months, I could handle "no" and not at all take it personally. Sometimes when a guy said no, I could actually "feel" his thoughts: he preferred blondes, I was not his type, he didn't feel like dancing, he was in a low mood or he did not want to get serious. I found out that a cute, snappy comment could often change the course of his decision. When he looked up at me in that split second of decision, I might say: "Come on, it's only a dance. You don't have to marry me." If that did not melt him into good-natured laughter, I had other comments I could make like: "I'll show you my moves, if you show me yours," with an added wink or twinkle in my eye. This comment usually got a yes.

Eventually, I was more than ninety percent successful at getting dances. I was far ahead of the rest of the ladies. What also helped was the fact that I was an excellent dancer. I was cute and sexy and once I was noticed on the dance floor by guys, they generally were happy to dance with me, provided I chose the right time to approach them. Plus, it became known, as I became more of a R.I.B.C. regular, that I was willing to dance if a guy asked me.

Now I sat by the dance floor with my housemate and eyed my new "prey." Mr. "John Travolta" looked like he had a shy streak. I made my move and he and I were together the rest of the evening. His name was Brent. He, like many local guys, worked for one of the huge farm implement companies in the area as a welder. Brent, like myself, had been permanently separated for over a year, from his wife. He owned his own home and drove a pick-up truck. Brent was quiet and more shy than I had anticipated. He made it clear right away that he was very interested in me, and that he had no intention of looking further at any of the assorted women who filled the R.I.B.C.

That night, my friend went home by herself and Brent took me home. We became an instant item. He dated only me, but I continued to date other men and honestly told him about it. Brent was not the jealous type. He was happy just to spend time with me. I enjoyed his company and kindness – he had a heart of gold. But there were times when Brent's sparse dialogue led to boredom for me. I needed other guys around me to give me the conversation my hungry mind required. However, Brent was attractive, pleasant and comfortable to be around and he adored me earnestly. He did not put me on a pedestal.

I enjoyed Brent's company, besides which, he had a loving heart and generous nature. It felt good to be around him.

I WONDER

You look at me
With eyes that seem to see me.
I wonder how much
Those eyes of yours can see?
I wonder how much
Your soul knows?
I wonder how much
Your heart Loves me?
Are you true enough
To stay near me?
Can you hold me
And still allow me to be free?
Between us can a lasting
Love – ever be?

Several weeks after I became sexually involved with Brent, I began to experience some serious health problems. I feared that I might be pregnant again as I had sharp pains and sensations in and around my sex organs. I had been more careful than in the past with birth control, but apparently it had done me little good.

If I was pregnant, it could only be Brent's baby. I approached Brent one evening with the possible news, and to my surprise he was delighted. We had planned a short holiday in Chicago the following weekend and he was now even more anxious for us to spend that time together. Brent and I drove the two and a half hour trip to Chicago the following Friday afternoon for a two-night stay at a fancy hotel and to see the city sights.

We enjoyed the John Hancock Center, the Chicago Conservatory, Old Town Chicago and the then famous Pickle Barrel Restaurant. All in all, it was a lovely weekend, except that I was sick, and felt very tired. I could tell I was in trouble. I planned to head for a doctor's office as soon as Brent and I returned from our little weekend getaway. But when we returned Sunday night, Brent had a little confession to make to me. He had gotten V.D., Gonorrhea to be specific; from the last girl he had dated before me. He had gone to the doctor to get treatment and had not taken it all. Maybe I should get checked for V.D., he suggested?

I was speechless for a while after he told me. What if I was pregnant and also had V.D., I worried? I tried not to jump to conclusions until I saw a doctor. Brent was very apologetic, so it was difficult to be angry with him, especially when I did not know exactly what was going on in my body, yet.

I found a doctor the next day, and underwent a complete round of tests. The doctor's tests quickly showed I was not pregnant but V.D. did not come up positive either. The doctor felt there was no evidence of Gonorrhea but I could take some penicillin anyway if I wanted to. I was confused. Something appeared to be seriously wrong, but I was not anxious to shove a lot of drugs into myself without being sure I needed them. My liver was not especially fond of prescription drugs. The side effects I suffered from them were sometimes worse than the problems they were supposed to help heal.

"We could wait a few days or a week," said the doctor, "and do another test. I could give you a prescription at that time, if necessary," he suggested.

"I'm not sure what to do," I replied. "I am having some problems now, but it could just be stress and a new relationship. I will wait another week to be sure."

However within a week, I was oozing pea green fluid and I was in serious pain. Not a good sign. I called the doctor. I saw him at his office and he gave me shots of penicillin pronto and a prescription for more besides. It took three rounds of drugs to wipe out the infection that had already spread to my inner organs. Brent had to take another round of drugs too, even though he had no symptoms.

My health declined. My digestion and elimination tracts were clogged from taking all the antibiotics and I started to gain weight for the first time in my life.

One thing worried me. Pablo had come back to Palmer that summer. We had one quick fling – one passionate night – while I was seeing Brent. I had used protection to prevent pregnancy but not to prevent disease. Never before (or after) in my life did I have intercourse with more than one man during the same time frame. I had been honest with both Brent and Pablo and told each of them about the other, and they both had accepted the truth without jealousy or repercussions. But now, what if Pablo was infected?

He was! Pablo was in trouble and he refused to see a doctor. He wanted to treat the disease – naturally – with fasting.

This was crazy I thought. I, of all people, was opposed to drugs of any kind, but to take chances with a disease of this magnitude was, I believed, suicide. This was a horrible, communicative disease and drugs were a necessity. Pablo was unshakable in his decision. He fasted for seven days plus, on water alone, and it was pitiful to see him agonizing in the communal kitchen and in the church hallways. My heart bled for him but I could not help him or convince him to take the drugs. Eventually, after weeks of agony, he improved and appeared to heal.

I felt terrible about it all, but I was no more to blame than Brent, and I did not have the heart or the right to be pointing any fingers. Pablo totally forgave me and I completely forgave Brent. After a couple weeks, most of my symptoms had disappeared, and I took acidophilus to implant friendly bacteria in my intestines and help my digestion and bowels. So I was improving. However, back then, I did not know how to remove drug residues from my body with cleansing, and my health suffered for years with side effects from this disease and its cure. Brent was deeply remorseful. He had not found out about his own V.D. until after he and I had gotten together. His last girlfriend had called him up on the phone to drop her bombshell. Brent did everything in his power to make things up to me including paying all my prescription and doctor's bills and he bought me flowers and gifts. Brent was so sincere and apologetic that I forgave him instantly.

However, the minister's wife, in particular, was not so forgiving when word leaked out that Pablo was fighting V.D. and I had given it to him. She had heard the past rumors about a woman living in the church who brought home a different man every weekend for sex, and now she assumed it was me. The secretary was long gone, and the minister's wife was totally unwilling to consider it had actually been the secretary who was "screwing the neighborhood." Most people do not realize that nice people get V.D., often from the nicest people. Sometimes, the sexually loose are luckier than those who make one mistake. But had I really made a mistake? Had I not been loving and honest with all involved? Was this bad karma or the universe's way to push me onto a different path? Perhaps both.

The minister and his wife put me on restriction at the church, and would not allow any men to enter my rooms or even stand on my private staircase. Even Brent, whom they knew, had to wait downstairs to see me. All our overnight dates now shifted to his house. In the following couple of weeks, church relationships were strained to say the least.

During this time, my outdoor garden was thriving and magnificent. The church had made tons of extra money doing garden weddings all summer because of all the beautiful flowers I planted. Now an engaged couple wanted a garden wedding with one condition. The vegetables I planted around the pretty concrete birdbath among the flowers had to be dug up and replaced with more flowers. They did not like the vegetables. The minister ordered me to dig them up and move some of the other yard flowers into that special concrete planter as a sort of punishment for me and I heartily refused. A transplant this time of year, I told him, would damage all of the fully-grown plants. He did not care.

Since I would take no part in aggravating the existing garden, the minister himself dug up the lush vegetable plants and discarded them! He then shoveled other garden flowers into the special, concrete central plot for this garden wedding.

The bride and groom got their wedding all right, but three days later, all the flowers were dead. They had been ripped up uncaringly, then roughly transplanted for the wedding and did not survive. The nature spirits were angry! They did not appreciate unloving treatment, nor did I. There were no more garden weddings that summer. In ripping up my garden, the minister had killed the goose that laid the golden eggs, so to speak. And I was furious. The beloved garden I had planted, nurtured and protected, was now destroyed.

I also felt humiliated by the church for a "crime" I had not committed. I was blamed for bringing multiple guys home like a slut, and the minister and his wife were never going to believe me innocent. Shades of my teen years! Was I continuing to pay for indiscretions in a past life? Nevertheless, I was not going to put up with more unjust treatment on that score in this life.

The garden disaster was the final straw. Brent had asked me numerous times to move in with him. Now I packed up my bags and loaded Brent's truck and left the church forever. I "shook off the dust of my heels against them." I was a woman scorned and I was going to make sure they paid!

If I had one drop of patience…

Though I was against swearing or vengeful actions, I was boiling inside. I cursed the church by decreeing with all the power of my being, that it be closed down within a year. My insides were still on fire, so I closed my eyes and "in my mind" I pushed with all my might and overturned the concrete birdbath in the center of the garden, breaking it into hundreds of pieces. Then I just let go. I allowed my fiery anger to cool and decided that God and the law of karma would give the minister, his wife and the church, their just punishments for accusing me falsely and judging me so harshly. After all I had done and given to the church in work, money and support, this was truly outrageous treatment they had given me. They did not trust me, nor had they even been willing to listen to the truth.

Though I had been angry enough to allow myself to send negative energy to the church – I had aimed my fury at a humble birdbath, not at people. Hurting people was something I could never do. It was against everything I was and everything I believed in. I could never harm another human being except in direst need of self-defense. I chose the birdbath as a symbol and an outlet for venting what I felt would be harmless anger.

Three days after I had pushed over the birdbath – in my mind, I found out from a church member that at the exact day and time I had "mentally" pushed it over, several children had actually shoved over the birdbath while playing nearby and broken it into hundreds of pieces. I fully believed that I had been responsible for this. I was actually quite surprised at my own power. Though I had harmed no one, this was the first and last time I allowed myself to use my mind in such a way.

Afterwards, I remembered a story from Paramahansa Yogananda's book: *Autobiography Of a Yogi*, wherein his guru states that simple minds, like children's and the feeble minded can be implanted with ideas easily from another stronger mind. A powerful mind can send out thought projections and vulnerable minds can pick up those projections intuitively and act upon them – if they choose to. (This does not override free will.) In the autobiography, a simple man is inclined by

Yogananda's guru's mind to steal a cauliflower for the purpose of teaching his chela (spiritual student) to be more responsible and remember to lock the ashram doors. (I love the stories in this book. They impart potent spiritual lessons, like parables. I have read the entire book over ten times.)

I had put out powerful thoughts, and I believe that subconsciously the children picked them up and decided to act upon them. This happens much more in the world than most of us realize. "Thoughts are things." Plus, from the Huna: "You get what you concentrate on. You are unlimited," and "Your moment of power is now." We are all part of creating the world around us and need to be very careful what we create in our minds and give energy to.

I never returned to that church and in less than a year, about nine months later, the church ran into serious financial difficulties and had to be sold. It appeared that my curse had manifested. Once again, church ownership returned to the Catholics and this time became a monastery for monks. The bad karma of that new age church had caught up with them – in more ways than one.

Still, I believe I had been meant to live in that church when I did. My several past lifetimes as a nun must have been calling me back to that old Catholic nunnery. Something deeply spiritual was stirred up within me in those walls, and I believe that I completed some old karma there in this lifetime.

In a world that is not as free
As I must be...

YOUR SILENT LOVE

You Love me gently,
Like a summer breeze.
You Love me easily
And your Love is free.
Your Love is silent,
But I say it speaks to me.
It never says I Love you,
But you give more
Than all the Love You's
Ever said to me.
Your Love is gentle
And it soothes me so,
That I could curl up
In that Love
And feel at last at peace.
I could right now
Be more content
Than anyone could ever be.
I feel you near and feel
That gentle Love surrounding me.
Your silent Love is more of Love
Than I may ever see;
Your silent Love says more
Than words can ever be.

Chapter Fifteen – The Writer's Life

"Heaven is not gained at a single bound;
But we build the ladder by which we rise
From the lowly earth to the vaulted skies,
And we mount to its summit round by round."

Josiah Gilbert Holland
Gradatim

Moving in with Brent was not a difficult transition for me. He owned a two-bedroom ranch house on a corner lot with a lovely backyard and a large basement, about a mile or two from the church. It was across the street from a grade school, about halfway up a little hill. All my possessions easily assimilated into Brent's living space. Soon I felt right at home.

Brent had a huge black Labrador retriever that he called "Night" who, luckily for me, stayed in the backyard and was not a housedog. I was still not too comfortable around large dogs and I also have some allergic reactions to animals that sleep in the same house I reside in. Night was rather ferocious and it took months before I could pet him or take him for a walk. Rather, Night took me for walks. He literally dragged me when he got a rare reprieve from his tiny backyard pen. I admit that I felt sorry for him. A large dog like that needed a whole yard to play in, not a six-by-four fenced-in cage.

I quickly set up housekeeping at Brent's, and baked our bread and filled the refrigerator and freezer with great food. I continued my book writing, and almost right away, I felt it was time for me to get a new job. The Holiday Inn was fine, but the place drew me into drinking more. Though I had given up my few cigarettes a week several months ago and I spent less time in the lounge, I felt it was time to surround myself with a more positive, healthful atmosphere. Also, Brent worked in the daytime and I no longer wanted to work so many nights away from him. I had my car now, my standard Dodge Colt, so I sought work in my happiest, most familiar field – floral design.

I found a great nine-to-five floral design job at a very busy and prosperous shop in Moline, on the Illinois side of the river. I would have to drive over the bridge every day, above the mighty Mississippi, but that made the job even more appealing to me in some ways. This flower shop had many designers and extra employees, as well. I knew I could learn a lot more there, and develop new skills as well. I actually spent a couple years in this shop that helped me fine-tune my designing skills.

Besides my florist shop job, I also continued to teach my Iowa Community College classes that had just increased in September. I taught yoga, meditation, cooking, nutrition and bread-baking classes a couple nights a week and occasionally on weekends, as well.

Brent was a good man, kind and generous but also a little boring. He was a poor conversationalist who rarely spoke about anything. After work, he did a few household chores or yard work or repairs and took Night for a walk. He then watched TV or went downstairs to the basement to his tool shop to work or read magazines. Once in a while we went out to eat, to a movie or dancing at a club. Occasionally, we went out with friends from his work or my friends, but Brent remained quiet and spoke very little.

I buried myself in my book work, teaching and florist job so I would not be bothered by Brent's extreme silence. I could hardly complain. Brent was devoted to me and basically gave me anything I asked for. My health was suffering. The V.D. and drugs had messed up my digestion and bowels and I had constipation problems for the first time in my life. Our sex life also suffered because of my health. The sex had been good, but never fantastic. Sometimes it was much better than at other times, but the V.D. had caused me some internal damage and it affected Brent's and my relationship as well as our sex life much more than I realized at the time.

Our first Christmas together was quiet but warm and cheery. I finally met Brent's family: his mother and father, older sister Linda and her husband, their baby girl Jenny and Linda's two step kids. I was totally surprised that Brent did not even know his own niece's name or age! Jenny was one-and-a-half years old and adorable. It turned out that Brent only saw his family twice a year – at Christmas and Easter time. Well, I was about to change that!

Brent's family took me to their hearts and I took them to mine. I made sure to talk to his mom and sister often, and soon we were visiting each other every two or three weeks. They were simple, kind and generous people – like Brent, but not nearly as quiet. It was nice to be around them and feel like part of their family.

After our first Christmas together, I began to have severe internal pains and I sought a good doctor. He recommended a specialist who declared that I required surgery. My right fallopian tube had been blocked up by fluids from the V.D. and now it needed cleaning or removing. More damage might also be involved. The surgery would reveal what exact procedures were required. My surgery was scheduled at the hospital in Iowa City during cold February. I remember that I was in the midst of taking belly dancing lessons at the time and had to miss a couple of them for the surgery.

Brent drove me to Iowa City, a few hours away, where I was to be hospitalized and he helped to comfort me and sooth my fears. Luckily for me, the surgery was minor, only a laparoscopy. The doctor was able to clear the blocked fallopian tube easily and no other major surgery appeared to be required at the time. I stayed in the hospital only a few days before I was released. Still, it took weeks to recuperate and I began to gain more weight.

During this time, I continued my book work. It was slow going, with lots of hand writing, research and then typing with a carbon copy, which made the work even more time consuming. Mistakes had to be "whited-out" or typed over with white cover up sheets, on both copies. If more than a few words needed changing or if a paragraph needed switching around, pages might have to be retyped. Yes, it was a tedious, awkward, rather primitive way of writing before computers had their heyday. It was only 1978 after all.

I was blessed to find a lovely, little old lady named Esther, a retired schoolteacher, to help me edit my book. Typewriters do not have grammar or spell check! Esther spent many hours teaching me grammar and sentence structure and she went over everything I wrote with the care and attention to detail that can only be described as a labor of love. I visited her every four to six weeks or so, and she guided me through many difficult chapters. Her kindness and generosity gave me strength and determination to continue my book even during trying times when I felt physically and mentally or emotionally unable to continue. She inspired and believed in me, even when my own family and some of my friends felt I was unequal to my writing task. Thank you to Esther, who is now in "heaven" or reborn. Your good karma is sure to follow you.

That winter, I also began to attend a Greek Orthodox Catholic Church. I was not Greek and had not been a practicing Catholic for many years, but I had many Greek, Palmer College friends and I went with them to this Church a couple times to fill the gap left by ending my association with the new age church I had recently moved out of. I loved the Greek priest, who was married and had several beautiful children, unlike the Roman Catholic tradition I was brought up in, wherein priests were never allowed to marry. Father George, I'll call him, was a distinguished, fatherly man full of warmth and understanding. He had an open heart chakra and spoke his sermons straight from his loving heart. Father George was a joy to be around as were all the Greek friends I came to know and love all those years that I was in the Quad-Cities.

The gorgeous Greek Church building, its intricate architecture, the ornate altar, the fine Greek art and the ancient Greek traditions, also enthralled me. The people and the place made me feel warm inside and I felt right at home. My latent memories of my Greek lifetimes also came flooding back to me and I became a regular Church member for the next five years that I remained in the Quad-Cities.

Winter turned to spring and my life continued: the writing, teaching, cooking, baking, and trying out new recipes for my book and my florist shop job. Brent got out his camera as the weather turned warmer. He had a good eye for shots and was a very gifted photographer. Brent's work was fantastic and his portfolio of photographs still stands out as one of the best I have ever seen in my life. Soon he set up a new dark room for himself in the basement.

Once spring was underway and my Community College classes were reduced, I stepped up my writing efforts and wrote many additional hours on weekends and nights as well. I also began to baby sit Brent's niece, Jenny, one day a week. I took her to the beach, the zoo, the playgrounds and I induced her to eat some healthier foods, too. Jenny had been raised on total junk foods and she needed to be weaned off colas and corn chips.

In the summer, when I did writing work on hot days, a trickle of sweat formed a little puddle under my chair as I worked at my typewriter on the kitchen table. Few people had air conditioning in those days and Brent certainly did not. We used floor fans to create a little air flow which gave just a bit of relief from the eighty to ninety degree Fahrenheit days that offered few breezes as refuge from the persistent heat and still, dry air. I experimented with multitudes of recipes and Brent and I ate royally – a little too royally. I kept gaining weight.

When Brent's three-week summer vacation rolled around in July, I took my own extended vacation from the flower shop and Brent and I took a long distance trip in his yellow pick-up truck that had an oversized camper top. We drove to Canada first of all, to visit God's Land and then to Winnipeg to see my friends there. I knew in advance, from my friend Sara, who was still living at the farm with her husband and small daughter, that Mata was away. I never could have visited if Mata had been there, as I had no desire to ever see her again. But I was determined to see my friend Sara, who still lived at God's Land. Sara's lovely daughter Melissa was four now and very much the little lady.

Brent and I stayed at the farm a few days, and I climbed Holy Spirit Mountain one last time with him. On the way down the mountain, Brent, who was not much of a hiker, strayed off the path and disturbed a hornets' nest. We both ended up running the rest of the way down the path with the annoyed creatures in hot pursuit. I only received two or three bites, but Brent got the worst of it and received multiple stings all over his bare chest, arms, hands, neck and face. We drove into Thunder Bay that night for a private sauna at one of the many public saunas common in the area. Both Brent and I were relieved that the stings left no marks and ceased to hurt after a healing, penetrating, relaxing, long, private steam sauna. It helped make the rest of our stay at the farm more enjoyable.

Soon it was time to leave God's Land and Brent and I said our good-byes. I bid a final farewell to my farm friends and to my past home of nearly two and a half years that was the scene of so much pain and growth for me. I planned never to return. There was nothing left there for me. Even my friend Sara and her family left the farm later the following year.

Brent and I continued on to Winnipeg and enjoyed visiting my many friends there, including my dear Ronnie and his sister. I was surprised that Brent and Ronnie hit it of so well that Brent talked more to Ronnie than I ever heard him speak to anyone. I believe that Ronnie's open heart chakra put Brent so much at ease he was very comfortable with him. The three of us enjoyed a lovely day at a Manitoba lake, and took in some of the local Winnipeg sights, including its terrific Man and Nature Museum and the trendy shops on Osborne Street.

A few of my casual friends in Winnipeg did not yet know about my break-up with Gopala and were a bit shocked, but they understood and accepted what had happened when I told them all that had transpired between us.

In a few more days, we were off, heading back to the U.S., to Yellowstone National Park in Wyoming. We enjoyed seeing Old Faithful and other geysers of hot water that leaped so high in the air, like fountains. There were also numerous hot springs to bathe in, huge waterfalls and the multi-colored hot sands to view that were common in the park. The surrounding lush forests and mountains gave Yellowstone a rustic quality that awakened nostalgic images of past Western days.

Then we went on to explore Mt. Zion National Park in Utah. Here we viewed different colored stone formations layered in whites, rusts, gold, and black slabs of rock piled up on each other, and forged together by the weather for thousands of years to paint visually stunning displays. These mountains of rock housed hidden cold and hot springs and tree groves that held magical allure. Breathtaking views could be seen from almost any part of this park that captured my awe and kindled inspiration. I especially loved Mt. Zion Park. One could easily see God's handiwork in this natural masterpiece.

Brent and I also took in the sights of Salt Lake City and the spectacular Mormon Temple with the unforgettable statue of Jesus chiseled by a famous Danish sculptor named Thorsen. We also swam in the Great Salt Lake with the rest of the tourists. None of the local people would swim in that lake as it was full of billions of tiny orange brine shrimp. But we were not above the experience, though I took care not to swim underwater so none of them would get in my ears.

Then it was on to South Dakota to see the colorful rock layers and canyons of the Badlands, the rugged Needles with tiny to large crevices that opened in the rocks that a body might barely slip into or a truck could drive through. Then there were the splendid, fertile Black Hills and the mountains of Mt. Rushmore with their impressive carvings of honored presidents. Here I purchased some of the famous Black Hills gold jewelry that is commonly found in the area as well as many other parts of the United States. Black Hills gold is mined in the surrounding hills and small mountains.

A pioneer religious group, seeking to escape persecution in the Eastern states, finally settled in the Black Hills. They were the first to create unique designs of jewelry from the gold found in these hills. To thank God for finding such a rich and bountiful land for them, the religious group chose to make all their jewelry with a particular pattern that included grapes and grape leaves, which were a sign of abundance and thanksgiving. Usually the jewelry contains a red grape leaf and a green grape leaf around the golden grapes. They make the red leaf by adding copper to gold and the green by adding silver to gold. To this day, most Black Hills gold jewelry is still made the same way with identical patterns. I treasure my small collection and wear it with appreciation for its inspiring origin.

It was a glorious trip. My eyes were overwhelmed by so many luxurious sights. My heart and soul felt nourished by the abundant beauty that was everywhere present. I felt awe-struck by our entire journey and reveled in the magnificent sights and varied lands that were included in lovely Canada and the amazing United States of America. It was so good to be able to enjoy some of the many native wonders of North America.

Speaking of natives, Brent and I encountered a number of local Indians on our holiday and I was impressed with their stateliness and noble bearing. There was powerful strength, calmness and depth of character about them that spoke

volumes about their history and struggles in what has now
become "white man's" land. I have a tremendous respect for
all North American Indians. I wrote this poem for one Indian
we came across on our travels.

DAKOTA

Dark,
Proud,
With raven-black hair —
Sure, but not arrogant,
Eyes piercing —
Seeing everywhere:
Tall, quiet Indian,
Standing there.

Brent took multitudes of excellent photographs of our travels, and we both relaxed and savored our surroundings as we
drank in the warm sun and fresh air. Unfortunately, I was not
much of a long distance driver, so Brent had to do most of the
driving. I could only drive two-hour shifts when he got really
tired. But we both loved exploring new places. In my heart, I
still treasure this special trip and hold fond and detailed memories of it, every time I reminisce and view the photographs.

Seeing so many wondrous things gave us a feeling of
vitality, strength and renewed resources. I felt healthier than I
had in some time, yet I felt tired upon our return to the Quad-
Cities. I lost a bit of weight on our vacation and then I gained
it right back. I never looked especially heavy or overweight. I
practiced yoga postures almost daily and my extra pounds
were mainly muscle. (11) It was strange to gain extra weight
during this time period for the first time when I had been
anorexic for so many younger years of my life.

Footnote: (11) The physical practice of yoga that some people call exercises are actually
called "postures" because they are not intended to be like exercises and generally do not
include movement. Each "pose" is meant to be held steadily for a period of time like thirty
seconds to three minutes to build strength and stamina. The easygoing style of yoga
postures that can be done at any age is called Hatha Yoga. Moving into different yoga
positions helps to strengthen the body, make it more flexible, firm and tone the muscles,
and it helps to expel poisonous toxins from the body by breaking up toxic deposits in the
cells, tissues and joints. There are other styles of yoga based on specific teachers or
methods like Iyengar Yoga and Kundalini Yoga. The later is a type of vigorous yoga
practice that is meant to help raise the kundalini energy up the spine through the seven
chakras and is often accompanied by quick or powerful breathing techniques like "breath
of fire." Meditation techniques are a different type of yoga.

Soon Brent and I were back to work and at our perspective jobs. But I did not feel quite right. I seemed to be tired all the time now, since our trip, and a few weeks later I found out why – I was pregnant. Though I had been quite careful about birth control since my abortion, Brent and I had been a bit careless during our vacation and it was then I had become pregnant, at the God's Land farm no less. Interesting karma! Suddenly I felt trapped.

Though I loved and cared for Brent, I knew, in our early months of living together, that I did not want to spend my life with him. I needed vibrant, "alive" conversation with a man to keep me with him. I needed more sparks, more fire, and more passion. Now I felt stuck "between a rock and a hard place." What should I do? I spent weeks debating with myself and going over and over again options in my mind. Now that I was healthier and most likely could keep a baby full term, I wanted to take the baby and leave Brent. I wanted to live with the child on my own.

After my older sister Trixie found out I was pregnant; she wanted me to give up my baby for adoption if I planned to leave Brent. She had a plentiful income and told me she'd give me all the money I needed if I did this, but not "one red cent," she said, if I kept the baby and moved out of Brent's house.

Brent of course, was overjoyed about the baby. He wanted to marry me and begin our family. I was absolutely torn apart inside. I saw no escape for me. I pined and fretted, but I was too divided inside myself to make a clear decision. Finally, in my third month, I knew what I "had" to do. I had to have a miscarriage. There was no other way out in my mind. But I believed I was too healthy at the time, so I began to let myself become run down. I lost sleep, worked too hard, carried heavy loads and I wished with all the strength of my determined being for this child to leave and come back at a later time if it cared to. I knew I could not be a mother now. I had a book to complete and I wanted a truly happy, stable life for my baby and myself with a man whom I saw myself spending a lifetime.

It was not long after I made my firm decision that my wishes became a reality. One hot autumn day, I began to have contractions. I called my doctor and he said to remain at home until and unless the contractions grew worse. Brent was noticeably upset and did all he could to support and relax me. He propped me up on pillows and rubbed my shoulders and back and intermittently he massaged my feet. Whenever he touched me, my contractions stopped. It was as if his wishes for the baby to stay took over my body and I began to heal. When he stopped touching me and went off to make me a cup of tea or rested a bit, my will took over and my contractions returned.

After thirty-six hours of this madness, I called the doctor. I was in pain and I could not take any more. I told the doctor that if he did not do a D & C immediately, I would jump off the Mississippi River Bridge. I would not tolerate more of this agony. I had been bleeding pretty regularly for several hours then, so the doctor decided to go ahead with the D & C. I was relieved. My many hours of labor were penance enough for my thoughts. I needed peace and release from this pain.

Brent was so heartbroken about the baby; I never did have the nerve to tell him the truth. I did not want his baby and most particularly, I did not want to spend the rest of my life with him. As kind and as loving as Brent was – he was not enough for me. However, I still grieved over our loss.

Both Brent and I had planted a large garden in his backyard in the spring and that fall, we had a bountiful harvest of squashes, cucumbers, carrots, peas, cabbages and much more. Next year (provided I was still around) we planned to plant an even larger area for addition vegetables. I had also planted daisies, marigolds, rockroses, zinnias and other flowers that I enjoyed gathering throughout the summer along with the purple violets that grew wild everywhere, that I treasured most of all.

Let Hearts do, what flowers do – They Bloom!

Autumn quickly turned to winter. Our lives continued without any dramatic changes. It was actually nice to live quietly without the unusual surprises my life had previously contained. But I knew, inside myself, that this private world of ours could not last forever. I was honestly bored – with Brent, his quiet demeanor and an existence that held little stimulating conversation or ideas. Brent's and my sex life was on and off again. The V.D. left emotional as well as physical scars that dulled my sexual appetites for Brent. I knew our days together were numbered. I brushed aside thoughts of boredom and unhappiness as I buried myself in my floral job, writing my book and in time spent with Brent's family and adorable niece Jenny. I treasured watching Jenny bloom into a gorgeous little girl full of charm, though rather spoiled, but infinitely lovable.

When springtime rolled around again, I began to realize that it was nearly two years since I had begun my book: *For the Love of Food* and it was now getting nearer to completion. It was over three hundred typed pages long and contained over fifteen chapters, yet I still had a long way to go. At the rate I was writing, I felt like I would never be finished. It was time to make some major decisions. I cut down my full time job at the flower shop to three days a week.

Now, I thought, I can really make some progress! I chiseled away at my manuscript. I molded each page and section of my book with utmost care and precision. This book was my baby – my contribution to society and the world. It was my chance to create something and bring it to life as my legacy. This book was, to me at the time, the most important thing in my life. I could not have children now, but – by God, I would create my own offspring of books. I knew this book was only the first of many. I prophetically saw that I would write many books in my future.

In late spring, I witnessed one of the largest rainbows I had ever seen. Both Brent and I took a multitude of pictures of this phenomenon that filled nearly the entire sky and surrounded the sun. Like Noah, I perceived this rainbow as a sign of blessing from God and a promise of good things to come. Inside myself, I had total faith in my future. I knew that good things were coming to me and my destiny was happiness and love. I wrote this brief poem about the occasion:

RAINBOW

I've seen a rainbow 'round the sun
– An illustrious one.
I'll never forget I was privileged to see
A rainbow 'round the sun.

One day in early summer, I woke up to a loud crashing noise and looked out the window to see my Dodge Colt totaled by a hit-and-run driver as it sat in front of the house, part way up our little hill. I was temporarily crestfallen, but a friend of mine named Carol, who worked at my florist shop, had a used gold Ford Maverick to sell me. The insurance money from my Colt covered it all, so I was content that I had a nicer looking car to drive that was automatic. No more clutch!

My work friend, Carol, was an older lady in her late thirties with two teenage children. We shared hours of conversation and gossip about our lives, the flower shop folk and every other subject imaginable. Her son was a renegade and always in trouble. He was unhappy with his lot in life and felt it was unfair. Carol and her husband had been unable to reason with their son to help him with his frustrations. I sat in Carol's kitchen one day as her son, Kevin, raved about how unlucky he was and how badly he was treated. His life was "too unfair." I could not help but speak up.

"Unfair," I told him. "You think life should be fair?" I informed Kevin briefly of my own abused childhood and life and let him know that: "Life is not fair. It is not supposed to be." I told him about karma and reaping what you sow and after a hearty explanation of my strong convictions; Kevin was quiet and actually paid attention to what I said.

Soon Kevin's tune changed. He became different at home and school, and finally took responsibility for his own actions. Carol thanked me. It had not been my intention to interfere in a parent/child dispute, but my inner sensing led me to dive in and "tell the truth" or at least to tell my truth. I believe that my sincerity and lack of personal investment in his emotional situation, allowed me to reach Kevin and give him a firm talking to. That opened his eyes to some of life's realities. Sometimes, a teen just needs answers from someone other than parents. I was thankful that I could help. Though it all appeared to be a seemingly accidental encounter, I was glad Carol's son received important life lessons that changed him for the better. After that first conversation, Kevin and I often chatted about life, and his feelings and views.

One day, out of the blue, Carol and I were chatting over lunch in the flower shop back room, and she looked up at me and said, "Jeanne (I had gone back to my given name in the Quad-Cities), if I keep talking to you, I'm going to have to leave my husband."

"What," I said. "We were not even talking about your husband. Why would you say that?"

"It's just that lately, whenever you and I talk," continued Carol, "I see how exciting and different your life is and I want to experience the same things myself, but I can't as long as I am married to my husband."

I was flabbergasted! What an unusual deduction. "Well,' I replied, "I certainly would not encourage you to leave your husband. My life may seem exciting, but I have not been all that happy. My experiences have been full of tragedies. I've had very little peace and contentment in my life."

"Your life still looks better than mine," Carol continued. "I would like more things to change in my everyday world."

"Be careful what you wish for," I told Carol. "You have no idea what kind of trouble you could stir up in your own life if you keep wanting it to change. For myself, if Brent was just a little more of a talker, if we had some kind of interesting conversation, I would probably be content to stay with him indefinitely. As it is, I am totally bored. I need something, someone – more."

That ended our revelations for the day. It was time to get back to work.

That second summer that Brent and I spent together, he bought a brand new red and white Ford pick-up truck with a streamlined, sleeker camper top. It was his pride and joy. Together we planted another, larger vegetable garden. I planted more flowers. We took a nearly identical summer vacation in the U.S., but skipped Canada this time. Brent and I loved our trip the previous year so much. We decided to repeat most of it. Only this year we spent more time in Yellowstone National Park. We decided to do some hiking and camping there. We bought backpacks and equipment for a four-day camping trip in Yellowstone, including "bear bells" to scare away the ferocious bears who might approach and to keep them from attacking. Bears had mauled several people early that summer in Yellowstone, so the park rangers gave us explicit instructions on how to avoid bears and how to deal with them if they did approach. This educational talk alone was enough to scare me. But I had survived the "farm," so why not this, I thought?

In early morning, just after a glorious sunrise, we hiked into the woods along a specified trail for more than five miles to reach a campsite that had been designated for us. It was deep in the wilds, and we passed a large field wet from a recent rain containing several inches of water. The sun was still in the midheavens when we arrived at our destination and set up our campsite. We enjoyed a leisurely afternoon. The sun was warm and comforting and before long, the recent rain was dried up on the plants and grass around us. We basked, naked in the bright sun's rays, and enjoyed a little tanning session.

Wanting kisses from the sun....

Before dark, we gathered firewood to cook a special supper. We enjoyed a pleasant evening and turned in for the night just after admiring a panoramic sunset of oranges and deep purples that filled the sky in every direction and could not be viewed in one glance. After the last rays of color disappeared under the horizon, Brent and I climbed into our tent and quickly prepared to sleep. We were both quite tired from our hike and all the fresh air. But we had hardly gone to sleep when we were stirred awake by the sound of a large bear approaching our tent. His loud, awkward, swaying movements and low growl alerted us immediately through the surrounding silence. All night long, he remained near us and circled and circled our tent. At any moment we expected our night visitor to burst in upon us. The rangers had warned us to tie all our food up in a tree and we had done this. Why wasn't the bear circling the tree instead of the tent? Also, the rangers had warned us not to have sex as that attracted the bears. We had avoided that completely as we had been too tired anyway.

There was nowhere else for us to go in the dark. It was impossible to find our way back to our camper at night. We could not even find the trail that was barely visible in the daytime as it was. Besides, how could we go anywhere with that huge bear, circling and circling? We could hear his breath as he paced around us, hour after hour, the entire night through.

I breathed deeply and slowly and said my prayers. That night was one of the scariest of my life. Tales of ripped-apart campers came to both our minds as we whispered nervously in the dark, very softly, so as not to disturb our night stalker. But the bear seemed content to just circle our tent. He was so close he touched it a few times, but he never came nearer. The angels I called upon must have protected us. Finally, after a night of little sleep, in the first rays of morning light, the bear left us and wandered back into the woods. Both Brent and I were so exhausted — and relieved, we fell asleep almost instantly and slept an hour or so. Soon after, we peaked out of our tent and cautiously surveyed our surroundings to make sure that the bear had truly departed. Once sure of his retreat, Brent and I gobbled up a hasty breakfast and packed our gear.

Our camping trip was over, we decided. Daytime tourist attractions were more in our league. As we began our trek back to civilization, Brent and I made a few wrong turns and ended up on wrong trails. Many hours later, we were on the right track – but it was raining now. We had yet to come to the large field with several inches of water in it. What would happen to it in the rain? Would that field become a lake of water? We did not want to find out.

It was raining harder now. We hurried along and finally came to the field, which must have been at least a half-mile across, as the water level was steadily rising. The water was just under a foot deep and our hiking boots were flooded and soaked as we trudged cautiously through the slippery grass and water. It felt like it took an hour to cross this small lake of water when in reality it was hardly fifteen minutes. The water continued to rise, and was over a foot deep by the time we stepped up to slightly higher ground on the other side. As we turned to view our escape route, we watched the water rapidly rising. In another hour or two, that field could be impassable. I said a little prayer of thanks for our protected retreat.

Brent and I relaxed a little bit now, and proceeded more slowly to our camper truck. The worst of our obstacles on the path had been overcome. We were still more than a mile and a half away, but we were both truly tired now. The two of us slowed our pace enough to feel our lack of sleep as we trudged along with our heavy packs, cold, exhausted and wet to our skin. It was nearly dusk before we reached our camper.

That night, we both took hot showers and went to the park lodge for a good hot meal and a little dancing. It was a precious reward after our fearful night and day of events. After this, I lost all desire to ever again hike in bear country. That night, we slept like peaceful babies in our camper. We enjoyed a couple more days at the park, sleeping in our camper of course, and then headed for South Dakota. We decided to skip Utah this time around, so we could enjoy more of Yellowstone and the Black Hills plus a trip to Detroit to see my family.

Visiting Detroit and my family was wonderful. Even Trixie loved Brent. We took in my hometown attractions and especially enjoyed the famous Detroit Zoo where Brent took some amazing photographs. Greenfield Village was also a special treat. I always loved watching the glass blowers, blacksmith and skilled craftsmen in that rustic, old world pioneer village. The green trees and woods always made me feel comfortable, even in that primitive setting that was at least better organized that God's Land Farm had ever been. Besides, it was only a one-day visit of watching "others" live off the land. After a warm, affable visit with my relatives, Brent and I headed back the four hundred miles plus to Iowa.

Once again, shortly after our return from our vacation, we enjoyed a bountiful harvest of our even larger garden we had planted that spring. I now began working rather frantically on my book, determined to finish it soon. Little puddles of my sweat formed under my work chair nearly every day now as I put forty hours of work a week into my book besides my part-time job at the flower shop. (Three ink pens have just given out on me today. I have written The River Daughter book chapters out in long hand first as I am having computer problems. [It turns out I have a "worm" that is worse than a computer virus.] Even my pens know this book will end soon and that ink is running out on this project!)

In the late fall, I quit working at the flower shop completely to focus more on my book. I still taught many classes a week at the Iowa Community College. But the rest of the time, I delved into the book up to sixty hours or more a week. I continued to bake all our bread and make all of our meals. Now I was suffering. My health had been declining again since my miscarriage over a year earlier. I was overweight, the highest weight of my young life – one hundred and forty-nine pounds and my digestive and elimination organs were clogged. For the first time in my life, I was constantly constipated.

My writing was like a healing meditation to me. Whenever I worked on the book, I was out of pain and happy. When I stopped, I felt my body pain and mental agony at my living situation with Brent. I was becoming more and more uncomfortable living with him. I had to leave soon. I did not belong with Brent and I knew it throughout my being. I had to finish my book, move out and get on with my life.

I pounded on the typewriter day and night now. I no longer slept with Brent; I slept on the sofa in the living room. Winter passed, and finally I met with Esther to go over my final book pages. I had started with a thirty-two page mimeographed book that I wrote in Winnipeg, Canada and now it had become a thirty-two chapter book that I completed writing in the U.S. It was about five hundred and fifty double-spaced, typed, carbon-copied pages, which I typed with two fingers at about forty-to-fifty words a minute. I pre-sold copies of the book for fifteen dollars each to hundreds of friends and students of mine in the surrounding Quad-Cities, elsewhere in the U.S. and also in Canada. This advance money contributed to the cost of self-publishing the book. Brent also helped me out with a loan of a few thousand dollars and finally, I was ready to get it printed!

The printer took my pages and drawings, and typed and printed them on sticky-backed sheets that I had to cut out and apply to blue-lined graph paper sheets. (I cut and set up the pages myself to save money.) Then they photographed my pasted pages for the final print copy. The printer said I did a professional job of cutting and setting up the pages. It cost me $15,000 all together to make three thousand copies of my book. It was a fantastic price in 1980 but it was worth it to me.

I had several friends and students help me to make the index for my new book. It was far from an easy process in those days without computers. We spread out over five hundred index cards on Brent's living room floor and hand wrote every topic and cross-referenced item on each card that connected to every food, utensil and recipe in the book. It was a painstaking job that took more than a week of day and night documenting. Finally, this last piece of the book was ready and I shipped the alphabetized index cards to the printer for my last contribution to the book.

Another, more quiet event, occurred that December 1979, before I finished my book, my divorce from Gopala became final. We had a simple, cheap, uncontested divorce that I arranged. Now I was really single again. Well, almost – my days with Brent were numbered. Gopala had called me only once after I had moved in with Brent. When he found out that I was living with another man, he had finally given up on us and did not call me again.

I ran into Gopala a couple times at Palmer after that, but our meetings were cool and stiff, and Gopala usually shuffled off in the opposite direction when he saw me coming. I was actually relieved at this. I did not want to hurt him more. Our time together was over, and there was really nothing else we had to say to each other. More than twenty years later, I saw Gopala one more time. He was living in the Southwestern United States with his wife and children. He said he was happy and I sincerely wished him well. We had very little else left to say to each other. I found out though, that he was still writing to Mata Eloise regularly and sending her money! No real surprise here – Gopala had always been in love with Mata. Perhaps Mata was Gopala's mother in a previous life incarnation?

For months, during the following spring of 1980, when the book came out, I pounded the pavement to promote my books and sell them to local health food stores and bookstores. I learned to write very rough press releases, and ended up in every local newspaper and on every radio and TV station in the Quad-Cities area. I became a resident celebrity.

But still, this was not enough. I wanted a real book publisher and international book distribution. I sent letters and copies of my book to as many book publishers as I could in New York City or anywhere they would take a look at the book. I approached publishers in Colorado, California and New England, too. Mostly, I got rejection letters. It was a bittersweet time of both success and failure for me.

Now, it was finally time. I had to make my move. I told Brent it was time for me to move out and be on my own. I needed my own space for a while, I told him. Though I still loved him dearly, I had to go. I was suffocating in our life together. Only my work on my book had allowed me to tolerate our living situation as long as I had.

Brent was very sad, but I assured him we could still spend time together. By summer, I had a one-bedroom apartment in Davenport, just a few miles from Palmer, an easy bike trip or car ride. At last, I was on my own again. I had time to reflect on my life and promote my new book. Somehow, I would get a publisher!

ALONE

Alone, Alone,
For the first time
In my life
I'm living alone.
Thinking alone,
Feeling alone,
Knowing and
Being Me –
Alone.

Alone, I can see me.
Alone, I can be me.
Time alone,
Getting to know me.
So next time
When I'm with you,
Instead of dissolving
Into you,
I'll just be me –
Looking at you,
And you'll be you –
Seeing ME.

BELOVED

You are like a warm wind.
You set my mind at ease.
– But more than this,
You set a fire in my heart
And with your Love of life
You make the flame leap high.
– But more than this,
You reach my soul and give it joy.
You share a part of you with me
That others would not sell or give.
You feed my soul with truth.
– But more than this,
I see myself in you;
You live as I would live.
You Love and you are beautiful.
– There is no more than this!

Chapter Sixteen – Homecoming

"Serene I fold my hands and wait,
Nor care for wind nor tide nor sea;
I rave no more 'gainst time or fate,
For lo! my own shall come to me...
Nor time, nor space, nor deep, nor high,
Can keep my own away from me."

John Burroughs
Waiting

It was a brand new decade. The year was 1980. I had been recently divorced, was newly single, and glad to be. I lived in an adorable one-bedroom apartment in a fairly large, nicely land-scaped complex that included a swimming pool. It was right next to a long bike path that wove through Davenport and Bettendorf on the Iowa side of the Quad-Cities. This scenic pathway, lined with grass and colorful flower gardens, kept me riding my bike on a regular basis. I was trying to lose the extra weight I had gained while I experimented with all those cookbook recipes. Luckily for me, I held my extra weight well and still looked pretty and even a bit voluptuous.

Summer was in high gear and I was enjoying my freedom. Instead of a job, I was peddling my books and teaching more classes. I had already scheduled sixteen classes and several day-long courses for my fall line-up at the Iowa Community College I taught for regularly. In summer, I now taught at the Unitarian Church – both yoga and meditation classes. I held a few nutrition classes at the local health food store, as well.

Since my new self-published cookbook came into print, I was in great demand as a local speaker all around the Quad Cities area. I had already given Sunday sermons on the topics of health, nutrition and fasting at seven different denominations of churches in the area including: Unitarian, Unity, Science of Mind, Seventh Day Adventist, Greek Orthodox Catholic, Methodist and Baptist Churches. I felt privileged to be so honored by such a variety of faiths.

Catering was also a source of excellent revenue for me at the time. I had done some catering jobs with Nancy (Reid's wife) at the church, and now I prepared foods for parties and weddings on my own. With my new book as advertising, I did more catering and was becoming well known for my delicious, natural wedding cakes, usually carrot cake or carob – a chocolate substitute. My cakes were decorated with lovely pictures and silk flowers and they were always beautiful to look at, as well as tasty. I also prepared all kinds of appetizers and snack trays, and served several types of main dishes at each event.

Around this time, I planned a large smorgasbord supper at one of the local church kitchens and sold tickets to students, friends and interested newcomers. All the Quad-City newspapers gave me full-page coverage on the event, and I spent weeks preparing all sorts of main dishes and delectable desserts. Some of my students assisted with the supper, but I did most of the work myself. The supper was a huge success and I gained more business for my catering, as well as students for my many cooking and yoga classes.

With my cookbook completed and summer in progress, my days were actually my own to mainly play and relax for a change. I sat by my pool, rode my bicycle and "hung out" at Palmer more often. I still saw Brent every week or two, but we were only friends. He and I shared a close bond for many months after I moved out. He surprised me by becoming a very good natural cook. He missed my cooking and baking so much after my departure that he even baked his own bread for a while. Eventually, Brent and I saw less and less of each other and he married another. I was happy for him. My path in life led in another direction and I knew we were best parted.

I joined a Palmer volleyball team that was all men except for myself, and we played other teams that also included only one woman. I learned a lot about the game during these months, as I had to work hard to keep up with the guys I played with who were all tall, strong and buff, and far more athletic than me. Even my health was doing very well these days. I was enjoying my new life so much that I believe my happy psychological state easily overrode any minor health concerns I had. At this time, I also decided to see a counselor, once a week, who was innovative and a bit unorthodox with his psychology practice. He was assisting me in learning to express my emotions verbally in ways that made my interactions with friends, family and men more comfortable and fulfilling for me.

William was one of the guys on my volleyball team that I became great friends with. He was good-looking and sweet natured. William and I played together every week on the team and soon we began to hang out with each other. We saw movies, rode bikes, and shared meals at my place or local restaurants. One day, after many months as friends, we were resting together on my bed, after a volleyball game and before long we were cuddling as we chatted. Hugging turned to touching, and before long, sweet William and I were in the midst of foreplay. Before William could enter me, let's say his inspiation disappeared. He was most apologetic and noticeably embarrassed. I was not disheartened; rather I was more concerned about his feelings as he very special man and a wonderful friend to me. Sometimes, I had my own amorous reservations or lost desire due to past experiences or fears, so I could certainly accept his hesitations.

"It's no big deal," I said. "We can make love another time. Why don't we just hold each other and cuddle for a while."

"I have had some problems in the past," William admitted cautiously. "It has been a long time since I have made love to a woman. But I would like to make love to you," he continued with a rather apologetic tone.

"It doesn't matter," I assured him. "I find it difficult myself to make love with someone the first time. You don't know them well, and I often feel shy and a little embarrassed. Just hold me for a while and we can try again later or another day if that feels better. We don't have to rush."

William looked me square in the eyes, almost in disbelief, as if to see if I really meant what I said. He saw that I was sincere, and he thankfully leaned into me for a wholehearted kiss that stirred us both to new passion. We both continued on into a gentle, tender lovemaking session that culminated into satisfying orgasms for us both. I was certainly surprised at this quick change of events, but also pleased and happy that William trusted me enough to let go and enjoy making love to me.

Weeks later, William admitted to me that his last love had made fun of him for not being able to have sex with her a couple times, and he had been impotent for some time after that. He believed that my acceptance of him, regardless of his performance, had allowed him to relax enough to enjoy sex again. After that, he was especially thankful and appreciative of me for the rest of the time he stayed in Davenport and we shared intimacies. William graduated from Palmer a couple months later and I only saw him on a few occasions after that when he returned to Palmer once a year for Homecoming. The last time I saw William, he was happily married, and still greeted me enthusiastically with warm hugs and a friendly kiss on the cheek.

After William graduated, I continued my life comfortably. We were primarily good friends and our short affair was more of friendship sex than anything. It is usually easy for me to part with someone when I know that good feelings between us – live on. William will always claim a loving spot in my heart for his sweetness, kindness, honesty and gentle lovingness. He is a rare being, whom I continue to wish all the best in life.

I still hung out at Palmer College frequently, and continued to sit in on many of their nutrition classes. A lot of my Palmer friends could not understand why I did not just go to the school and become a chiropractor, but I was more in love with nutrition as a profession and I preferred to attend some nutrition classes at the Iowa Community College instead. I enrolled and completed one of their certificate courses. Besides the college course, I attended nearly every local nutrition lecture and seminar that came to Palmer, and there were many. I delved into every aspect of holistic nutrition that I could find in books, magazines and local classes as well as taking seminars in other cities by famous doctors like: David Mendelson, Abram Hoffer, Lynden Smith, Emmanuel Cheraskin, master herbalist John Christopher, and many others.

B.J. Palmer, the son of the man who first created or discovered chiropractic (named Daniel D. Palmer) had been known as the developer of chiropractic. He had traveled the world for art treasures that he filled his mansion with, on Palmer Campus. "B.J." also built an enchanting conservatory full of hothouse plants, lovely stone statues and international artifacts that he called: "Little Bit O' Heaven." This was a place I loved to frequent. The white, graceful statue of Venus rising out of a pool of water surrounded by lush tropical plants was favorite eye-candy for me as well as the many statues of Buddha and Hindu gods that B.J. Palmer had purchased and brought out of Asia to adorn his exotic collections of world art treasures. He shared these with all of Davenport and the surrounding areas, as well as with visitors from all over the planet. "Little Bit O' Heaven" was full of wonders: walls of purple amethyst, little gnomes and ladybug statues peeking out of tropical trees and bushes, huge seashells and more, arrayed this delightful place that was true to its name. Here I spent many delightful hours.

B.J. Palmer had been a very deeply spiritual man. His recorded words to live by were like a gentle sermon speaking truth principles that could be savored and applied to anyone. Everything and everyone had been sacred and important to B.J. who had honored all of life. He said: "We may never know how far-reaching something we may think, do, or say today will affect the lives of millions tomorrow." B.J. did indeed touch the lives of millions with his huge heart, mighty deeds and love of humanity. B.J. Palmer is considered to be one of the "Fathers of Chiropractic". His touch could be felt, even after his death, all over the Palmer Campus, throughout Palmertown and beyond.

Once a year, Palmer College held a homecoming extravaganza for alumni who wanted to return to their alma mater to learn updated and innovative chiropractic methods. There were inspirational and required seminars for the doctors and their spouses, and social events for student and doctor fellowship. Old and new Palmer students mingled at "Homecoming," to share friendship, ideas, techniques and more. Palmer College also scheduled famous and well-known doctors for lectures and debates. They also held several parties and provided showcases to sell chiropractic products during this event.

At this year's August 1980 Homecoming, I knew I had to attend to share my books at the booths that displayed and sold chiropractic related products. Something inside my being told me I had to be there! I listened to my inner voice and obtained a table for the weekend on Saturday and Sunday. I met many alumni chiropractors and sold dozens of my cookbooks. My cookbook, after all, supported chiropractic and I even talked about it in the beginning chapter and explained how important chiropractic was to good health. I even quoted Thomas Edison using a "Palmer familiar statement" of his that supports chiropractic and nutrition: "The doctor of the future will give no medicine but will interest patients in the care of the human frame, in proper diet, and in the cause and prevention of disease." This truth statement has always been among my favorite quotes.

One visiting alumni doctor, in particular, stood out in his praise and appreciation of my cookbook. He said his wife had just written a bread book and would love seeing mine. When Homecoming was over, I soon had an invitation to visit this Dr. Riverside and his young wife in upper Ohio, just three hours away from my hometown in Michigan. I accepted their invitation with relish as I sensed I would make important lifetime connections through them. I was right. The inner voice in each of us always knows. We have only to follow our truest instincts and the best that is possible in life will come to us.

I made instant friends with Mrs. Riverside, or Amber, by first name. Amber and I hit it off right away and had plenty to talk about. My visit of several days was a delight. Dr. Riverside introduced me to his associate clinic doctor – Dr. Jonah Merritt and we also found we had lots in common to talk about. Dr. Merritt invited me to lunch just before I left and we shared plenty of chiropractic stories. We talked about one long-standing joke or rather dilemma, that occurs in every chiropractic college town: Chiropractic students are under so much pressure with school, clinic work and part-time jobs that they either get married, divorced or have a baby while going to school to help alleviate some of the pressure.

I had seen this happen again and again in Palmertown. Married students divorced and often married another soon after. Single students married and both single and married students often ended up having one or even several children while in school. The rigorous school, clinic and work schedules drove chiropractic students to do other strange things as well. Dr. Merritt and I each shared a wealth of stories we laughed over as we ate. He was playful, easy-going and intelligent. Dr. Merritt and I thoroughly enjoyed each other and parted friends.

Since I was only a few hours away from my family in Detroit, I had arranged to see them next for a week after my Ohio visit. I casually invited Dr. Merritt to come up to my family's place for supper that week if he was interested, so he could sample some of my delicious vegetarian cooking. (Detroit was only a two-hour drive from the main Chiropractic clinic Dr. Merritt worked at in Michigan most of the time.) Since my offer was a casual suggestion, I was thoroughly surprised when he accepted. In Detroit, I spent several days enjoying my family's company and then I borrowed my sister's apartment for a night to prepare a special meal for Dr. Merritt.

At the time, I remember I was very self-conscious about still being overweight. Though I was by no means unattractive, I chose a flowing, blue, East Indian print dress to cover my roundness. Dr. Merritt, or Jonah, I should say, once again surprised me when he arrived at my door with a bouquet of flowers. Jonah was quick to put me at ease in his company. He was a Cancer, astrologically speaking, and very comfortable to be around. I could talk to him about anything I felt and he always managed to understand exactly what I was trying to say. Being with Jonah continually felt like being with my best friend. (I later wrote this poem for him:)

TRUE FRIENDSHIP

You who give me honesty,
Are the truest friend
Who could ever be.
You give it with integrity
And gentleness
And love for me.
The beauty and power
Of your friendship will be
Imprinted on my soul
For all eternity.

Jonah and I shared a leisurely supper and never stopped talking about our lives, Chiropractic, health and nutrition, our families, our work and any and everything that was of interest to either of us. We talked for hours. It was growing late but he was making no move to leave, though he had a couple hours' drive on his return trip.

My third surprise occurred when he reached across the sofa and drew me to him for a long, sensuous kiss that would have melted me to liquid wax if I had been a candle. I had expected friendship from Jonah, but not passion. He was exceptionally handsome and could have his pick of ladies, I was sure. Now, I was not ready for him to take such a personal interest in me.

One of the genuinely wonderful characteristics of Jonah was that he never noticed my extra pounds. I could tell he was looking inside me and seeing who I really was. I had not expected this. Now he let me know that he wanted me – all of me. I felt shy, virginal and as modest as a schoolgirl, beside him. Jonah was serious. He looked into my eyes with warmth and tenderness that melted me again into liquid. His arms surrounded me and he pulled me to the floor. He wanted me – now. I was afraid and full of apprehensions. I held back and avoided Jonah's eyes.

"Why are you resisting," Jonah whispered, at he lifted my chin and looked deeply into my eyes again.

"I did not expect this," I murmured. "Everything between us is happening so fast."

"It is right," Jonah continued softly. "Give in to what you really feel inside."

I hesitated for a long moment and then surrendered. It was too late to make rules. How could I resist the truth? I was as comfortable with Jonah as I was with myself. Only my illusory fears stood between us.

I was clumsy and virginal in my acceptance of him, but he took control and with total gentleness, he touched all the places in me that released my heart and soul to soar with his. Ever so softly, I opened to Jonah's tenderness, like a flower blooming before the sun. I melted again and again to his mastery of me. Jonah played me like a master musician plays a flute. There was no sound or sensation he could not extract from my being.

Wave after wave of gentle, heartfelt love flowed over me

and washed my doubts away. His touch and his tongue knew me over and over. When he entered me, it was like making love for the first time. I knew only him. Together, Jonah and I rode the river of love's delights into the early morning light.

With Jonah, it was all right to talk and love. We spoke of many things throughout that long night. I felt an inward bond surface between us that had lasted beyond centuries. Faint memories of loving Jonah in lives past surfaced in a new way, like transparent bubbles that grew in size and gained depth, color and dimension as they rose above us and burst quietly about us in the room. This powerful man with the strength of a lion was gentle as a lamb and he exuded tenderness like no other man I have known before or since.

In the early hours, we slept. I woke to more love play that did not stop to bathe or comb the hair out of our eyes. Jonah was making love to the very soul of me and outer perfection had no power to disrupt what was flowing inside of him or me. I felt completely enfolded and caressed. Each and every part of me was held sacred by Jonah. Our merging together as one was like a sacrament. God was never spoken of by either of us, but God was fully present in our love's Communion. The beauty, love, truth and powerful presence of God were evident in the profound union of our bodies and souls. Jonah and I had been fully present in the moment of now. Making love with him was meditation in action.

Later that day, after Jonah had departed amid kisses, caresses and plans to meet again, I found that I did not feel alone or deserted by him. A part of Jonah remained with me. I felt him deep inside. This feeling never left me and carried me until he and I next met.

A couple of days later, I left my family in Detroit and returned to the Quad-Cities. September was coming to a close. Fall was slowly blooming into reds, golds and browns. My cooking and nutrition classes increased at the end of September and I was busy and full of a new confidence and power.

I was determined to lose weight now and delved into dieting research for the first time in my life. I had never needed to diet before; after all, I had been anorexic. Now it was good to understand and empathize with others who constantly fought the "battle of the bulge." This experience broadened me and helped me to extend my knowledge of healing and healthy living.

Jonah and I kept in touch by phone. We talked long hours on occasion. Both of us had agreed to date other people. We lived four hundred miles apart. I was newly single and Jonah was separated after a ten-year marriage. We soon arranged to meet in Davenport for our first reunion. Jonah loved to fly small planes, so he flew himself into the Quad-Cities to share a long weekend with me in late November.

For four days, Jonah and I barely ventured beyond my apartment. We did spend one afternoon taking in the local sights, but other than that, our world revolved around my bedroom. We lay in bed most of the day, intermittently talking, playing, laughing, caressing, spooning, touching, eating and making love for exercise. We slept little and needed little from the world outside. Jonah could lick me to a frenzy and I would feel like I totally exploded inside and could feel nothing further, then ten or twenty minutes later, he did it again – then again, and again. Jonah's appetite for loving was insatiable and he made me feel that nothing was too much. The more he gave, the more I took and the more I gave in return. Giving and receiving were one and the same. Both were synonymous to each of us.

YOU AND I

We can fly together
– You and I.
We can reach the stars
Without having to try.
We can play together;
Write our names
In the sky.
We can love forever
– You and I.

I could confide anything to Jonah. He knew my deepest secrets, my darkest fears, my greatest longings and everything was good to him. He saw only beauty and love in me. I was incapable of being anything else with him. Whatever our past karma, it all manifested into good in the present. Both of us basked in the wonder of what we shared that was a constant stream of delight.

I never did find any formidable flaws in Jonah's character or actions except perhaps that he was too generous in nature, and others sometimes took advantage of this. Perhaps too, he was too slow to realize what he really wanted and needed in life and others, here again, directed him away from his own best interests. He liked to drink, but did not do it excessively.

On Jonah's last night at my place, we went dancing at a local club called the Longbranch. I'll always remember it as he bought us both long-sleeved T-shirts with the name of the club imprinted across the front. I still have mine. That was a special evening. Alone or in public, Jonah was the perfect date, the perfect gentleman. He was always kind, considerate and affectionate. He loved to hold hands and walk arm in arm, constantly. Jonah was not however the perfect dancer, except in slow dances, proving that the best lovers are not always the best dancers.

Later the next day, I dropped Jonah off at the airport and my world returned to its regular routine. I saw Jonah briefly at Christmastime when I visited my family in Detroit. We also kept in touch by phone often. Jonah and I shared another visit at my place the following spring.

One of the highlights of my life occurred around this time period. Mother Teresa of Calcutta came to Iowa for a lecture at a local school to raise funds for her charity work. She was the holy nun who took care of the sick and dying on the streets and in poverty-stricken hospitals of India. What a gift it was to hear her speak on that humble stage where she stood before hundreds of people who shed multiple tears at her loving words. She said: "You do not have to go to India to do God's work. You can do it right here where you are right now. Look at your neighbor, the person beside you, on your left and on your right. They need your love now. Give your love to everyone you meet. Then you will be doing God's work in this world. Love everyone who touches your life, no matter who they are." Mother Teresa's loving presence and words melted hearts that night. The entire audience embraced, and most left with tears in their eyes.

I had the rare privilege of meeting her in person, touching her and holding her in my arms. Mother Teresa said precious words privately to me that I will always treasure. She helped me to see that I was capable of doing great work for God – just by loving in the moment. Nothing else was or is required

– just love. I did not have to "do" anything – or "go" anywhere – just "be" love, in the now.

That winter, I concentrated on getting a publisher for my cookbook: *For the Love of Food.* I was more determined than ever to get my book into the mainstream of publishing activity. But all my efforts came to dead ends. My stack of rejection letters kept growing and I was beginning to lose faith in my dreams of becoming a famous writer one day. I was in the deepest of slumps when I visited a friend of mine, Val, who owned a local bookstore in Bettendorf one afternoon. She understood my frustrations and pain over not finding a publisher. There was a sales representative from a major publisher in Val's store at the moment and she suggested that I give the "rep" a copy of my book to bring back to her publisher, which was Ballantine Books – one of the top publishing houses at the time. I felt I had nothing to lose by doing this, even if it came to naught as my other efforts had, it was worth a try.

Just a few months later, I got the surprise of my life. Ballantine Books wanted to publish my book! I was overjoyed. My frustration turned to relief and excitement. God did want my book published in a big way. Now I knew I was on the right track!

Jonah came for a visit that spring and we savored each other as before. He was thrilled at my publishing news. This visit, we delved into some new aspects of each other and finally talked about – God. Jonah believed in God but had no particular beliefs about God. He could take or leave any practice or worship of God. Living life according to his highest ideals was enough for Jonah. I fully respected Jonah's views. I knew people who talked about God but did not live a Godly life. Jonah was a loving, genuine, giving person who exuded more of Godly actions in his expressions than others who talked a lot about doing so.

What was amazing about Jonah was his openhearted acceptance of my views and beliefs. Many others had laughed at my visions of past lives and my love of chanting. Jonah accepted and admired both of these beliefs in me. He enjoyed hearing me sing my chants and songs and was totally willing to explore some of our past lives – together. I had already seen a procession of past life visions with Jonah – all loving and positive. Now Jonah was willing and wanting to explore these with me himself.

Jonah and I sat across from each other on the floor of my living room and I explained to him how to do a special type of breathing technique along with an eye meditation and our bodies touching. He wholeheartedly participated and soon both of us were seeing the same visions of our past. It was a rare treat to share this with a man I loved and honored.

Memories and visions of many former lives surrounded us both, as our faces changed to assume other identities our souls had known through the ages. When it was over, we discussed our experiences and found much of what we had seen was in unison. Jonah was more than a friend and lover to me, he was now part of all I was. He had embraced every part of me and I felt truly "known" by another human being for the first time in this life. Even when Jonah was not physically present with me, part of him – his essence or spirit – was with me. During the time I knew him, I was never completely alone.

SOUL CONNECTION

The beauty
That you are to me,
Is imprinted forever
In my soul
And in my memory.
A part of you
Will always remain
– Inside of me.
Everywhere I go
And everything I do
Will bring me closer
To the destiny
I share with you.

That summer, I hooked up with a local spiritual group that had a center right next to the Palmer Campus. I found a wealth of friends within this group and some comradery of spirit as well. I began to work part-time waitressing at a local restaurant for extra money, during the warm weather, with a couple of the guys from that group and they opened up a new world for me. One of them played guitar and we began to sing together regularly.

One day I was talking to Jonah on the phone for one of our long chats that we had every couple weeks or so, and our talk grew very serious. For the first time since I had known him, Jonah admitted to really loving me. I had felt this all along, but I was delightfully overwhelmed by his declaration, just the same. Jonah said he loved me and he loved everything about me. My heart soared to a place it had never yet been in this life. What came next was equally astonishing for me.

Jonah felt he had to go back to his separated wife and tie up loose ends with her before he could be with me. I was shocked. Go back to her! Why? For how long? He did not know. He felt it was the "right" thing to do and I could not dissuade him. My elation quickly turned to consternation. I remember I was leaning against the door of my bedroom while speaking to him on the phone and I literally crumbled against it and folded into a crying heap on the floor. My tears would not stop. He tried to comfort me and tell me that everything would be all right, but I knew better. I knew this was the beginning of the end for us. There would be no quick divorce. I *knew* and *felt the truth* of my concerns. I was losing Jonah to his past. He embraced my tears and fears but he could not erase them. I cried a long time after our conversation ended. I had lost the love of my life. I knew it!

In the weeks that followed, I was occupied with my new friends at the spiritual center, busy with my jobs, classes and my new contract with Ballantine Books. The publishers and I spent several weeks negotiating a contract that was signed in late summer. My book was due in print about one year later.

That summer, I visited my family in Michigan again. I was getting much better at long distance driving since I had met Jonah, and had taken a number of four hundred mile drives by myself. I saw Jonah for a day of my Detroit visit and we sat on his boat and talked heart to heart – as we always did. I had lost an amazing thirty-five pounds over the last several months and was now a trim one hundred and fifteen pounds. Jonah only commented on my weight loss after I mentioned it. He saw me the same as he always had done. I was beautiful before and beautiful now to him.

Jonah had returned to his wife two months previously and now they were living together again – just as I had feared. Jonah said it would end soon, but I did not believe him. He was slow to leave anything – even what was not good for him.

That day Jonah held me and once again I cried. He wanted to make love to me but I said no. I could not make love to him knowing he would be returning to his wife that same day. If he wanted me, he had to leave her. But I knew he could not and would not. We parted, both in tears. It was to be a long time before I saw him again, but I knew we would be together again – later.

JEWELS

Even you cannot take away
The love that had grown inside.
I am surrounded by golden daffodils,
Acres of diamonds and sapphire jeweled skies.

Ruby roses with emerald leaves,
Lilies-of-the-valley in opalescent seas,
Remain in the garden
You planted in me.

The diamond, dew-drenched morning
Whispers your name.
You have touched me deeply.
I will never be the same.

I went back to Iowa, my friends and my jobs and felt a growing unrest. A couple months later, when I received my first royalty advance for my book: *For the Love of Food*, I decided I would travel for a year before the book came out. I bought myself a brand new car for the first time in my life – a Ford Escort. It was a cute, little, bright blue, compact with a few white racing stripes on the sides. It was my mark of having "arrived" or having "made it."

One day, in the autumn of 1981, I loaded up my little car with my self-published editions of my cookbook and my personal luggage and headed out across the United States and Canada. I would sell and promote my own editions of my book even before the new Ballantine Books publication came out the next year. I would also explore and enjoy the many wonders of North America. This part of my travels was a solitary endeavor, and I relished this opportunity to further acquaint myself with my own unique self. Fresh adventures lay before me. It was time now for me to discover other worlds and prepare myself for a new life.

Glimpses of experiences from many future years to come – visions of this present incarnation, flashed across my mind's eye, and I realized that some of my most important journeys in this lifetime were barely beginning. I drove down the road toward my future full of hope and anticipation.

RESSURECTION

What once was a rosebud,
tightly sealed,
Is now a radiant blooming flower.

What someday will be
a mass of withered petals,
Is Myself – awakening in my brightest hour!

SOUL'S REPOSE

What part of me is wounded now?
I cannot tell.
My limbs are tired;
They refuse to dance.
My voice refuses to sing.
I cannot sleep, yet I am weary,
Oh what's the matter with me?
Life hangs like a burden.
Like a listless pool am I,
Divided from the sea.
I'll lie here till my worlds unfold
And dance like pictures in my mind,
Showing me where I have fallen
And lifting me again on high.
I will lie here but a moment
As I slip into my soul's repose.
Then I'll waken fresh and vibrant,
Shaking dew drops like a rose.

Epilogue – Answers/
The Mystery Revealed

"I hold that when a person dies
His soul returns again to earth;
Arrayed in some new flesh disguise,
Another mother gives him birth,
With sturdier limbs and brighter brain
The old soul takes the road again.

John Masefield
A Creed

I finished scribbling the final sentences of chapter sixteen and looked up to focus on my surroundings. It was now the month of September 2004. I lay propped up in bed supported by six huge pillows that nearly dwarfed me as I lay in their midst, pen in hand. My good friend Gloria walked into my bedroom and sat down in the chair next to my bed.

"I put your groceries away in the kitchen." I remember her saying. "How's your book coming along?"

"Thanks so much Gloria! You're amazing. I don't know what I'd do without you. I've just completed it, I believe. But something is missing," I added thoughtfully. "I'm at the place where I just head out across the country to sell my self-published copies of *For the Love of Food*. The book's already enormous, so I need to end it here but I'm only thirty-one years old at this point of the story. There are twenty-two years yet to write about my travels and living in Vancouver and also here in Virginia Beach. That should be another book."

"That makes good sense," offered Gloria. There is so much covered in the book already. It will give people quite a bit to think about as it is. There's so much information in it. I'll need to read it several times just to process all the spiritual facts and stories."

She had been the first person to read my entire manuscript so far.

Four and a half months after the accident, the neck brace was off, but my neck was still stiff and I could barely move it right or left. I still slept flat on my back in what I jokingly referred to as my "coffin pose." Friends like Gloria had done everything for me, from shopping to laundry to cleaning. They also visited me and kept me company.

I recall looking up at her appreciatively as I continued. "I've decided to call the second book, *The Ocean Daughter*. After all, these years were spent living by the Pacific and Atantic Oceans. *The River Daughter* talks about a river of spiritual energy and a river turns into an ocean before too long."

"Of course, that's a perfect title for your sequel. I'll look forward to reading that too," declared Gloria. "But you started *The River Daughter* taking about your accident and wondering why it happened and I think you need to end it with an explanation. You need to write about your experiences with Neil!"

I looked at her thoughtfully and knew she was right. Gloria was not only a friend; she was my confidant as well. I told her everything. The last several weeks had been a powerful and exciting time despite my injuries and the nearly constant neck pains, that only subsided for brief periods. I now knew why my car accident had occurred, at least in the spiritual sense. I *had* to include the karmic reasons for it, in *The River Daughter*, even if it took another chapter to reveal.

When your present life reflects your past or when an old chapter of your life (or past lifetime) is focused on and produces a parallel new chapter, then the past and present become joined. In actuality, past and present are already one and occurring simultaneously. In most of our present states of consciousness, it only appears that time is linear and consecutive. It is possible to flash back and forth between lifetimes – past, present and also future ones. I myself have done it. This is exactly what has happened to me on many occasions.

I am a powerful woman. Many times in my life, I have created in the present, actual events that were born out of my intense concentration on something or someone for the purpose of understanding and healing. I have seen, heard and felt all the emotions and even touched other moments of lifetimes that are both connected to the present and interrelated. Not only can the past affect and create the present, but also *the present can be changed by changing the past* and *the past changed in the present!* Past lives can not only be viewed now, they can be fully experienced, lessons can be learned and the seemingly distant past can be altered to help heal the present. Author Richard Bach talks about this in his spiritual book entitled: *One.*

I took Gloria's advice to heart and began reflecting over the last two months, back to early July 2004. At that time, I had barely finished putting Chapter Six – the "Union" chapter about my marriage with Gopala on my computer and the next day my psychic friend Virginia did a tarot card reading for me. I was in a slump that day and very depressed. My neck had been out of the brace only a few weeks and though I had many friends around me helping me and visiting, I was lonely. I wondered how long I had to wait for love to stay in my life.

Virginia's reading gave me surprising and optimistic news. A new man was on the horizon for me, whom she said I would meet right away. She described him physically and told me we would have an intense love bond that would last at least a year and a half. Virginia went on to say that my relationship with him would bring me a whole new circle of friends here in Virginia Beach.

It took only two more days for Virginia's predictions to come true. I met him at the Heritage Store deli (two blocks from the ocean) on the following Saturday afternoon. I was talking about this new book I was writing with my dear friend Mary at the food service counter and Neil was next in line and overheard me discussing the book's contents with her.

"What book is this, that you're talking about?" said Neil. "It sounds very interesting."

"It's my book," I said. "I am writing a new book about my life with a metaphysical twist. It is an exciting spiritual journey and the book discusses some of my nearly five hundred visions of past lives. It's called *The River Daughter*."

"I'd like to read that," continued Neil. "Tell me more about it."

Neil and I gathered our food purchases and found a table. It only took me a few more minutes to realize that this was the exact man that Virginia had just predicted I would meet. He fit her description to a tee. In fact, Virginia's description of Neil's physical appearance and a past life of his were instantly verified by myself. I "saw" immediately the past life she said Neil had experienced – so deeply – that it showed up in his facial features and in his aura in the present. It was a powerful life as an American Indian. Though he looked as if it were his genetic heritage in this lifetime, it was actually a physical remnant of an incarnation predominant in Neil and it had far-reaching effects that were obviously epitomized in his present life.

When a person looks the part of a particular previous life, then it often overshadows the present in such a way that shows they have lots of past karma still left from that incarnation, that they are working out now. Or the characteristics of that past life are so strong that they surface and reflect strongly in the present, as well.

Virginia had also told me that Neil would be dark complexioned, with dark hair and would be Jewish. Also, that he sweat a lot, not in an unpleasant way, but certainly more than average. He also had "musical interests" and he was in a health-care profession. Well, Neil was all she described.

As we munched on our snacks in the deli, Neil and I dug immediately into a very deep conversation. I was amazed at where we "went" with it so quickly. Since he was a chiropractor and I, a nutritionist whose ex-husband was a chiropractor, we found we had tons in common. Neil also played guitar in a couple of bands.

In one hour of conversation, he and I were so engrossed, neither of us wanted to end the conversation. Our energies immediately wrapped around each other and we could both see and feel our mutual interest. I do not ever recall getting so deeply acquainted – with anyone – in so short a time. I felt right away as if I had known Neil all my life.

After an hour and a half of rapid conversation, we both noticed we had to get on to other engagements. Neither of us wanted our time together to end. So he invited me to a kind of small party/music practice he was having with one of his bands that night. I immediately accepted. I spent a good part of the late afternoon and early evening resting so I would have enough energy to go out for a social evening for the first time since my accident. A friend of mine dropped me off at the practice house later that night. Neil was obviously pleased to see me and introduced me to the band as well as other friends who were there and then he and I got started on a lively conversation, just the two of us.

We shared an hour or so of deeply engrossing discourse and I felt as if I had known this man forever – life after life. My heart and mind were entirely open to him. I felt like I could say anything to Neil. We seemed to be two kindred spirits. He was so easy to relate to and open up with. I felt my heart chakra open easily to a warm, comfortable embrace of his endearing charm and personality. He displayed a generous and caring nature. Actually, I realized later that I had been totally in love with him since that first hour we had met in the health food deli. It was a spontaneous feeling I had no control over. I just loved him! (Much later, I remembered that I often tap into emotions from other lifetimes – instantly – and feel them, in present time. Also, each of us is attracted to the energies of those whom we have karma with that needs to be worked on or completed in this lifetime.)

After our talk, the band set up and began playing. Their repertoire included soft rock, top forties-type tunes. These were some of my favorites. I reveled in their music. It continued into the early hours. It was three a.m. before we made a move to leave. Neil and his group drove me to his place, surprisingly, only one block from where I lived. Then Neil walked me the short block home. At my place we hugged and I felt the urge to ask him to stay. I did not want to say goodnight.

"I do not want to seem too forward," I told Neil, "but would you consider spending the night with me? No sex," I continued. "I'd just like to hold you and sleep in our clothes. Would that be all right?"

"That would be perfect," said Neil. "I would love to," he added. Neil appeared to be having similar feelings as myself.

We talked until nearly five a.m. and then slept innocently in each other's arms. We never even kissed. But it was the perfect continuation of an amazing day. We had just met twelve hours previously and now it felt to me like it was twelve hundred years ago. The next night, Neil and I took a long walk on the beach and slept together again in the same fashion as the night before, only we were asleep by two a.m.

The third day was Monday and a holiday. Neil was playing music at a huge party that I was also invited to. There was plenty of food and exciting people and Neil was very affectionate, giving me constant hugs and dancing slow dances with me during the breaks. It was an idyllic night. The party ended at four a.m. and Neil and I parted that night to get some sleep, as he had to work in his office later that morning. I did not see him that Tuesday, but he called me twice on the phone.

I saw him again on the following day, a Wednesday night. We slept at my place again and this time we took things a step further and got naked but agreed not to rush into sex. We frolicked together playfully for several hours, exploring each other but not consummating. It was an amazing night. It was like practicing Tantra yoga wherein all manner of foreplay is indulged in without the final sexual consummation. We caressed, fondled and savored each touch and sensation, yet we never kissed. Neil told me that the first two nights we had been together, it had been so nice just to hold someone, but tonight he was especially glad that he was with "me." He felt it was so right for us to be together that night.

As we embraced, our energies mingled and I was transported to what felt like another plateau in time. I viewed a procession of lifetimes with Neil and me that were so vivid; it was as if there was a three-dimensional TV screen all around us projecting rich, living colors of scenes from dozens of other lives. For the first time in my life, my visions had full depth and vivid colors. The images were not transparent projections superimposed across the present. These visions appeared to be as real as we were. Neil and I were living these lifetimes – now!

Throughout our love play, these lives danced around the two of us and I described bits of some of them to Neil: Biblical, Greek, Roman, Persian and Egyptian lifetimes flowed in a steady stream before my eyes with Neil and me at the center of each life. I saw bedrooms and battlefields. The Egyptian lifetime in particular flooded the room with detailed precision from the swaying palm trees to the courts of royalty, from the desert sands to the marketplace. I saw Neil in particular as a kind of scribe writing with a stylus on papyrus paper. I was a member of the royal household. Past Neil and I were lovers.

The scents of sweet jasmine and spices were thick in the air. I smelled them *now*, in the present! A wave of hot breeze caused the hanging lamps to sway and flicker. The sound of my own sandals shuffling across the stone, tile floor as my garments rustled like music to past Neil's ears, was rhythmic. My nearly transparent, gossamer-like clothing nearly floated to the ground as I undid the simple clasp. The others had gone; Neil dropped his stylus as I folded, naked, into his arms. There was more, but I could not see it clearly for weeks to come.

Some men and especially women, often see past lives when engaging in sex. Heightened energies either from love, love making, a high voltage relationship, happiness, prosperous feelings or any kind of positive connection that increases normal energy levels can easily lead to past life visions for anyone who is more sensitive or aware of such possibilities. Many people see these past lives and assume they are "imagining things." Trust the vague impressions you "see, feel or receive" and they often intensify and increase in frequency.

These visions are nothing to be afraid of. They offer powerful insights into past lives and present relationships. Note the overall feelings of such perceptions – good, bad, happy, sad and you will get glimpses of what you can expect with a present love in terms of future experiences with them. But remember, past circumstances can be changed though not usually instantly, they often require time and conscious effort for changes to be effective, on the parts of both (or all) people involved. *Observe and learn the lessons given in visions but: Do not become obsessed with past lives! We still have to live in the "present."*

Many excellent psychics will tell you that real psychic messages or visions seem as if we are "making them up in our minds" yet they are real impressions from the subconscious or higher conscious mind (or god-self) that appear dream-like but are often more real than how we live each day in this physical world. Keeping track of your dreams or visions in a journal helps to increase your awareness of insights that you receive. As you focus more conscious awareness on accepting and understanding messages from the subconscious and superconscious, you will open the doorway to more messages and guiding experiences as well as increase the clarity and strength of what you perceive from *this lifetime* or past incarnations.

In the present, I relished each moment in Neil's arms. His embrace felt like a healing balm to my accident injuries, and I knew he also was receiving healing as I saw his aura glow a rich, vibrant, healing green in the dark. This third night together, was utter magic. It was worth a dozen nights of passionate love making to me. Healing energies surrounded us both. We were both in serious need of many days of love-filled moments to heal our abundant psychological and physical wounds. I would savor each moment of this divine remedy.

As I write these words, a ladybug, an omen of good luck crawls down my window, and I open it to release her to a sunny day outside. (An Egyptian perspective, no doubt!)

In the next several days, Neil and I slept together sometimes, shared nighttime ocean walks and healing energies. On the eighth day, I heard him play across town with another band in a public mall. We cuddled during his breaks and then held hands under the table as we shared a meal with his band. Neil held my hand in the car most of the way home. Then when we arrived back at his place, as he walked me the block home, he told me good-bye. We were through, he said, and could be friends. I could not believe my astonished ears. I was shocked. It just did not make sense after our week together and this evening in particular, he had been so affectionate. He left me bewildered at my door and walked home without a backward glance.

I was dumbfounded, confused and deeply hurt. After less than an hour of torment, I walked right over to his place, his roommate let me in, and I walked right into his bedroom and confronted him. In the weeks that followed, I realized that Neil had a sexual problem. His aura was somewhat dark, distorted and wounded. My friends thought he was gay, but he had been married twice and had two children. However, his aura was not typical of a heterosexual. His hormone balance was off. I finally noticed this for the first time. I saw this clearly, now that my visions of our past lives and the "light energy" Neil and I shared no longer blocking my present view of him. I had been only vaguely conscious of this before. I had chosen to blind myself to certain present realities. This is so easy to do when one feels the initial power of love energy.

Neil and I spent a second week talking and trying to understand and possibly alter the present realities of what we actually shared. He had admitted ending our relationship that night because he felt sure I expected sex and he had little appetite for it except with rare women, and he felt I was not one of them. He did not even like kissing. We spent one last night cuddling together and in the morning, I had this dream: Neil and I were in a bedroom that was filled with only water and a plain, uncovered mattress with a box spring under it. The water surrounded the bed that rose just about a foot above the water line. I sat on the mattress while Neil jumped into the water and began to swim around.

Neil said, "Come on in. The water is fine."

I looked at the water, which was murky and looked like sewer water. "It's dirty," I said.

"It's fine," repeated Neil. "There's nothing wrong with it."

But I could see that the water was filthy and scummy. I stuck my legs in it but would go no further. The water was too disgusting to me.

Neil kept swimming around. Now he was actually under the bed, floating on his back in the water. He let go of a stream of water from his mouth, with only his head sticking out from under the bed, in the water, just like they do on cartoons. "The water's great!" he declared.

I was totally unconvinced and would not enter it.

He continued to swim around.

I stayed on the bed and woke up. Later, that morning, I told Neil my dream. He saw no value in it. I knew it was a clear message to me from my super conscious – higher self, of our present situation. Neil was happy as a pig in mud with the distorted sexual energies he played in. They appeared normal to him. I however, preferred "clean energies" and healthy, wholesome male/female relationships. His sloppy energies were physically reflected in the way he kept his own bedroom and his car. They were both beyond messy and dirty.

After this last night together, and my following dream, we agreed to stay away from each other for a couple weeks or so, to help alter our relationship to "just friends."

When we first saw each other after ten days apart, it was like a loving reunion. We had lunch at my place and chatted for hours. Five times Neil told me how much he missed me, and I told him I missed him too, as much if not more. A day later, we passed each other at the Heritage Store with only a brief wave, and then he moved on. I knew immediately something was wrong. It was subtle, but I felt it.

We had agreed to "just be friends" now and I was content with that. He would see other women; I would see other men.

I was okay with that after having ten days to switch gears. But inside myself, I hoped that down the road, more might one day be possible for us. Time would tell.

I believe my fairy tale desires allowed me to hope that he would one day change, improve and become the man I envisioned psychically that he could be. It is hard to let go of sharing energy with a man. I, like many women fall in love with a man's energy and potential rather than the realities of what he actually is. I trusted God and the universe to bring us together later if that was right, if not, I could move on now with complete happiness, knowing – trusting that the best possible would happen for both of us.

The next day, Saturday, Neil and I were to attend a couple of parties. I did all I could to get another date or ride to the party. Two guys I called would be out of town; one guy had his mother in town. None of my girlfriends was available to drive me. (Remember, my car had been totaled in the accident and I was still unable to move my neck well enough to drive yet anyway.) My lawyers had all my insurance money still tied up and I had not been working. I was too broke to afford the long cab ride.

Though I felt uncomfortable relying on Neil for a ride, we "were" supposedly friends. He had agreed to drive me after all. He could have said no. Neil came by to pick me up for the parties dressed very casually. I, on the other hand, had decided to dress up as I always did and put on a blazing red, floor length dress that was fancy/casual and would suit an outdoor party.

On the way to the party, Neil appeared agitated and finally burst out that he felt I had been lying about my perceptions of our relationship and other things I told him and that I was arrogant as well. He refused to tell me exactly what he felt I had lied about. He himself admitted lying to me and said he was after all a Scorpio – a scorpion, and did sting. What did I expect from him but lies? He said it was, after all, his true nature!

He said these things so viciously; I could not believe my ears. I was stunned. I felt attacked and as if he had just slapped my face a few times or beaten me. I felt sore and bruised inside after his verbal attack. We fought like a couple that had been married many years. I wanted to discuss these matters he had just thrown at me so callously, but we were at the party now and he said that our conversation was over. I argued that it was unfair for him to hit me with such statements and then run away. Neil retorted, "This is a party and I intend to have fun," as he walked away from me.

I was crushed. I felt as if Neil had just unloaded a truckload of manure on me. He just dumped it and walked away, leaving me to dig out from under it. I was miserable the entire night. Though I appeared the "belle of the ball," I was broken inside. I spent two more days without much sleep – digging out of Neil's manure, and then I confronted him. It happened over the phone. It took one and a half hours to clear up this mess and finally arrive at a mutual resolution. Neil promised not to dump on me again like that, and he apologized for his behavior. Some of my friends said I should not have forgiven him. His behavior was inexcusable and he would probably do it again, they said. But I wanted to forgive him if at all possible and remain friends. I cared about Neil, but now my love feelings had been destroyed, like a large bubble that had finally burst, and could not be made whole again. A distance had been created between us by his actions, and I would not trust him enough to let myself love him again.

Okay, I thought, we got through this. Hopefully now we can be friends and put all this behind us. But a day later, he was to come to my house for lunch and changed the time – three times. As I tried to explain my frustration at this to Neil on the phone – he hung up on me. I was furious. He called an hour later with apologies. What was happening? Why was he doing this and why was I putting up with it? Again, I forgave him though I had allowed him to ruin my lunch and my day.

The next day we were to take a walk by the ocean to finally talk and see each other in person as we had mainly only talked on the phone since the party. Neil picked me up after my nutrition class and we both made a late supper together at my place. Then we went for a walk. I wanted to clarify our "friendship" and talk more about what happened between us at the party and that week, and this infuriated Neil. It was over, he said. Let's move on! I needed more resolution after the intense events of this week. But Neil was brutally opposed. Then we both backed off and attempted to lighten the conversation, but it was fruitless.

When he dropped me off at home, I spent a sleepless night and realized I could not go on this way. We could not, obviously, be friends. I wrote him a kind but determined note and said good-bye. I would not suffer another time at his harsh words.

He had a major cruel streak and he was unleashing it on me. I had finally had enough! I told Neil in the letter to stay away from me.

At this point in my story, I had just finished writing Chapter Twelve – the "Being of Light" chapter wherein I separate from my husband and also say good-bye to Jesse. Now, just like a reflection of that past, it was time to say good-bye to Neil in present time!

But inside myself, I was still crushed and bruised by this week's encounters with Neil. I felt emotionally and physically as if I had been beaten by Neil's fists, and left bloodied on a pavement somewhere. I was falling apart. I could not sleep or work. I headed to the Heritage Clinic to see a friend of mine, named John. He is an energy worker, psychic, hypnotist and extraordinary being. John and his lovely soulmate wife Melissa were, and are, good friends and tremendous supporters of my career and me. Like many of the people at the Heritage, John, Melissa and I were old Atlanteans, part of a healing circle of individuals who are assisting in healing planet earth today.

I only called upon John for his special services when I was desperate for help and could not progress through intense life and spiritual situations without assistance. As I waited for an energy treatment, I fell apart in the waiting room and could not stop crying. The pain in me was horrific. Loving friends there comforted me as best they could. They had all seen me with Neil and knew I was upset about him. Two people then told me that Neil's first wife had come crying to the clinic on more than one occasion, years ago, claiming that Neil abused her by shutting her out emotionally.

This was news to me, but not really a surprise. "Once an abuser, always an abuser." I wished this was not true – but it usually was. Abusers may need many lifetimes to change unless they sincerely work at it. Neil was totally unwilling to change himself. He was too busy blaming others for his short-comings. He could not face his own impotence – emotionally or physically. I found out, from several firsthand sources, that Neil had bedded many women but could not come across sexually, and then he blamed them for being sexually unattractive to him, as he had me.

This new information about Neil fit in with another recent vision I had regarding him. It was a continuation of the Egyptian lifetime I had envisioned with Neil during our third night together. We had been lovers in that life wherein he was a kind of scribe and I, royalty. We shared a unified passion and our affair lasted many moons. One day, the two of us were caught in the act of lovemaking and Neil was put to death for his "crime" – for defiling a daughter of the royal household. I sincerely mourned him then. Neil's punishment in that life made him wary of loving me, and led him to block the flow of sexual energy to me in following lifetimes. This may have been the root of our sexual problems in this life, or it may only have been part of the problem. Neil may have had lifetimes with other lovers, who hurt him, to add to the pain of the Egyptian incarnation.

My energy worker, John, was ready for me now and I continued to cry as he led me to his treatment room. As powerful energies in me were being balanced, by currents from my body worker's hands, another past life with Neil flooded into my conscious memories and I saw us together in a lifetime I had viewed nearly twelve years previously. Neil was my father in a "past" Polynesian lifetime in Hawaii. He was the leader of our tribe, a Kahuna, and he was powerful, cruel and controlling. In that life, I was like my younger self in this lifetime: weak, fearful, quiet and obedient. In that life, I tolerated Neil's cruelties as my father, and later married a man who continued my father's cruel and controlling treatment of me. I saw everything in that life, as I lay on my body worker's table.

Nearly twelve years previously (in this life), I had another serious car accident while I was dating the man I had been married to in that same Hawaiian lifetime. He is presently a doctor, a surgeon in this lifetime, as Neil is a doctor now too. I "saw" that their present karma in this lifetime is to do good works and help others to heal, to pay for past life cruelties to many. This is easier said than done. Changing bad habits that have lasted for lifetimes takes tremendous awareness that often surfaces slowly in individuals through the intuition.

After my other car accident, twelve years previously, I saw other details of this Hawaiian lifetime. In it, my husband and I were arguing – again. He grabbed my wrists tightly and was hurting me. My husband was angry because I was so weak and vulnerable. I pulled away from him and ran off, towards the waterfalls. He was in hot pursuit of me. I reached the double waterfalls and the pool of water it fed into and I dived into the pool to escape from him. As I did so, I asked the gods to take me away from him and his abuse of me, and they did. I crushed my face on a huge underwater rock. (The same injury I received in my car accident twelve years ago – a crushed face – I received in the past Hawaiian incarnation.)

I died instantly in that past life. My bloody body floated to the surface of the pool of water and as two men lifted my broken body from the water, my husband then (the surgeon in this life), cursed my dead body. My soul floated above my dead body watching that scene and I was glad the gods freed me from my husband's cruelty. I was happy to die and get away from him and my father's controlling treatment of me as well. I was then free – though my freedom was temporary. I still had to come back into earthly form and face both of them – again, with strength, courage and power – in another lifetime (this present one) and say no to their abuse. This has not been an instant realization for me in this lifetime. Little by little I have learned to accept better treatment from men by increaseing degrees. Changing past life patterns, as previously stated, is not an instant process. It may take dozens or hundreds of re-peat situations and many lifetimes, to learn an important life lesson and move beyond an old state of consciousness.

Now, after viewing more scenes from this detailed past life, on the energy worker's table, I finally felt relieved and like I knew the truth. I am like a curious child who "takes apart a clock to see why it ticks". *I must see the truth for myself.* Only then can I be satisfied. I, as well as everyone else, have the power to inquire, see and learn from these previous or rather other life experiences. *We can "ask" and receive answers to every question.*

This lifetime, I eventually learned to stand up to both my past father (Neil) and husband from that incarnation, and said "no" to their abuse. I would be willing to die rather than be abused again. But much more importantly, I was willing to live, without them! I was willing to live as I deserved and accept loving, kind, wonderful treatment from a man who honored and loved me for all the beauties I am today.

Throughout this lifetime, I have been learning how to interact with men and hold my ground while saying no to physical and emotional abuse rather than to run away in fear, confusion and with feelings of self-blame. It is imperative for every woman to recognize abuse, let the abuser know that bad treatment is unacceptable and stand firm in refusing further bad treatment. This may mean staying and teaching the abuser and yourself new ways of behaving, or it may mean leaving them, or if necessary, restraining an abuser with legal action.

It takes time and practice to change patterns that have often continued for lifetimes. I had to learn to recognize many of my habits and the multiple ways I had of interacting with men. Then slowly scrutinize each one to see how I was contributing to the way men treated me. I helped to create their behavior towards me and now I had to change my expectations to accept the better treatment I deserved. I also had to change the "signals" I gave to men as well as state my allowances or boundaries, and alter my own behavior to stop abuse as it was happening.

After my experience on the energy worker's table, I felt like I was in a daze, half in this physical world and half in the spirit world, so I *knew*, from former experience, that my past life visions were not completely over yet. The next day, John worked on me again, but there were no more visions that day. However I knew there were more related lifetime experiences to "see" that would surface in their own time.

Three days later, my girlfriend Pam picked me up to go to a talk given by a Huna (Hawaiian) priest, a Kahuna, at one of the local churches in Virginia Beach. Somehow, I did not pay any attention to the significance or connection this might have to the Hawaiian past life vision I had only days before. The talk was actually more like a religious ceremony and each person who came into the meeting room had sage smoke circled around them for purification and sage smoke burned the entire time of the talk and ceremony. I enjoyed the priest's words and the rituals and felt a special rapport with him, but I had to leave halfway through the evening as the smoke was too thick and made breathing difficult for me. I am allergic to smoke, and have been for two and a half decades now, since I gave up smoking and smoky bars completely. I left the Huna talk early and walked by myself, the mile and a half home.

That night, I was restless and sleep was uncomfortable for me. Sometime after two a.m., I woke in the early hours with a powerful vision that caused me excruciating physical and mental anguish. In my vision, the smoke was so thick, I could not breathe. My body lay on a Hawaiian funeral pyre, covered in layer upon layer of flowers. Every inch of my body was draped in flower leis, except for my eyes, nose and mouth areas. My father in that life (Neil) stood beside my flower adorned body. My spirit or soul body hovered close above him as he spoke aloud, softly, to me in spirit.

"The twilight is not to be feared my daughter," said my father as he sadly gazed upon my body as flames began to rise below me and smoke circled my lifeless form. He regretted then how badly he had treated me. His heart ached. I felt it in my spirit form. "You will come back to me," my father continued.

I was beside him in spirit; the smoke seemed to terrify me. I finally realized that I could not reach my father and return to him. I began to regret my hasty departure from life. "The smoke, the flames," I cried in a silent voice my father could not hear. "I cannot return to you my father. My body is consumed." Though I was in spirit, the smoke frightened me and I felt trapped in the smoke.

"I will be reborn my father. Reborn, reborn! To awaken another day!" I heard my echoing voice struggling to be heard by my father. "I will return to your arms, to your arms. Do not turn away from me my father! I am here! I am here with you. Let me come back to you – my father," I pleaded. "I am here beside you!" My fading voice was impassioned and anxious. The smoke seemed to choke me, though I was out of my body, I felt as if I were still alive and being consumed by the smoke and flames. My spirit was actually in the process of departing for other realms and leaving that lifetime behind.

In the present, as I lay in my bed, I felt like I was choking from the burned sage I had inhaled only hours before. I felt like I was suffocating. I was in immense pain and felt like I was dying – again. It was all so real and it was happening *now!*

I felt my own anguish and my father's in that Hawaiian life. My husband's heart was cold and he still scoffed at my leaving him in death and blamed me. He was angry. I forgave my father and realized he really loved me but did not know how to express it. My father's heart ached and my own spirit felt as if it was breaking.

Now in this life, in the early morning, I felt *all* the pain of the Hawaiian life. It was real and excruciating. I relived my burning, the smoke and all the pain I felt in spirit form then – *in the present time!* For a few hours I lay in my bed and relived every "past" moment. Thankfully, as the early morning light streamed in my window, I fell asleep for a couple hours out of sheer exhaustion. But my sleep was tortured and I woke, distraught and incredulous of my experiences. My body felt twisted and I was in terrible physical pain. My lower back ached and my legs were numb. I knew I could not go on this way and sought my old chiropractor whom I had visited before my accident. The adjustment did me little good.

As I walked home from his clinic, still in pain, a friend of mine, Mary, from the Heritage Store deli, pulled up beside me in her car and offered me a ride. She drove me to the Heritage and I found someone to give me a short back massage that I hoped would help alleviate more of my back pain. Also, I felt as before, like *I was half in this physical world and half in the spirit world*. I *knew* there were still more visions waiting to unfold before me.

I hung out in the deli, with my head drooping over the table, because I was still in quite a lot of pain. Eventually, I met another massage therapist friend there who also offered me a massage. I still felt badly, so I agreed to a second massage. I was desperate for any and every kind of help I could get. As Nancy began to work on me in the massage chair, I felt a deep spiritual peace descend on me. I felt drawn inward to my spirit realm and felt like I was in a deep state of meditation.

Suddenly, I saw Neil and myself in an East Indian lifetime. In it, we were married and had been for some years. I had on a long, cotton, gauze-like, ruby red dress with a very thick band, at least six inches thick, of gold threads on the borders, a sari, and Neil had on an orange, light cotton shirt and loose orange draw-string pants (similar to pajamas) and a red dot on his middle forehead over his third eye chakra – to enhance energy there. (Orange denotes sexual self-control and celibacy and red, passion and blooming sexuality. The gold band is elevated spiritual awareness.) I could tell that I was upset in that life. Past Neil had decided to be celibate to enhance his spiritual life and he was imposing celibacy upon me, against my will, in our marriage. He was actually doing it more as a punishment to me and to distance himself. He was blocking out his emotions so he would not have to feel his own heart.

After I viewed this scene, I felt greater understanding dawn on me, in regard to my present relationship with Neil. He did not want sex with me in this life and I wanted sex. We were recreating the same feelings of that former East Indian life and perhaps some of his disinterest for sex with me was also because he still remembered (subconsciously) the pain of being killed in the Egyptian incarnation for loving me. Neil was still blocking his true emotions in an effort to be outwardly "spiritual." *We always pick up where we left off with each other in past lives.* We do not get to "escape" anything. We eventually have to face our pasts – over and over again – if need be, until we deal with all we have avoided and left unhealed! Would Neil and I ever heal this past rift in this lifetime? I did not know about him. But I knew I wanted to heal this rift for myself, and never have to face it again in this or any other incarnation. I pondered these thoughts for the rest of the day.

Interestingly enough, Neil walked into the deli shortly after my visionary massage and ended up sitting right behind me at an opposite table. I sat with a friend, Zippo, who had offered to drive me home, as I was far too weak to walk. After an uncomfortable silence between Neil and me (we did not speak or look at each other) that seemed to shout itself around us, Zippo and I departed from the store. As we headed to my home, I was feeling a little better than earlier. But I asked him to give me one of his famous energy treatments anyway when we arrived. He did so for ten minutes and left me to rest.

The next day, I was somewhat better but still in a low energy state wavering perilously between two worlds. The second day following, I was growing more uncomfortable and knew that I would keep regressing. I had to do something to help myself so I prayed. I did deep breathing too. My inner guidance spoke to me then: "Call Neil."

"Oh no, not that!" I protested inside myself. I kept praying most of the day. Two more times my inner guidance said to call Neil. Forgive him, it said. Give him another chance. I was weak, tired and still on the edge of pain. I knew Neil could help me, yet I resisted. A few hours later, I surrendered to the truth within me and called him. He did not answer my call and I was relieved. I left him a message and told him I needed help. If he wanted to help me, I would be thankful, if not, I said I would never call and bother him again.

Neil called back soon after, and arranged to visit me at home and give me a chiropractic adjustment and some extra body energy work as well. When he arrived a few hours later, I had to speak to him first. I told him how much he hurt me, and asked him to please not be abusive to me again. I could not take any more pain. He apologized sincerely and promised to be caring of my feelings in the future. I told him of my visions and he listened politely, though I doubt that he believed me. He dared not offend me, though, by calling me a liar again. He said he believed that I believed what I said, and he was very gentle with me and actually kind.

As I lay on his portable adjusting table, looking up at him, I felt myself sucked back into our Hawaiian lifetime again. I was lying on a dried grass cot and he was standing above me waving sacred smoke over me with a large brown and black almost stripped, feather. I said, in that past life: "Heal me O my father." I flashed back to that Hawaiian incarnation and saw and felt myself as a young woman, lying ill on my bed. Past Neil, the headman or Kahuna of the tribe, was also the healer. I could tell that I completely trusted him to heal me. He was brushing sacred smoke over me to cast out evil spirits and heal me.

I flashed back to present times as Neil continued to lean over me to work on me. Late that same night, I was in excruciating pain. I called Neil on his cell phone, after his musical gig ended at midnight, and he came over to work on me again. He worked on me for over an hour and even rushed out to find supplements to help me. He was certainly making up for his recent cruelty to me. I forgave him wholeheartedly, and was thankful for his help. Neil returned in the morning with more supplements for me.

Later the second day, he came back to check on me. As I lay on his adjusting table again, I had one more final vision. I saw myself in the Hawaiian life as a little girl playing happily beside my father, past Neil. I knew with this vision that the Hawaiian lifetime was now healed for us. Neil and I had changed our bad karma with forgiveness and caring. We had helped heal each other. I rapidly grew better after this last vision, and *I returned to feeling fully "present" in this lifetime.*

Also, shortly after, I did a thirty-day cleanse to remove drug residues from my body from the prescription muscle relaxants and pain killers I had taken for nearly two months after my neck was broken in the car accident. After this cleanse, I felt significantly healthier and my car accident injuries were noticeably improved.

To thank Neil for helping me, I also altered his diet, put

him on several special supplements and directed him to do a rejuvenating cleanse. Within several weeks, his impotence disappeared and he became fully functional in the bedroom again, though not with me. In our time apart, he met someone new and I was not disappointed. *Now that our past karma was completed, I no longer found myself attracted to Neil!* Who he was now was not someone I was physically drawn to or wanted a sexual relationship with, in present times. I myself had other love aspirations I preferred to focus on – now. Both Neil and I then continued to enjoy a warm friendship.

At that time, I had begun dating a man whom I eventually recognized as a German commandant of the prison camp I was confined to at the end of my last earthly incarnation. This brought up some of my issues leftover from that lifetime. It also gave me hope that I was about to complete karma from that last lifetime and be able to soon carry on beyond my past lifetimes of karmic loves into a higher dharmic relationship that would finally allow me to pursue my present life's real purposes. My story with this past German love and final letting go of that lifetime's pain and karma, is recorded in this book's sequel, *The Ocean Daughter.*

Back in the present of September 2004, I also see that my last earthly lifetime in a German prison camp was another reflection – a ripple in the stream – of that Polynesian lifetime in Hawaii. I suffered and was abused in the prison camp and finally died trying to escape, torn apart by two German Shepherds. The two dogs are a similar "ripple" or reflection of my dying by a double waterfall in Hawaii and my being abused by two men – my father and husband in that life. I tried to escape the prison camp just as I tried to escape in my Hawaiian lifetime by running away from my husband and "choosing – asking" to die, so I hit my face in the water. In the German lifetime the dogs prevented my physical escape to teach me I could not run away from: my past, my pain and my inability to say no to abuse. I had not overcome the abuse in my German prison camp lifetime any more than I had overcome it in the Hawaiian lifetime – until now. I had to face my abusers in a strong place inside myself and say no to abuse – once and for all. I had to forgive and love them while keeping true to myself, to dissolve the past. *This karma is now finally resolved.*

Eventually, all bad karma is healed and dissolves. Then only good karma remains and even this must be "healed" and let go of. Then and only then, can one proceed to fulfill one's dharma, or life purpose, in serving God or the universal force in a final lifetime on earth. This puts an end to the "wheel of birth and death" and one no longer experiences lifetimes on planet earth or any other physical planet for that matter. The spirit is finally returned to fully being a true son or daughter of the divine. For me, I become once again: *The River Daughter*.

ALWAYS FREE

Who can cage me,
Chain me, tie me?
Nothing in this world can bind me.
For I shall always be –
Infinite and Endless –
Eternally Free...

. . .

Great seers and saints like Edgar Cayce and East Indian Swami Paramahansa Yogananda say that people who we know well or intimately in this life are people we have known well in past lives. We are all connected on one level or another, but those closest to us now in this life, have been related to us as lovers, parents, children, siblings, friends or enemies in many lifetimes. This is a fact.

I myself was married to my father, spent time as nuns with my mother and also was mother to my younger brother in past incarnations, among other familial relationships I discovered later in this lifetime.

One of the things that has been hardest for me to bear in this present life is that I have experiences with people and soul mates I have known for lifetimes and I only get to spend days, weeks and rarely, if I am blessedly fortunate, months with them – then they are gone! The scenes of my life change, like a movie set – too quickly. I am left spinning in the dust. I cannot hold onto these people and I only seek to, because it is all moving so fast! My speeded-up karma, like "instant karma," does not allow me the pleasure of too many long acquaintances. My head sometimes spins from the constant change of scenes. *I am thankful when other people help me – by giving me energy.*

It has been impossible for me to explain this to others. I can meet someone and within an hour – as with Neil – feel all the love and emotions I have felt for them in dozens of lives – right now, in the present! Others I meet do not feel as I do. No wonder they think I am a little crazy and hold on too much. They are running on to new experiences while I am still struggling for answers – reasons why I feel as deeply as I do. I need to dissect and understand how and why the past affects me so deeply now – before I can move on to other life experiences. My mission or dharma, this life, is to unravel hundreds of my past incarnations, tie up loose ends – and heal them. Thus healing the present simultaneously.

What I shared with Neil was one example of how I "picked apart the inner workings of that clock" I mentioned earlier in this chapter, to see why it worked the way it did – and now I knew. I could put it back together now, let it go and move on in my life because I now understood the reason why as well as how to fix or heal the situation.

As I have worked out old karma from many past lives, I have realized that *karma must be dealt with at the level on which it is created!* This means that old grudges, enemies, angers, hurts and negative things from past lives have to be "recreated" (at least in energy) in this life in order for them to be overcome or risen above. I have found myself being slapped down energetically many, many times in this life to work out old, bad karma. (Not the good stuff – called good karma – that is much easier to overcome at higher energy levels!)

The serious car accident I mentioned in my "First Words" of this book, that I had just experienced months ago, wherein my neck was broken, was part of a continuation of that Hawaiian lifetime just like the other accident where I smashed my face, twelve years previously. I had to be weakened and low to meet Neil at the level we left each other at in the Hawaiian life, so I could overcome the same level of conditions and rise above and heal that old situation.

When I complete or heal an old hurt, my energy levels rise up higher and I enjoy God ecstasies and happiness in my life. But these good times are short-lived by me. I get momentary tastes of joy and am soon slapped down in energy to deal with more past bad karma. To onlookers it appears that I keep screwing up my life. But I know inside of me – that I am actually healing my life. I get tired, frustrated and occasionally angry about my constant struggles on lower energy levels, but I know throughout my being, that this is part of God's divine plan – to heal me. God wants me to become strong so I can help others to also carry their own crosses and heal their lives.

All pains, all challenges, all crosses we bear – can and will eventually be transformed into good for each of us. "All things work towards our own good." We must trust, believe and know this! All that seems bad or evil in our lives can eventually lead us to our own good. There is a silver lining in everything; even what appears to be "bad." We are God beings! And we must return to who we really are. The light in us may become surrounded by darkness but "the light will *never* be the darkness." *We are light and we have only to discover and know this in every moment to stay in the light forever.*

So many times in my life, I thought I was free; when my father left home, at the yoga ashram, when I left the farm and Mata, when Gopala and I separated, when I got my first car and other times as well. But now I know that true freedom is inside myself – not found in outer conditions. To be truly free, I need to heal and release my past karma so I can live fully in the moment of today. As my past heals, my energy levels rise and I see a more intimate view of my own soul and God. I am presently in the process of becoming free – truly free.

"I KNOW"
I know "who" I am.
I Know!
I've met myself
And I Love what I see.
I find,
Now that I Know me –
I Know everybody.
And I Love them
And want all to see,
Who they are
And that they are free.
I Know you –
Do you Know me?

Look for the sequel to *The River Daughter* entitled: *The Ocean Daughter*. See Jeanne Marie Martin's website for more information at: www.jeannemariemartin.com

Every day, in little ways, we need to be moving
progressively towards improving ourselves –
mentally, emotionally, physically, energetically,
and spiritually. If we are not forging ahead,
we are going in the opposite direction towards
digression, delusion, disease, pain and death.
Our mission on earth is to live fully and express
our magnificence! Only then can we become who
and what we are truly meant to be
– shining lights in God's eternity!

Jeanne Marie Martin

Our deepest fear is not that we are inadequate. Our
deepest fear is that we are powerful beyond measure. It is our
Light, not our darkness that most frightens us. Actually, who
are you not to be? You are a child of God. Your playing small
does not serve the world. There is nothing enlightening about
shrinking so that other people won't feel insecure around you.
We were born to make manifest the glory of God that is
within us. It is not in some of us; it is in everyone. And as we
let our own light shine, we unconsciously give other people
permission to do the same. As we are liberated from our own
fear, our presence automatically liberates others.

Nelson Mandela 1994 Inaugural Speech

ABOUT THE AUTHOR

Jeanne Marie Martin
(At age 47)

Jeanne Marie Martin is the author of twenty-four books and over five hundred magazine articles. She is a clinical nutritionist as well as an international speaker, workshop leader, consultant. Jeanne Marie has worked with hundreds of doctors and health care specialists in Canada and the U.S. As a Holistic Health Consultant she specializes in lifestyles and diets for individuals with: allergies, candida albicans, chronic fatigue syndrome, high or low blood sugar, cancer, parasites, digestive/bowel problems & weight problems, plus vegan, vegetarian & partial meat diets.

For over thirty years, Jeanne Marie has worked in the health care field developing nutritional and medical intuitive abilities. She also gives past life and soulmate readings and teaches yoga and meditation classes. Jeanne Marie has trained yoga teachers and recently became an ordained minister. She is also a singer, published poet, professional floral designer and arts and crafts expert who has produced her own line of greeting cards and an array of poetry bookmarks and love messages as well. Over one million copies of her books are in print and a number of them are best sellers.

See her Website at: www.jeannemariemartin.com

Lead us from the unreal to the real.

Lead us from darkness to light.

Lead us from death to immortality.

Hindu Prayer

ๅ Personal Closing Message from Jeanne Marie Martin

January 26, 2006

Each story in this book was carefully scrutinized and prayed about to be sure it contained life lessons and spiritual principles that would make it a worthwhile contribution for readers that could enhance your own spiritual journeys. Ultimately, it is not what we "do," it is what we "are," that makes us children of the river of light. No matter what your past has been, it all dissolves into a faint dream as you step into the light of your true beingness in the Divine. *"Even if your sins be as scarlet, they shall become as white as snow."* Because sin is merely error or "missing the mark."

When sailing or flying a plane, it is said that one is off course ninety percent of the time. Each of us goes back and forth over our true course in life as well. Keep your sights on the goal of union with your true self, which is simultaneously union with the Divine. For we are indeed one. But relax your pace and enjoy your journey. Let nothing be so important as to take away your peace and trust in your higher self and God.

Neale Donald Walsch, in his book: *Conversations With God*, says that our human judgments consider a soldier dying silently on a battlefield to be superior to a woman making love with a whimper. God does not judge, nor view such situations so erroneously. Respectable outer appearances do no assure inner quality. Outer actions do not always reflect inner intentions!

Some day the people of planet earth will discover that lessons learned are more important than their packaging. With practice, we can step out of an ugly experience as easily as we step out of an article of clothing. (My book: *Soulmate Realities*, gives you techniques to assist this process.)

Once again, keep focused on the light – no matter how many times you fall or seemingly fail. Ask for Divine and angelic help and grace will lift you beyond the past into the eternal present. This is your true home, your destiny – in NOW. I will meet you here!

Blessings and Love, Jeanne Marie Martin

ISBN 141208363-X

9 781412 083638